MW01039512

The Eden Narrative

The Eden Narrative

*A Literary and Religio-historical Study
of Genesis 2–3*

Tryggve N. D. Mettinger

Winona Lake, Indiana
Eisenbrauns
2007

The preparation of the manuscript for this book was aided by a grant from the Royal Academy of Letters, History and Antiquities, Stockholm.

Cataloging in Publication Data

Mettinger, Tryggve N. D.
    The Eden narrative : a literary and religio-historical study of Genesis 2–3 / Tryggve N. D. Mettinger.
        p. cm.
    Includes bibliographical references and indexes.
    ISBN-13: 978-1-57506-141-2 (hardback : alk. paper)
    1. Eden. 2. Bible. O.T. Genesis II, 4–III, 24—Criticism, interpretation, etc. I. Title.
    BS1237.M48 2007
    222′.1106—dc22

                              2007037248

To Solvi

my "favorite wife"
who is more than an echo of Eden to me

Contents

Acknowledgments ix

Preface xi

Abbreviations xv

1. Introduction 1
    1.1. The Agenda of the Present Study 1
    1.2. One or Two Trees? A Survey of Opinions 5

2. A Narratological Analysis of the Eden Narrative 12
    2.1. Unifying Elements 13
    2.2. Time and Location 14
    2.3. Scenes and Plot 16
        1. Scenes 16
        2. "Plot Segments" 18
        3. The Overall Plot 21
    2.4. Characters 29
    2.5. Focalization (Point of View) and Voice 32
    2.6. Narrator and Characters:
        Omniscience and Restricted Knowledge 34
    Summary and Conclusions 41

3. The Theme of the Eden Narrative 42
    3.1. "Theme" in Literary Theory 42
    3.2. The Theme of the Eden Narrative 47
        1. Death versus Immortality 47
        2. The Test of Obedience:
          Disobedience and Its Consequences 49
        3. Theodicy 58
        4. The Two Trees 60
    Summary and Conclusions 63

4. The Genre and Function of the Eden Narrative 65
    4.1. The Genre of the Eden Narrative 66
        1. The Genre: Myth 66
        2. A Sociofunctionalist Interpretation
          of the Eden Narrative 70
    4.2. Excursus: Structuralist Approaches 74
    4.3. The Nature of Genre and How Genre Works 76

4.4. The Eden Narrative versus the
      Chaos Battle Drama of Creation 80
Summary and Conclusions 83

5. Traces of a Tradition: The Adamic Myth in Ezekiel 28 85
  5.1. The Contents of the Adamic Myth 87
  5.2. Wisdom and Immortality in the Adamic Myth 90
  5.3. The Innovations of the Eden Poet (Genesis 2–3) 94
  Summary and Conclusions 97

6. Wisdom and Immortality in *Adapa* and *Gilgamesh* 99
  6.1. The Myth of *Adapa and the South Wind* 100
      1. Adapa: Wisdom, the Gift of Ea 102
      2. Adapa: Immortality Forfeited 104
      3. Adapa and the Eden Narrative:
         A Comparison 107
  6.2. The *Gilgamesh Epic* 109
      1. Gilgamesh: Wisdom from the
         Antediluvian Age 112
      2. Gilgamesh: The Quest for Immortality 116

7. Synthesis 123
  7.1. The Two Main Traditions Alloyed 124
  7.2. The Conceptual Framework 126
      1. The Ontological Boundary 126
      2. Wisdom 129
      3. Immortality 130
      4. Theodicy 132
  7.3. Date and Literary Integrity 134

References 136
Indexes
  Index of Authors 156
  Index of Scripture 160
  Index of Other Ancient Sources 163
  Index of Terms, Mainly Literary 165

Acknowledgments

I am grateful to Oxford University Press, Oxford, for permission to quote from Andrew R. George, *The Babylonian Gilgamesh Epic* (2003); to SCM-Canterbury Press, London, and Westminster John Knox Press, Louisville, for permission to quote from Gerhard von Rad, *Genesis: A Commentary* (1961); and to Professor Lars-Håkan Svensson for permission to use his translation of Gunnar Ekelöf's poem "Poetik."

The Bible translation I quote in this book is the New Revised Standard Version (NRSV), unless otherwise stated. I use normalized spellings without diacritics in ancient Near Eastern names (Uta-napishti, Gilgamesh, and so on), even when I quote from translations in which diacritics are used.

Preface

"*About conditions in Paradise, opinion has been divided for millennia, owing to, among other things, the troublesome lack of eyewitnesses.*" Anders Palm, Professor of Comparative Literature and my colleague at Lund, makes this irrefutable observation (Palm 2004: 15). Thus, the situation arouses one's curiosity. The ancient Romans used to say *habent sua fata libelli*, which means "books have their fates." And so does this book.

It all began during a very rainy summer in Sweden a few years ago. My wife, Solvi, and I had moved to our summer house in the province of Småland, the district of lakes and forests. In my despondency over the weather, I decided to resort to some Akkadian reading and found the *Gilgamesh Epic* a suitable choice. Like Uta-napishti in his boat, I sat in my summer house hoping to reach land in a world with more pleasant weather. It so happened that before I embarked on *Gilgamesh* I had just finished a rereading of the myth *Adapa and the South Wind*.

I found that the two protagonists, Adapa and Gilgamesh, were figures who were exceedingly wise, their wisdom ultimately deriving from the god Ea, but also persons who forfeited immortality by a narrow margin. The idea dawned on me that the biblical story of Eden is a text in which we find the same combination of knowledge and immortality, here symbolized by the two trees. Might the combination of motifs in the two Mesopotamian texts be able to shed light on the Eden Narrative?

Back in my library in my home in Borgeby, outside Lund, I decided to look into the matter and see what biblical scholars made of the trees in Eden. When I found that ever since Karl Budde (1883) a number of scholars had contributed to a deforestation of Eden, running the tree of life through the chipper of classic source criticism—the tree of life being regarded as a late intruder in the text—the spirit of suspicion came upon me. I decided to determine for myself how many special trees sound exegetical ecology could tolerate in the Garden of Bliss and, above all, what the Eden Narrative is really about: what is (are) its theme(s)? The present book was born out of this curiosity.

I felt a strong need to employ a consistent method—a method, moreover, that meets the needs of the material, a piece of verbal art that takes the shape of a narrative, which has become one of the most precious pieces of world literature. Consequently, I found it natural to approach the Eden Narrative armed with the methods used by literary scholars. There appeared to be reasons to question the source-critical approach (*Literarkritik*) to the Eden Narrative. I must add that this does not mean that I question this approach in the study of other texts.

My investigation proceeds as follows. After a brief survey of the relevant research and a statement explaining my agenda (chap. 1), I first undertake a narratological analysis (chap. 2). The text appears to make excellent sense on the assumption that both trees belong to it from beginning. A striking insight from my analysis is that the man and the woman do not share the knowledge possessed by the narrator at all. They are informed about the existence of one tree only. But this does not necessarily mean that we must eliminate the other tree from the text.

The next chapter (chap. 3) discusses the theme of the narrative. I argue that the text is about a divine test, related to the passages about God's testing of Israel, Abraham, and Job. The thesis of the Eden author is that obedience to the divine commandment leads to life, and disobedience to the forfeiture of the possibility of immortality. In important respects, the Eden Narrative repristinates significant elements of Deuteronomistic theology (the Law and obedience).

Only in chap. 4 do I arrive at the question to which genre the narrative belongs. My conclusion here is that the narrative is a myth. Of the various methods of investigating myths (structuralist, semiotic, functionalist), I opt for functionalism, because I want to come to grips with the question of what the poet wanted to accomplish in his reader. This issue calls for a functionalist approach.

The last two chapters are devoted to material prior to the work of the Eden Poet. Chapter 5 analyzes Ezekiel 28 with the aim of recovering the basic elements of an Adamic myth used by Ezekiel. It is thus a discussion of tradition history. On the assumption that this basic myth was known to the Eden Poet who produced the narrative that we now have in Genesis 2–3, I raise the question what the Eden Poet did with his material, looking at how he changed it, and finally focusing on the purpose of these changes. After this study of the biblical narrative, I proceed to a discussion of the prime ancient Near Eastern material, *Adapa* and *Gilgamesh* (chap. 6). In spite of considerable differences with regard to plot, I find in these narratives—one a myth and one an epic—a stable thematic marriage of wisdom and immortality, two concepts that are essential both to the oldest form of the Adamic myth as known from Ezekiel 28 and to the Eden Narrative in Genesis. The book ends with a synthesis (chap. 7), in which I discuss some implications of my findings.

To me this enterprise has been an invigorating experience. For many years, I have taken an interest in literary theory. The present project grew out of curiosity, and in the course of my explorations I learned a number of new things. I needed to apply perspectives and techniques I had never used before. This inspired me to take on a pedagogical task: I try to explain my various methodological steps, making it clear to my fellow students what it means to carry out a narratological analysis and what we may learn from the discussion of phenomena such as genre and theme among scholars of comparative literature. Every chapter finishes with a brief summary and a recapitulation of its conclusions.

I have a confession to make. There are a plethora of works on the first chapters of Genesis. I decided from the outset that I was not going to spend the rest of my life on this project, however fascinating it may be, and thus there may be studies, even important ones, that I have overlooked. Should this be the case, I want to express my sincere apology. There was no intention of negligence.

There is one contribution that has been a constant companion of mine, and this is Terje Stordalen's *Echoes of Eden* (2000). Reading and reviewing (Mettinger 2003) this rich resource aroused my keen interest in Genesis 2–3. Moreover, Stordalen's work did the best thing that a book can do: it inspired me to do work of my own. For this, I am profoundly grateful.

It is a pleasure for me to thank colleagues and friends who have helped me with advice and comments on various chapters.

Aspects of literary theory are important in my work, and so are Assyriological matters. Both fields are full of pitfalls for the biblical scholar. I received valuable comments on my "literary" chapters from some eminent specialists. Thus, Greger Andersson (Örebro) and Anders Palm (Lund) read and commented on my chapter on narratology, and at the very outset of my project Anders Palm gave me expert advice on what to read in narratology. Eva Haettner Aurelius (Lund) read my chapter on genre. Torsten Pettersson (Uppsala) read and gave valuable comments on all of chaps. 1–4.

On Mesopotamian texts, I have had the great privilege of being able to consult outstanding Assyriologists, with documented competence also in the West-Semitic ambit. Manfried Dietrich (Münster) read chap. 6, and Peter Machinist (Harvard) read chaps. 6–7. Both colleagues gave valuable comments on my material. Earlier in my project, Edward Lipiński reminded me of important references and sent me his review of Chrostowski's monograph (Lipiński 2001). I discussed some matters of Egyptology (eventually not included) with Lana Troy (Uppsala).

I have also received inspiration from my own intellectual milieu at CTR (that is, the Centre for Theology and Religious Studies, Lund). My thanks are thus extended to Tord Olsson for a session in the Senior Seminar on Comparative Religion (on chap. 4) and Sten Hidal for two sessions in the Senior Seminar on Biblical Studies (on chaps. 2–3). Sten Hidal also provided information about the interpretation of the Eden Narrative in the Early Church. Göran Eidevall and Irene von Görtz-Wrisberg gave me valuable comments and tips on literature. Irene also shared my proofreading burdens. Ola Wikander has been an inspiring conversation partner throughout the project.

Tomas Lind (the University Library) and Leif Lindin (the Theological Library) provided indispensable help on a number of bibliographical matters.

Magnus Zetterholm, specialist in New Testament Studies *and* computers, enhanced my dexterity with the last-mentioned resource to unforeseen heights.

Scrutiny of my English was made possible by a grant from the Royal Academy of Letters, History, and Antiquities, Stockholm. A grant from the same source financed the proofreading.

From beginning to end, it has been a pleasure to work with my publisher, James E. Eisenbraun, and his staff. I am especially grateful to my editor, Mrs. Beverly McCoy, for the skill and care that she has invested in my book.

Working my way into the Eden Narrative was to me an experience of sheer intellectual enjoyment. It also reminded me of the privilege of being a biblical scholar: the gift of spending one's years on the narrow peninsula of time in close contact with texts of unmatched existential dimensions.

Borgeby, on Candlemas Day, February 2, 2007
Tryggve N. D. Mettinger

Abbreviations

General

BM	registration number of cuneiform tablets in the collections of the British Museum
col.	column
frag.	fragment
DH	Deuteronomistic History
Dtr	Deuteronomistic
GE	*Gilgamesh Epic*
LXX	Septuagint
MB	Middle Babylonian
MT	The Masoretic Text of the Hebrew Bible
NRSV	New Revised Standard Version
OB	Old Babylonian
P	Priestly source
RSV	Revised Standard Version
SB	Standard Babylonian
VA	Vorderasiatische Abteilung Thontafeln

Reference Works

AfO	*Archiv für Orientforschung*
AJSL	*American Journal of Semitic Languages and Literature*
ANET	*Ancient Near Eastern Texts Relating to the Old Testament*, ed. J. B. Pritchard. Third edition. Princeton: Princeton University Press, 1969
AOAT	Alter Orient und Altes Testament
AUSS	*Andrews University Seminary Studies*
BaghM	*Baghdader Mitteilungen*
BDB	*Hebrew and English Lexicon of the Old Testament.* F. Brown, S. R. Driver, and C. A. Briggs. Oxford: Clarendon, 1907
Bib	*Biblica*
BibS(N)	Biblische Studien (Neukirchen, 1951–)
BJRL	*Bulletin of the John Rylands University Library of Manchester*
BKAT	Biblischer Kommentar, Altes Testament
BN	*Biblische Notizen*
BO	*Bibliotheca Orientalis*
BWL	*Babylonian Wisdom Literature.* W. G. Lambert. Oxford, 1967. Reprinted, Winona Lake, IN: Eisenbrauns, 1996
BZAW	Beihefte zur Zeitschrift für die alttestamentliche Wissenschaft
CAD	*The Assyrian Dictionary of the Oriental Institute of the University of Chicago*, ed. A. L. Oppenheim et al. Chicago: Oriental Institute, 1956–

CAT	*The Cuneiform Alphabetic Texts from Ugarit, Ras Ibn Hani and Other Places*, ed. Manfried Dietrich, Oswald Loretz, and Joaquin Sanmartín. Münster: Ugarit-Verlag, 1995 [second, enlarged edition of *Die keilalphabetischen Texte aus Ugarit*]
CBQ	*Catholic Biblical Quarterly*
CBQMS	Catholic Biblical Quarterly: Monograph Series
CDA	*A Concise Dictionary of Akkadian*, ed. Jeremy Black, Andrew George, and Nicholas Postgate. Wiesbaden: Harrassowitz, 1999
ConBOT	Coniectanea Biblica: Old Testament Series
CTM	*Concordia Theological Monthly*
ER	*Encyclopedia of Religion*, ed. M. Eliade. 16 vols. New York: Macmillan, 1987
FRLANT	Forschungen zur Religion und Literatur des Alten und Neuen Testaments
GKC	*Gesenius' Hebrew Grammar*, ed. E. Kautzsch; trans. A. E. Cowley. Second ed. Oxford: Oxford University Press, 1910
HKAT	Handkommentar zum Alten Testament
HSS	Harvard Semitic Studies
HUCA	*Hebrew Union College Annual*
IBHS	*An Introduction to Biblical Hebrew Syntax*. B. K. Waltke and M. O'Connor. Winona Lake, IN: Eisenbrauns, 1990
JAOS	*Journal of the American Oriental Society*
JBL	*Journal of Biblical Literature*
JCS	*Journal of Cuneiform Studies*
JJS	*Journal of Jewish Studies*
JNES	*Journal of Near Eastern Studies*
JSOT	*Journal for the Study of the Old Testament*
JSOTSup	Journal for the Study of the Old Testament: Supplement Series
JSPSup	Journal for the Study of the Pseudepigrapha: Supplement Series
JSS	*Journal of Semitic Studies*
JTS	*Journal of Theological Studies*
LB	*Linguistica Biblica*
OBO	Orbis Biblicus et Orientalis
OBT	Overtures to Biblical Theology
OLP	*Orientalia Lovaniensia Periodica*
Or	*Orientalia*
OrAnt	*Oriens Antiquus*
OTG	Old Testament Guides
PTMS	Pittsburgh Theological Monograph Series
RA	*Revue d'assyriologie et d'archéologie orientale*
RB	*Revue biblique*
RENT	*Routledge Encyclopedia of Narrative Theory*, ed. David Herman, Manfred Jahn, and Marie-Laure Ryan. London: Routledge, 2005
RHPR	*Revue d'histoire et de philosophie religieuses*
SAACT	State Archives of Assyria: Cuneiform Texts
SBB	Stuttgarter biblische Beiträge
SBS	Stuttgarter Bibelstudien
SBT	Studies in Biblical Theology

SBTS	Sources for Biblical and Theological Studies
SEÅ	*Svensk Exegetisk Årsbok*
SJOT	*Scandinavian Journal of the Old Testament*
SSN	Studia Semitica Neerlandica
STK	*Svensk Teologisk Kvartalskrift*
SubBi	Subsidia Biblica
TB	Theologische Bücherei: Neudrucke und Berichte aus dem 20. Jahrhundert
TTKi	*Tidsskrift for Teologi og Kirke*
TUAT	*Texte aus der Umwelt des Alten Testaments*, ed. Otto Kaiser. Gütersloh: Mohn, 1981–
TWAT	*Theologisches Wörterbuch zum Alten Testament*, ed. G. Johannes Botterweck and Helmer Ringgren. Stuttgart: Kohlhammer, 1973–
TZ	*Theologische Zeitschrift*
UF	*Ugarit-Forschungen*
VT	*Vetus Testamentum*
VTSup	Supplements to Vetus Testamentum
WBC	Word Biblical Commentary
WMANT	Wissenschaftliche Monographien zum Alten und Neuen Testament
WO	*Die Welt des Orients*
ZA	*Zeitschrift für Assyriologie*
ZAH	*Zeitschrift für Althebraistik*
ZAW	*Zeitschrift für die Alttestamentliche Wissenschaft*
ZDPV	*Zeitschrift des deutschen Palästina-Vereins*
ZTK	*Zeitschrift für Theologie und Kirche*

Chapter 1

Introduction

1.1. The Agenda of the Present Study

In the present work, I aim to answer two specific questions:

1. What is the theme of the narrative in Genesis 2–3 (to be exact: 2:4–3:24)? This entails a study of the Genesis passage as a self-contained piece of literature.
2. Did the poet use a preliterary story about the first man in Eden and develop this material into something new? If so, what do these changes tell us about the interests of this poet? This entails raising the tradition-historical question.

I will proceed in the following manner: First, I subject the Eden Narrative to a narratological analysis, whereupon I move to a discussion of theme and genre. I then deal with the tradition history and the revealing changes made by the Eden Poet. Finally, because the two trees symbolize knowledge and immortality, I discuss two Mesopotamian myths in which we find a thematic combination of these very phenomena.

Various labels have been used in referring to the story in Genesis 2–3.[1] To call it "the story of the fall" presupposes the idea of an original state of existence, the *Urstand* or prelapsarian state (a state before the "fall") of Christian dogmatics. The designation "Adamic myth" (Ricoeur) presupposes that a stance has already been taken on the issue of genre. Simply using "Genesis 2–3" is rather bland. I have opted for calling the story the *Eden Narrative*, a designation that does not imply any preconceived interpretation but nevertheless reminds us of the contents of the passage and forms an apt title for a piece of poetry by a master.

When we ask what a story is all about, we are speaking of its theme. The ensuing presentation of some previous, representative opinions is complicated by the fact that many exegetes do not use the term *theme*

---

1. See Jensen 2004: 41 n. 1.

in their interpretation of Genesis 2–3 but nevertheless seem to express an opinion regarding the central content or idea of the passage.[2]

In his classic commentary, Gunkel expresses himself fairly clearly about the message of the Eden Narrative. After his treatment of the many details, he devotes some five pages to an overall estimation.[3] He notes that the main point of the narrative appears at the very end: the expulsion from the garden (p. 33). Gunkel calls attention to the fact that the story seeks to answer an underlying question. If the story had ended with a "therefore" (as we have it in the subsection ending with 2:24), then it would be told with an eye to the events described: *Therefore*, humans now have knowledge of good and evil, but they no longer live in Paradise; instead, they suffer all sorts of toil and misery (p. 29).

Westermann calls attention to the span of events (*Geschehensbogen*) comprising the divine command → transgression → expulsion, finding "a primeval narrative of crime and punishment" in these chapters.[4] Like Gunkel, he sees the narrative as an attempt to answer a basic, existential question. This question is not "How did death come into the world?" but, rather, "Why is the human being, though created by God, a being limited by death, suffering, toil, and sin?" (p. 377).

Similarly, Gordon Wenham finds that Genesis 2–3 offers "a paradigm of sin, a model of what happens whenever man disobeys God."[5] It "explains through a story what constitutes sin and what sin's consequences are" (p. 90).

Gerhard von Rad, in his exposition of this narrative, finds "one of its most significant affirmations" in the serpent's insinuation of "the

---

2. A broad history of interpretation of the Eden Narrative from the Early Church to the early twentieth century is found in Feldmann (1913: 501–605), a work that Terje Stordalen kindly called to my attention. For a survey of the study of the Eden Narrative in early historical-critical study, see Metzger 1959. For surveys of the later scholarship, see Westermann (1976: 255–59, English trans. 1984: 186–90; 1972: 26–39); Stordalen (2000: 187–205); and Jensen (2004: 41–69). Space does not permit me to list works on the history of reception. I would like to mention the following, however: on Adam in early Judaism, Levison (1988); on Adam and Eve in early Jewish and Christian thinking, Gary A. Anderson (2001); and on Genesis 2–3 in Syriac Christianity, Kronholm (1978: 85–134) and Gary A. Anderson (1988). Note the handy compilation of excerpts from the Church Fathers in Louth and Conti 2001: 47–102.

3. Gunkel 1910: 28–33.

4. Westermann 1976: 259–67. Note p. 263: "eine urgeschichtliche Erzählung von Schuld und Strafe." English trans. 1984: 190–96; the quotation above is from 1984: 193.

5. Wenham 1987: 90.

possibility of an extension of human existence beyond the limits set for it by God at creation."[6] Von Rad appears to regard human hubris and its consequences as the thematic focus of the narrative.

In his 1970 monograph, Odil Hannes Steck argues along similar lines, laying heavy stress on the etiological nature of the narrative. According to Steck, it is to be understood according to its conclusion, which speaks of the expulsion from Eden. It is a story that tells of the reasons for the present human predicament, with its shortcomings and damaged relations between human beings. To Steck, the very root of the evil is "the human endeavor to form one's own existence autonomously."[7]

The Eden Narrative contains two prominent symbols: the tree of life and the tree of knowledge. Two scholars who take these symbols as points of departure for their different interpretations of the theme of the narrative are James Barr and Terje Stordalen.

According to Barr, the two themes articulated in the story are knowledge and immortality.[8] He adds provocatively: "The person who comes out of this story with a slightly shaky moral record is, of course, God." Barr goes on to ask: "Why does he want to keep eternal life for himself and not let them [the humans] share it? Even more seriously, why does he not want them to have knowledge of good and evil? What is wrong with this knowledge, that they should not possess it?"[9] Barr's thesis about the Eden Narrative is that this is not, as it has commonly been understood in the Christian tradition, basically a story about the origins of sin and evil. To Barr, the Eden Narrative is "a story of how human immortality was almost gained, but in fact was lost" (p. 4). The humans were expelled from the garden, "not because they were unworthy to stay there, or because they were hopelessly alienated from God, but because, if they stayed there, they would soon gain access to the tree of life, and eat of its fruit, and gain immortality: they would 'live for ever' (Genesis 3:22)."[10]

---

6. Von Rad 1961: 87.

7. Steck 1970; on the genre as "etiological narrative," see pp. 66–73; on the endeavor for autonomy, including the quotation above, see pp. 124–25: "das menschliche Bestreben nach autonomer Selbstgestaltung des eigenen Daseins."

8. Barr's monograph has the title *The Garden of Eden and the Hope of Immortality* (1993). It is based on his Read-Tuckwell lectures, a funded lectureship designed to deal with human immortality and related matters.

9. Barr 1993: 14.

10. Barr 1993: 4.

In his monograph *Echoes of Eden* (2000), Stordalen also recognizes the importance of the two trees and their symbolism but takes a different approach.[11] He suggests making a basic distinction between the story and the story's meaning. The first he calls "story narration" and the second "story significance" (pp. 64–65). In a reading that is primarily focused on the first of these but even so comes close to an overall understanding, he discovers "the fundamental conflict of the story, that of Life and Knowledge" (p. 241). To him, the Eden Narrative is "a story where the human party at first had less knowledge but free admission to the Tree of Life, and in the end attained more knowledge but was exiled from the garden" (pp. 241–42). It is a story about the impossibility of having both: knowledge *and* life. Basically, the text presents itself as "a narrative formulation of the need to keep and guard Wisdom and Torah" (p. 474).

An interpretation that increasingly attracts attention is the Eden Narrative as a story about human maturation.[12] In her semiotic analysis, Ellen van Wolde argues that this is in fact the central thematic aspect of the story.[13] She sees Gen 2:24 (the man leaving his father and mother) as presenting "man's process of development in a nutshell" (p. 217). Van Wolde takes the four narrative episodes as referring to the subsequent stages of "before birth" (2:4b–6), "childhood" (2:7–25), "adolescence" (3:1–7), and "maturity" (3:8–24, p. 218). The tree is the tree of the knowledge of good and evil. The same type of knowledge is mentioned in connection with children in Deut 1:39, "your children, who this day have no knowledge of good or evil" (rsv), as van Wolde notes (p. 218). She concludes: "[T]he reader gives the (iconic) qualities and possibilities of the text their maximum due when he arranges the text from the perspective of 'the growth towards maturity of man'" (p. 223).

The maturation exegesis is an understanding that has won sympathy among feminist theologians. Lyn M. Bechtel develops this interpretation in two studies.[14] A well-known feminist approach that moves in a different direction is the approach of Phyllis Trible.[15] What she offers is a close reading in the spirit of James Muilenburg. She

---

11. Stordalen 2000: 229–49, especially pp. 240–49, 457–71.
12. See, earlier, Gunkel 1910: 18.
13. See van Wolde 1989: 216–29.
14. Bechtel 1993 and 1995. Note that Bechtel worked out her interpretation unaware and independent of van Wolde; see Bechtel 1993: 83 n. 1. Stordalen also views maturation as an important aspect of the text (Stordalen 2000: 242–49).
15. See Trible 1985: chap. 4, pp. 72–143.

notes that "Life and Death is the subject of the narrative" (p. 74). Her overall interpretation is, as her chapter heading indicates, "a love story gone awry." Her subheads speak of "eros created" (2:4b–7, p. 75), "the development of eros" (2:7–24, p. 79), "eros contaminated" (2:25–3:7, p. 105), and "the disintegration of eros" (3:8–24, p. 115).

This brief survey shows one thing clearly: there is no consensus on what the Eden Narrative is all about—on its actual theme.

1.2. One or Two Trees?
A Survey of Opinions

The Eden Narrative in Genesis 2–3, in the form that we now have it, is a story about divine commandment, human disobedience, and the consequences of insurrection. This span of events has as its focal point the two special trees in the garden of Eden, which are the most prominent symbols of the narrative.

These two trees are connected with certain problems that have been solved in a number of different ways. The discussion about whether there are two trees or only one is not a discussion about a minor detail.[16] On the contrary, the trees stand for life (immortality) and knowledge (wisdom), two divine prerogatives. Is there an organic relation between wisdom and immortality, or are these two motifs unconnected? Indeed, the whole sense of the narrative depends on what we decide about the two special trees in the garden of Eden.[17] It should be noted that I retain the conventional translation "good and evil," though the real sense may actually be "good and bad."[18] A survey of the references to the trees looks as follows:

2:9 two trees: <u>the tree of life</u> *in the midst of the garden* and the tree of the knowledge of good and evil

2:17 one tree forbidden: the tree of the knowledge of good and evil

3:3 one tree forbidden: the tree *in the midst of the garden* (which is a tree that opens the eyes and gives knowledge of good and evil, v. 5)

3:6 the tree

3:11 the tree (which was forbidden)

---

16. As was pointed out by Humbert 1940: 21.
17. "Tout le sense du mythe en dépend" (Humbert 1940: 21).
18. See below, §3.2.4 (p. 63).

3:17   the tree (which was forbidden)
3:22   two trees:
    a.   implicit reference to the tree of the knowledge of good
       and evil
    b.   explicit reference to <u>the tree of life</u>, from which one may
       not eat
3:24   <u>the tree of life</u>

Four irregularities leap to the eye from this listing:

- The tree of life only appears in two places, at the beginning and at the end of the story. The rest of the narrative deals with one tree only, the tree of the knowledge of good and evil.
- The single tree in the "corpus" of the text is unnamed except in 2:17.
- The expression "in the midst of the garden" appears twice: the first time as the place of the tree of life (2:9) and the second time as the place of the forbidden tree (3:3), which the continuation identifies as the tree that gives knowledge. This striking variation needs an explanation. What are the implications of the woman's "mistake"?
- Only one of the trees is forbidden to the humans, the tree of knowledge. The prohibition does not pertain to the tree of life. Only at the end, after the eating of the forbidden tree, is the way to the tree of life barred. The text offers no explicit explanation for this difference between the trees. Why was the tree of life not forbidden from the beginning?

One is tempted to agree with Claus Westermann when he notes that the two special trees produced not only appetizing fruit but also a vast assortment of literature.[19] Many scholars from the last century seem to agree that, while the tree of life holds a place at the center of the garden, it somehow stands at the margin of the narrative.[20] Ellen van Wolde notes a corresponding tendency in the way that scholars deal with the two trees. Surveying the research, she points out that "the trees are almost always dealt with separately and not related to each other" and that "attention is almost exclusively directed to the tree of knowledge of good and evil, whereas the tree of life is paid hardly any attention."[21]

---

19. Westermann 1984: 211, German original 1976: 288.
20. As was noted by Winter 1986: 57.
21. Van Wolde 1994: 32.

The one-tree trend in critical research started with Karl Budde in 1883. Budde proposed a theory according to which the tree of life was a secondary amendment to a story that originally only contained one. The reference to both trees in the Masoretic Text of 2:9 is a main point in his argument. The wording is strange, he notes, because the locative expression "in the midst of the garden" is placed between the two, making the tree of knowledge a latecomer, not necessarily sharing the privileged position.[22] He also aptly points out that in 3:3 the tree in the middle of the garden is the tree of knowledge and not the tree of life.[23] Budde prunes the text and emends 2:9 to read: "Out of the ground the LORD God made to grow every tree that is pleasant for the sight and good for food. And in the midst of the garden the tree of the knowledge of good and evil."[24] Budde thus deletes the tree of life from the narrative. He also eliminates the other two occurrences of the tree of life—those at the end of the text (3:22–24).[25] There is only one tree in Budde's Eden Narrative, the tree of the knowledge of good and evil.

Budde's theory fared quite well in twentieth-century research. Gunkel took it up in his influential commentary on Genesis, finding only one tree in his "main source" (JE) but two trees in a later stratum.[26]

Westermann, in his magnum opus, expressly placed himself in the wake of Budde and magisterially declared:

> Does it [the narrative] deal with one tree or with two? A proper answer can be given only by looking at the narrative as a whole; it is concerned with one tree only. K. Budde has demonstrated this convincingly . . . and nothing has been advanced yet to refute him. He has shown that there is only one tree in the body of the narrative, 3:2, 3, 5, 11, 12, and that it is qualified in two ways—the tree in the middle of the garden, 3:3, and the forbidden tree: 3:11.[27]

This one, unnamed tree receives a name when the tree of life is incorporated; the unnamed tree now becomes the tree of knowledge (2:9; 17).[28]

In his monograph on the Eden Narrative (1985), Howard N. Wallace devotes an entire chapter to the two trees and makes a number of

---

22. Budde 1883: 51.
23. Budde 1883: 48.
24. Budde 1883: 58.
25. Budde 1883: 54–65. Budde deletes vv. 22 and 24 and has the text end with 6:3 (which he removes from its present location) followed by 3:23.
26. Gunkel 1910: 16 and 26.
27. Westermann 1984: 212, German original 1976: 289.
28. Westermann 1984: 223, German original 1976: 303.

observations. He notes from the outset that, "[w]hile two trees are mentioned in the present form of the narrative, it is clear that only one tree is essential for its development." Wallace then goes on to treat them separately. His discussion of the tree of knowledge leads him to conclude that the main concern of the narrative is the penetration of the divine realm by the couple.[29]

Christoph Dohmen, in his monograph on creation and death in Genesis 2–3, proceeds along the same path, endorsing Budde's main point about there only being one original tree.[30] To Dohmen, the original "Yahwist" story, which he dates to the time of Solomon, contained one tree only, the fruit of which bestowed the gift of opened eyes. A reworking from the time of Manasseh by the "Elohist" brought the two trees to the fore. The original, unnamed tree is now denoted the tree of knowledge.[31]

David Carr, in his turn, finds a three-step development: first an early creation account, then a creation-and-fall story with the tree of knowledge, and finally a layer that adds the tree of life.[32]

The venerable tradition from Budde is amply represented even in the most recent research.[33] Ever since Paul Humbert's 1940 monograph, however, a small group of scholars have defended the opposite position: that both trees have meaningful functions in the story and that this may be the case even if the process of growth behind the present story is a complicated and intriguing one.

Humbert's contribution (1940) is a major monograph on the Eden Narrative. Humbert did not feel convinced by the arguments for traditional source criticism in the Eden story. His perusal of the suggestions for doublets in Genesis 2–3 led to the conclusion that only a few are uncontestable: 2:8 and 2:9 are doublets, as are 2:8 and 2:15; indeed, the whole passage of 2:10–14 (the paradise rivers) should be considered a learned gloss (1940: 46–47). The text as we now have it combines the motifs of two originally independent myths: a myth of creation and a paradise myth (pp. 48–81). Budde's emendation in 2:9 should be accepted. This verse did not originally contain a reference to the tree of life (pp. 21–22). Nevertheless, both trees have a firm place

29. Wallace 1985: 101–41, esp. pp. 102 and 130. Quotation from p. 102.

30. Dohmen 1996: 208–14 (original pub., 1988).

31. Dohmen 1996: 208–14; see also 154–74.

32. Carr 1993: esp. p. 583. Pfeiffer (2001: 4–7) also assumes a single tree and connects this with the tradition of the world tree.

33. One could mention Witte 1998: 81; Rottzoll 1997–1998, esp. 1998: 1, 14; and Pfeiffer 2000: 491.

in the story. On the presuppositions of the narrative, the tree of life was there from the beginning *in the garden*. But it does not show up *in the text* until its very end (3:22–24, p. 128); that is to say, its existence was hidden until then. Humbert's thesis of the hidden tree of life ("l'arbre caché de la vie") is an original suggestion but seems not to have commended itself to subsequent researchers.[34] Humbert also offers a perceptive discussion of life and death in Genesis 2–3, listing various interpretational options for the tree of life.[35]

After Humbert, other scholars argued for the unity of the text and found textual "surgery" of the literary-critical type unwarranted, but Humbert played a surprisingly marginal role in the debate.

Odil Hannes Steck, in his monograph of 1970, defended the thesis that the text is a unified whole (p. 27) and suggested a tradition-historical development behind it. He found an older *Paradiesgeschichte* (Paradise story), with only one tree, which grew into the *Paradies-erzählung* (Paradise Narrative) of the Yahwist as we now have it, a narrative with two trees and the passage with the sentencing of the serpent, woman, and man.[36] Genesis 2–3 is an etiological narrative, to be read "from its end"—in other words, it should be understood from its etiological perspective.[37]

In his 1993 monograph, James Barr maintains that the tree of life has an essential place in the text. Barr underlines his readiness to imagine that there was an original story about just one tree, a nameless tree that then reappears as the tree of knowledge. His object of study is, however, the story as we have it; he takes a "canonical" approach. The final story testifies to a connection between life and wisdom that is also found in Proverbs (3:18). At this stage, the story tells "how human immortality was almost gained, but in fact was lost."[38]

In his major monograph on the motif of Eden in the whole Hebrew Bible, *Echoes of Eden* (2000), Terje Stordalen also provides a thorough treatment of all relevant aspects of Genesis 2–3 (pp. 185–301). This scholar goes into close combat with the defendants of the one-tree position, especially Budde and Westermann.[39] In recent literature, he notes a trend toward the final text—a position that has also become

---

34. Humbert 1940: 21–28, esp. pp. 21–22, 26, 129.
35. Humbert 1940: 117–52, esp. pp. 126–27.
36. Steck 1970: 41–58, esp. pp. 45–56.
37. Steck 1970: 66–73: "von hinten her will sie auch gelesen sein" (p. 68).
38. Barr 1993: 57–61; quotation from p. 4.
39. Stordalen 2000: 187–97.

his own.[40] Stordalen understands the text as a narrative about the two trees and suggests a fundamental conflict between life and knowledge. In the story, the human party at first had less knowledge but free admission to the tree of life but in the end attained more knowledge but was exiled from the garden with the tree of life.[41]

Konrad Schmid finds a unified and well-structured narrative, defying literary-critical "surgery." Only one tree was forbidden; the humans made the mistake of not taking the opportunity to eat from the tree of life, because they were more intent on attaining knowledge.[42]

Surveying the attempts chosen as representative, above, we can easily see that scholars working along literary-critical lines of the traditional, continental type usually find the tree of knowledge to be the original tree, the tree of life being a later development. Scholars working along tradition-historical lines sometimes find a similar development, albeit explained in terms of traditions or motifs.

A reverse perspective—first the tree of life and then also the tree of knowledge—has only been adopted by a few exegetes. The tree of life is thus seen as the original tree by Eduard Nielsen.[43] Jutta Krispenz, studying the Eden Narrative in light of the Egyptian tree goddess Nut, concludes that the tree of life is the basic motif of the tradition, while the tree of knowledge is a later blueprint of this motif.[44]

When I proceed to my narratological analysis, I shall have the following questions in mind, garnered from a first perusal of the text and from the preceding survey of major scholarly contributions. These questions are not narratological questions per se, but I hope to be able to answer them after a narratological analysis of Genesis 2–3:

1. Why are there two trees but only one prohibition? Notably, why is the tree of life not forbidden?
2. Why does the body of the narrative only deal with the tree of knowledge?
3. What are the implications of the "mistake" of the woman when she refers to the tree of knowledge as being "in the midst of the garden"?

---

40. Stordalen 2000: 197–98.
41. Stordalen 2000: 215–49, esp. pp. 240–49, and note pp. 241–42.
42. Schmid 2002: esp. p. 32.
43. Nielsen 1972: 13–22, esp. pp. 20–22.
44. Krispenz 2004: esp. p. 314. "Der Lebensbaum ist in alledem das tragende und von der Tradition getragene Motiv. . . . Der zweite Baum, der Erkenntnisbaum, ist dem Lebensbaum nachgeformt, ohne das [*sic*] er darum auf der literarischen Ebene von Gen. iif. sekundär genannt werden müsste."

It is my contention that only if these questions must be left un-answered may we proceed to literary "surgery" in the text and as-sume a combination of sources. I am speaking of the textual level here; that there might be a combination of various traditions is a different matter.

It is increasingly common in current scholarship to date the Eden Narrative to late postexilic times, even to the Persian period. I am con-vinced that this dating is correct and will not repeat the observations that have been made and that converge to support this conclusion.[45]

---

45. For the insight that the text presupposes Genesis 1, see especially Otto 1996. See also Sawyer 1992: 64–66; Stordalen 1992; 2000: 206–13. See also below, §7.3 (p. 134).

Chapter 2

A Narratological Analysis of the Eden Narrative

The narratological properties of the Eden Narrative have already been subjected to a number of analyses, resulting in valuable insights.[1] There is, however, room for further investigation of this important aspect of the narrative.

Regardless of the historical developments that produced the text as we now have it, it is this final product that must be the starting point of our analysis. Until a convincing point against this presupposition has been presented, the final text must be regarded as a unified whole.

First, some basic distinctions. The distinction between *story* and *discourse* seems to be indispensable to narratological studies. The term *story* designates "the narrated events, abstracted from their disposition in the text and reconstructed in their chronological order, together with the participants in these events."[2] While *story* is the succession of events, *discourse* is the discursive presentation of them.[3] With Genette, one may say that discourse is the "signifier" and story the "signified."[4]

Second, a comment on the tripartition so well known from modern narratological studies: author (actual writer), implied author ("the image of the author projected by the text itself as the creator of its art"[5]), and narrator. As Meir Sternberg points out, such a tripartition is not entirely unproblematic when dealing with biblical material; here the implied author and the narrator tend to merge into each other. For this reason, I will go along with Sternberg, who employs the more univocal term *narrator* "to refer to the master of the tale in general."[6]

---

1. For previous analyses of the narratological properties of the text, see especially Trible 1985: 72–143; Bal 1985: 31–42; White 1991: 115–45; Walsh 1994; and Stordalen 2000: 214–49.

2. Rimmon-Kenan 2005: 3.

3. Rimmon-Kenan 2005: 3; and Culler 1992: 169–70.

4. Genette 1980: 27.

5. Sternberg 1987: 74. On the notion of "the implied author," see Booth 1991: 70–77.

6. Sternberg 1987: 74–75. See also Rimmon-Kenan 2005: 87–90.

The Eden Narrative is a text characterized by simplicity.[7] There are a few short scenes, four major characters, a single location, and one time. There is a straight plot movement with a definite turning point. The first half of the text (2:4–24) is narrative without dialogue, marked by linear movement; the second (2:25–3:24) is marked by dialogue and uses more of a concentric arrangement.

2.1. Unifying Elements

I shall not devote much space to the delimitation of the text. It is obvious that it ends with 3:24. Modern scholars also agree that it begins somewhere after the conclusion of the Priestly account of creation in Genesis 1. In my opinion it is now clear, from the studies of Terje Stordalen and Eckart Otto, that Gen 2:4 forms a bridge between this account of the creation and the Eden Narrative.[8] The text to be studied thus comprises 2:5–3:24.

Before embarking on the narratological analysis proper, I will direct the reader's attention to some unifying elements in the texts. There are four recurrent motifs that form what amounts to inclusios, or literary framing devices that function to delineate and hold the text together.

1. The expression "there was no one to till the ground," found at the beginning of the text (2:5), strikes a significant note. The man was put in the garden of Eden "to till it and keep it" (2:15). When he was evicted from Eden, he had to "till the ground from which he was taken" (3:23). Occurring at the very beginning and end of the text, this motif forms an inclusio.

2. The formation of the human being from the dust of the ground is another motif that constitutes an inclusio. It is found at the very beginning of the narrative (2:7) and rounds off the section in the just-quoted 3:23 (and see 2:19 regarding the creation of the animals).

---

7. As was pointed out by Trible 1985: 72.

8. Stordalen 1992; and Otto 1996: 183–92. Stordalen argues as follows: Gen 2:4 is a literary unity; we should not treat 4a with what precedes (Genesis 1) and 4b with what follows (Genesis 2). The *toledot* formula always serves as the introduction to the following section; it is always followed by a genitive of the progenitor (never of the progeny). Thus it here refers to the product of heaven and earth, not to the story of the genesis of the two. The combination of the *toledot* formula and a *běyôm*-clause is found not only in Gen 2:4 but also in Gen 5:1 and Num 3:1. Moreover, the verse forms a chiasmus. Gen 2:4 thus presupposes Gen 1:1–2:3 and serves as a bridge between it and the Eden Narrative.

3. The notions *life* and *life-giving* have similar functions in the text. Having been formed from the dust and having received the breath of life into his nostrils, the man "became a living being" (2:7). At the end of the text, we find the woman being given the name Eve, "because she was the mother of all living" (3:20). The notion of life recurs in 3:22: eating from the tree of life implies that one will "live forever."

4. We should not miss what is perhaps the most important motif to connect the beginning and end of the text, namely, the tree of life (2:9; 3:22, 24).

Another noteworthy factor here is the divine designation used in the Eden Narrative: Yhwh Elohim (24 times). This designation occurs throughout, except for the conversation between the serpent and the woman, where we find only Elohim, used by the serpent and the woman alike (3:1b–7).[9] The double designation seems to indicate that the God of the Eden author is both Israel's covenant partner (Yhwh) and the God of all creation (Elohim).

Against the background of these observations, it becomes likely that the final part (3:20–24), which has so often been deemed secondary, also has a firm place in our narrative. Indeed, *prima facie* Genesis 2–3 stands out as a narrative that forms a meaningful whole. The ensuing analysis will determine whether this impression holds true or not.

2.2. *Time and Location*

Time and location in the Eden Narrative may be dealt with very briefly. Terje Stordalen provides an informative discussion of these aspects of the narrative.[10] The events take place in the very distant past, *in illo tempore*. The main events occur immediately after the creation of man and woman. Stordalen has made a good case for the conclusion that this aspect of "primevalness" is emphasized by use of the word *miqqedem* (2:8), which he takes to have a temporal sense, "in the beginning, in the old days," and not a locative sense, "in the east."[11] However, it is impossible to be entirely certain about this issue.

The location is the garden of Eden. What kind of reality should be ascribed to the garden in the narrative? Stordalen notes that "comparable

---

9. On this designation, see L'Hour 1974: esp. pp. 552–56. Note also Wenham 1987: 57; and Stordalen 2000: 287 and 457–58.

10. Stordalen 2000: 250–301.

11. Stordalen 2000: 261–70, esp. pp. 268–70. For this temporal sense, see, for instance, Deut 33:15, 27; Mic 5:1; Hab 1:12; Ps 68:34.

literature locates comparable gardens in cosmic border regions."[12] He points to the etymology of the name *Eden*, which provides connotations of 'luxuriance', 'bliss'.[13] Eden is an "emblem" of human richness and happiness.[14] After a 50-page discussion of all relevant aspects, Stordalen is able to conclude: "On the one hand, we are caused to construe the Eden Garden as a cosmic 'world apart', whose events are not conceivable in the ordinary realm. On the other hand, precisely its 'otherness' accounts for its symbolical relation to the everyday world."[15]

God "took the man and put him in the garden of Eden to till it and keep it" (2:15). It is tempting to understand Eden as "the private garden of God," as it seems to be in some other passages (Ezek 28:13, Isa 51:3), and to follow Edward L. Greenstein, who sees man's work in the garden as menial labor in the service of the deity.[16] There may well be, as Greenstein maintains, a remnant of the ancient Near Eastern notion of humanity created to take over the work of the gods; but if so, this connection is on the subliminal level, as Greenstein himself notes. What we have on the surface level in Genesis 2 is a garden planted for the maintenance of humans, and man's work here has the primary function of providing food.[17]

A sacred mountain, vegetation, and water together form a stock motif in ancient Near Eastern iconography. We find it in the famous wall relief in the palace of Assurbanipal.[18] As Manfried Dietrich has discussed in a thorough study, the motifs of the garden in Genesis 2–3 are depicted against a backdrop provided by the Mesopotamian temple garden.[19]

The passage on the rivers of paradise (2:10–14) has sometimes been taken to refer to a definite area in the east. Manfried Dietrich suggests

---

12. Stordalen 2000: 286.

13. See Millard 1984; Stordalen 2000: 257–61.

14. Stordalen 2000: 298.

15. Stordalen 2000: 301. See also Westermann 1976: 294; English trans. 1984: 215–16.

16. Greenstein (2002: 234), who suggests some interesting parallels to the creation of humanity in the service of the gods in Semitic literature (notably Atrahasis; pp. 219–39).

17. See Westermann 1976: 283–84, English trans. 1984: 208.

18. See Keel 1978: fig. 202, discussion pp. 149–51; Börker-Klähn 1982: no. 228, plates volume p. 228, text volume p. 217. An excellent discussion of the configuration mountain–vegetation–water is provided by Metzger 1983b.

19. For details, see Dietrich 2001.

southern Mesopotamia and refers to the traditions and iconography of Enki/Ea of Eridu, an important cultic center in the south, while John Day refers to Armenia instead.[20] The observations made by Stordalen make me less inclined to assume a real-world geography here. The rivers streaming forth in Genesis 2 seem to me to reflect the notion found in the tradition behind the Eden Narrative about Eden as situated on a mountain (Ezek 28:14, 16). Because this may be "the mount of the assembly" (compare Isa 14:13)—El's dwelling place—it is not impossible that the garden of Eden has some connection to the idea of the dwelling place of El.[21]

When all is said and done, the Eden geography may well combine various backgrounds in which, ultimately, connotations of both Enki/Ea and El are combined. In light of what has been said above, however, what is important for us is that we are not justified in placing the events of Gen 2:10–14 in a real-world geographical context.[22]

2.3. Scenes and Plot

1. Scenes

What are the criteria to be used in defining the scenes of a narrative? Basically, we may focus on change: scenes are small pieces of a narrative that are distinguished from one another on the basis of a change of person, place, or action.[23]

There is a fair amount of agreement about how the scenes in the Eden Narrative should be delineated. Terje Stordalen suggests a seven-scene arrangement, as do Jerome T. Walsh and Gordon Wenham.[24] Taking 2:4 as a superscript or redactional bridge and 3:20–21 as a piece of interplay, Stordalen suggests the delineation shown in the chart on p. 17. The main difference between Stordalen and the scholars mentioned above is that, while Stordalen takes 2:25–3:7 as a single scene, the others divide this section into two scenes (3:1–5 and 3:6–8) and take the whole of 2:5–17 as a single scene. It is worth noticing that Phyllis Trible also considers 2:25–3:7 to be a single scene.[25] Moreover,

---

20. Dietrich 2001: 302–20; Day 2000: 29–31.

21. Day 2000: 29–34. For a connection between first man and the divine assembly, see Job 15:7–8.

22. On this subject, I agree with Westermann (1976: 294; English trans. 1984: 215–16) and Stordalen (2000: 250–301).

23. Thus, e.g., Gunkel 1910: xxxiv.

24. Stordalen 2000: 218–20; Walsh 1994; and Wenham 1987: 50–51.

25. This scene forms the middle section in her three-part arrangement (which also comprises 2:7–24 and 3:8–24). See Trible 1985: 79–143.

1. Yʜwʜ God creates the first human being (2:5–7).
2. Yʜwʜ God plants the garden and locates the human being there (2:8–17).
3. Yʜwʜ God creates animals and the woman (2:18–24).
4. *The naked couple eat and gain insight (2:25–3:7).*
5. Yʜwʜ God conducts a hearing (3:8–13).
6. Yʜwʜ God issues sentences (3:14–19).
7. Yʜwʜ God expels the couple from the garden and the Tree of Life (3:22–24).

we find that this scene, which contains the climax of the plot, stands beautifully as the central piece of the whole scenic arrangement if we follow Stordalen.[26]

A few more reflections are in order. The first has to do with the way in which Stordalen and others interpret 3:8–13 (God conducts a hearing) and 3:14–19 (God issues sentences) as two different scenes. One might consider reading this as a single scene. Discourse time and story time are equal throughout 3:8–19. The place is one and the same, and the same persons appear. However, a change of action is observable: first, God conducts a hearing; then he issues a sentence. On the basis of the change of action, I prefer Stordalen's understanding: we have two different scenes here.

The second point has to do with the phenomenon of exposition. Stordalen does not identify any exposition in Genesis 2–3, though exposition is a common phenomenon in biblical narrative.[27]

By *exposition*, one generally means "the presentation of *indispensable* pieces of information about the state of affairs that *precedes* the beginning of action itself."[28] There are two different ways of bringing expositional material to the reader's attention. Either the material may

---

26. Trible (1985: 106–7) finds a contrived inclusio arrangement in 2:25–3:7, but her B and B′ do not correspond and neither do her C and C′. Auffret (1982: 23–68) has a five-scene arrangement, as follows: Gen 2:4b–17, 2:18–25, 3:1–13, 3:14–21, and 3:22–24.

27. See Bar-Efrat 1989: 111–21. A thorough study of various types of distribution of expositional material in fiction is found in Sternberg (1978: 41–128).

28. Ska 1990: 21, emphasis in the original. Similarly, to Sternberg (1978: 20–33), the exposition is what goes before the first scene. In the first scene, the action proper takes its starting point.

be offered at the beginning, or it may be revealed gradually in the course of the narrative.[29]

It is not easy to decide about expositional material in Genesis 2. Westermann seems inclined to take the whole of 2:5–24 as an exposition of the narrative in Genesis 3.[30] However, this would be going a bit too far. If we were to look for exposition in the beginning, then 2:5–7 might make sense. It is clear that in this section we are being informed about the state of affairs at the beginning: there are no plants in the field, no herbs, no rain, and no one to till the ground. The problem with taking vv. 5–7 as the exposition is, however, that we also find action here: God creates man. I therefore agree with Stordalen's tacit assumption that we do not find any separate exposition in Genesis 2–3.

2. *"Plot Segments"*

The term *plot* I understand, with Prince, as referring to "[t]he main incidents of a narrative; the outline of situations and events (thought of as distinct from the characters involved in them or the themes illustrated by them)."[31] An intriguing issue is the relationship between plot and story. Many would agree that, irrespective of the sequence of the discourse, plot is the arrangement of the events in temporal order.[32] Others would go along with Chatman, who says: "The events in a story are turned into a plot by its discourse, the modus of presentation."[33] This amounts to speaking of plot as "story-as-discoursed." In the present context, there is no need to arrive at a definite understanding of the relation between plot, story, and discourse.

In Genesis 2–3, the author uses various kinds of plot signals. He exploits the technique of stating a problem to be solved or a gap to be filled. Thus 2:5 refers to the lack of vegetation and of a human being to till the earth, and 2:18 refers to the lack of a companion for the human. The prohibition in 2:17 signals a divine trial of the first humans, arousing the reader's curiosity about the outcome.

In his penetrating study, Stordalen (2000) works on the basis of these plot signals, uncovering five "plot segments." (We should note that these are not identical with sections of the text; they are intertwined.) Stordalen finds four "announced plot segments" and one ad-

---

29. See Bar-Efrat 1989: 111–21.
30. Westermann 1976: 263, English trans. 1984: 192.
31. Prince 2003: 73. On plot, note the article by Dannenberg (2005), with bibliography; Rimmon-Kenan 2005: 6–28.
32. See, for instance, Bar-Efrat 1989: 93.
33. Chatman 1980: 43.

ditional plot segment as constituting the "emerging conflict." His "plot segments" are as follows:[34]

---

1. A Human Tiller to the World (found especially in 2:5–7, and also in 2:8–15 and 3:17–19)
2. A Counterpart for the Human Being (2:18–24)
3. Prohibition Test (2:16–17; 3:1–6; 3:14–19)
4. Human Knowledge (2:25–3:7; 3:8–13; 3:21; 3:22a)
5. Emerging Conflict: Life vs. Knowledge (2:8–16, 23–24 etc.)

The "emerging conflict" means: "Life but not Life and Knowledge."[35] This fifth plot segment is the only one that is actually related to all scenes in the story (p. 232).

This fact has certain implications for Stordalen's overall understanding of the text. He distinguishes between what he calls "story narration" and "story significance" (pp. 63–67). While Stordalen avoids committing himself with regard to the theme of the text, his definition of the emerging conflict as the fundamental aspect of the plot is important to his understanding of the meaning of the text.[36]

Stordalen thus assumes a fundamental conflict in the story, a conflict between "Life" and "Knowledge." In the narrative, "the human party at first had less knowledge but free admission to the Tree of Life, and in the end attained more knowledge but was exiled from the garden" (pp. 241–42). Contrasting Life and Knowledge in this way, Stordalen has to assume that Life in the sense of immortality was at hand from the beginning. The question is whether this overall understanding carries conviction.

There are two problems with the conclusion that the text presents a fundamental conflict between Life and Knowledge. One problem grows out of the fact that there are good reasons for a different understanding of the overall plot of the narrative, to which I shall turn in a moment. The other has to do with Stordalen's analysis of Gen 3:22.

In order to sustain his interpretation, Stordalen feels obliged to assume a rather special understanding of this verse. The Hebrew runs:

---

34. Stordalen 2000: 221–33 and 476.
35. Stordalen 2000: 229–33 and 240–49.
36. See Stordalen 2000: 465–74, esp. pp. 466 and 473. Stordalen expresses himself very cautiously.

וְעַתָּה | פֶּן־יִשְׁלַח יָדוֹ
וְלָקַח גַּם מֵעֵץ הַחַיִּים וְאָכַל וָחַי לְעֹלָם:

wěʿattâ pen-yišlaḥ yādô
wělāqaḥ gam mēʿēṣ haḥayyîm wěʾākal wāḥay lěʿōlām.

The anacoluthic construction used here is usually understood as meaning:

> and now, lest he put forth his hand and take *also* of the tree of life, and eat, and live for ever— (RSV; my emphasis)

Stordalen suggests the following translation:

> lest he *keep stretching out* his hand, and take *even* from the Tree of Life, and eat, and live forever. (p. 230; my emphasis)

The conjunction *pen* is taken to mean "lest [someone continue to do what they are already doing]."[37] Here Stordalen polemicizes against James Barr, who argued that 3:22b "must mean that the fruit of the tree of life had not been previously eaten."[38] Though Stordalen's interpretation has a long pedigree (as he points out, it was suggested by Obbink in 1928),[39] this interpretation has been refuted by Humbert. Humbert's main point is that the word *gam* 'also' must imply that they had not eaten of the tree of life before.[40] James Barr agrees with this, adding that the phrase "put out his hand and do something" is an inchoative expression and cannot easily mean "to continue to do what he has been doing all along." The phrase that states the reason for the expulsion thus "excludes the idea that they had been eating of the tree of life from the beginning."[41] In other words, the traditional understanding of the crucial verse is still valid.

Stordalen's plot-segment analysis builds on a number of accurate observations and is valuable in several respects. As one can see, however, I find it difficult to follow him in every regard. I am thus skeptical

---

37. Stordalen 2000: 231.

38. Barr 1993: 58.

39. Obbink 1928: 106. Obbink refers to Exod 1:9–10 and 1 Sam 13:19 in support of this. Stordalen adds 2 Sam 12:27–28.

40. Humbert 1940: 131–33. Was it this rejoinder to Obbink that gave Stordalen second thoughts and led him to say that "whether or not they have by 3:22 eaten from the Tree of Life is impossible to detect. At any rate, the new situation to be avoided is *not* the eating of the Tree of Life, but eating from the tree *after* having taken from the Tree of Knowledge" (p. 231, emphasis in the original)? Even so, his translation of 3:22 and his understanding of the fundamental conflict of the text fail to convince me.

41. Barr 1993: 58 and 135 n. 2.

of his idea of a fundamental conflict between life and wisdom. Besides, there is more to be said about the overall story line, the overall plot.

3. *The Overall Plot*

Peter Brooks, a comparative literature scholar, has pointed out that

> [n]arrative is one of the large categories or systems of understanding that we use in our negotiations with reality, specifically, in the case of narrative, with the problem of temporality: man's time-boundedness, his consciousness of existence within the limits of mortality. And plot is the principal ordering force of those meanings that we try to wrest from human temporality.[42]

To attain a proper grasp of the plot is thus of importance to the present enterprise. The ensuing analysis of the plot of the Eden Narrative will confirm a certain amount of traditional wisdom from previous scholarship; at the same time, it will outline and highlight certain important features that have been overlooked.

The fact that the body of the narrative focuses on the tree of knowledge should not cause us to overlook the fact that the tree of life is there too, right from the beginning, and that this tree reappears at the very end. Though seemingly disappearing from the scene, the tree of life has a very important function in the narrative.

Indeed, in this plot the two trees are suggestive of what is to follow.[43] The two trees represent divine prerogatives and stand for the chief divine qualities. One stands for Life, in the sense of immortality, the other for Knowledge. "Thus, the question is raised whether the Creator will allow the creature to attain equal status."[44]

Having created man from dust, as an "earth creature" (*ʾādām*), God prepares a garden and has a number of trees grow there, including two special trees. Though this is often blurred in translation, there is a particular type of stress on "both"–"and" in 2:9: "*both* the tree of life in the midst of the garden *and* the tree of the knowledge of good and evil."[45]

We note that the expression "in the midst of the garden" is directly linked to one of the trees only—namely, the tree of life. Does the position indicated apply only to this tree or to both of them? In the first monograph to be published on the phenomenon of "split

---

42. Brooks 1992: xi; see also p. 22.
43. White 1991: 119.
44. White 1991: 119.
45. Note the disjunctive function of the *zaqeph qaton*: וְעֵץ הַחַיִּים בְּתוֹךְ הַגָּן וְעֵץ הַדַּעַת טוֹב וָרָע.

coordination" in the Hebrew Bible, Andreas Michel devoted a whole
chapter to Gen 2:9, arguing that this verse is indeed an excellent example of this syntactic feature.[46] Two elements of the clause are separated by an intervening element. In the present case the two objects,
the tree of life and the tree of knowledge, are separated by a locative
expression ("in the midst"). In cases of this sort, the "inserted" element applies to both. The location indicated ("in the midst . . .")
therefore applies to both trees. Michel's arguments seem convincing.
His investigation demonstrates that what we have in Gen 2:9 is a phenomenon of the Hebrew language system and that literary "surgery,"
though possible, is by no means necessary. It thus transpires that the
woman does not make a formal "mistake" when she refers to the tree
of knowledge as being "in the midst of the garden" later in the text
(3:3). Michel's observation is important.

Another significant observation is that there are thus two trees but
only one prohibition:

> And the LORD God commanded the man,
> "You may freely eat of every tree of the garden;
> but of the tree of the knowledge of good and evil you shall not eat,
> for in the day that you eat of it you shall die." (Gen 2:16–17)

Thus the NRSV. This rendering calls for a few comments. The Hebrew
of the last line is worth noticing: *kî běyôm 'ăkolkā mimmennû môt
tāmût*. Two things should be noted here. First, the expression *běyôm*
'on the day that . . .' is not necessarily temporal. Here, and in some
other instances as well, it carries more of a conditional sense.[47] The
exact point of time for death is not the issue. Second, the present case
differs from the common Hophal constructions well known from le-
gal contexts in that here we have the verb in the Qal. In conditional
constructions, this refers to a threat of death, not to the formal proc-
lamation of a death sentence.[48]

This means that 2:17 is not to be understood in forensic terms as a
sentence to be executed on the very day of the eating of the forbid-

---

46. A. Michel 1997: 1–22. Michel's German term is *gespaltene Koordination*. The
type of syntactic feature used in Gen 2:9, with split direct objects, has many other
examples in the Hebrew Bible and is treated in a special chapter (pp. 171–306). A
case especially similar to Gen 2:9 is Exod 24:4: *wayyiben mizbēaḥ taḥat hāhār ûšětêm
'eśrēh maṣṣēbâ* 'He . . . built an altar at the foot of the mountain, and set up twelve
pillars'. Here, too, the location applies to both.

47. Thus Humbert 1940: 140, referring also to Exod 10:28; Num 30:6, 9, 13;
1 Kgs 2:37, 42; and Ruth 4:5. See also Illman 1979: 104–5.

48. Illman 1979: 104–5; on the Hophal formula, pp. 119–27.

den fruit. I suggest translating: "for *if* you eat of it you shall certainly die."[49]

With the prohibition of one of the two trees (2:17), God confronts man with a test, an important but surprisingly neglected feature of the text.[50] The Hebrew text of the Eden Narrative does not use the specific term for testing (Hebrew *nsh* in the Piel). One might therefore hesitate to speak of a test in the present text. The important thing, however, is not whether we have the precise terminology but whether the plot confronts us with what may be denoted as a test, and I believe this is precisely the case. God arranges an experiment with the first humans: he proclaims his divine commandment in the form of a prohibition, and then he waits to see whether the two humans will obey or not. In my next chapter, in which I discuss the theme of the narrative, I will dig deeper and adduce similar texts in the Hebrew Bible that contribute to putting this characteristic of a test in relief. Right here, I limit my perspective to the plot of the Eden Narrative.

In presenting a divine test for the first humans, the narrator creates suspense, and he does so in two different ways. First, the test entails the raising of suspense around the question "to eat or not to eat," which may be circumscribed as "to obey the divine commandment or not to obey." This suspense reaches its climax in 3:6, which records the act of disobedience just carried out: "and she ate . . . and he ate." The plot ascends to 3:6 and then turns to descend. The plot of the Eden Narrative nicely illustrates Gustav Freytag's well-known pyramid graph, used to describe the structure of a tragedy.[51]

Second, the reader understands that the outcome of the test may have certain consequences for man's access to the other tree, the tree of life, although this tree is not mentioned at all in what happens between 2:9 and 3:22.

---

49. I disagree with Moberly (1988: 4, 15) and Otto (1996: 181 n. 79) here, who both understand Gen 2:17 in the light of death sentences in the Hophal. Wenham (1987: 67) got it right.

50. The understanding of the Eden Narrative as dealing with a divine test does not seem to play any role in the history of exegesis. Begrich (1932: 114) makes an offhand remark, saying that there is a *Gehorsamsprobe*, a test of obedience. A "prohibition test" is used by Stordalen (2000: 226–27, 476–77) as one of his five "plot segments" but otherwise plays no role in his interpretation, which instead focuses on the surmised conflict between "Life" and "Knowledge" (pp. 229–33), on which see my discussion above (§2.3.2, p. 18). I have consulted some knowledgeable colleagues about the situation in the writings of the Church Fathers. No one has been able to find any references to a divine test taking place in Genesis 2–3.

51. Freytag 1894; see also Prince 2003: 36.

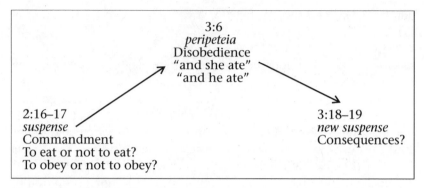

Fig. 1. The dramatic line of the plot moves upward, from the divine commandment in 2:16–17 to the peripeteia in the act of disobedience in 3:6, and then assumes a downward direction.

The central scene (2:25–3:7) contains a number of features worth noticing. As Phyllis Trible points out: "The serpent and the woman discuss theology. They talk about God" but "only using the general appellative God, they establish that distance which characterizes objectivity and invites disobedience."[52] The serpent, however, is hardly a respectable theologian. He distorts and misrepresents the divine commandment. A factor we should not overlook is the surprising "mistake" that the woman makes when she speaks of the divine commandment as having to do with "the tree in the midst of the garden" (3:3), although she is obviously referring to the tree of the knowledge of good and evil.[53] In 2:9, the tree "in the midst" is the tree of life. I shall revert to the "mistake" in 3:3 below, at the end of the present chapter.

Another important factor is that, in the words of the serpent, the act of eating of the forbidden fruit would make the man and the woman "like the gods" (3:5).[54] The expression hints at knowledge as a divine prerogative:

> for God knows that when you eat of it your eyes will be opened, and you will be like the gods, knowing good and evil. (3:5; my translation)

---

52. Trible 1985: 109.

53. It was noticed, however, by Schmid 2002: 31–32. Note my quotation marks around "mistake." See above about split coordination.

54. With Garr (2003: 17–92), I take the formulations here and in Gen 1:26, 6:1–4, and 11:7 to refer to a plurality in the divine world.

In 3:22, both knowledge and immortal life seem to be divine prerogatives:

> Then the LORD God said, "Behold, the man has become like one of us, knowing good and evil; and now, lest he put forth his hand and take also from the tree of life, and eat, and live forever"— (3:22; RSV)

These expressions in 3:5 and 3:22 point to the existence of a borderline, a sort of demarcation, between the divine world and the human—a border that God does not want the humans to pass. Passing this boundary is "transgression" in the deepest sense of the word. Though none of the Hebrew words for "sin" appears in the text, the notion is very much present.

After the peripeteia has been reached in 3:6, when the human couple eats of the forbidden fruit, there is new suspense in the text: What will be the consequences of their disobedience? To begin with, God conducts a hearing. The order of the interrogation is: the man—the woman—the serpent. This order is reversed in the pronouncement of sentences in vv. 14–19. We thus have an inclusio with the serpent in the middle:

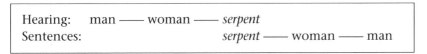

Fig. 2. The hearing and the sentences form an inclusio.

The phrase 'where are you?' (*ʾayyekkâ*) conforms with the rhetorical use of *ʾayyê* in "making an urgent appeal to someone's responsibility."[55] In the three sentencing pronouncements, we note the two curses, one on the serpent, the other on the earth. Man and woman are not under a divine curse; however, they are subject to penalties. In 3:19, we find an expression that is part of the very backbone of the plot, to the effect that man is made from dust and will revert to dust:

עַד שׁוּבְךָ אֶל־הָאֲדָמָה כִּי מִמֶּנָּה לֻקָּחְתָּ
כִּי־עָפָר אַתָּה וְאֶל־עָפָר תָּשׁוּב:

ʿad šûběkâ el-hāʾădāmâ kî mimmennâ luqāḥětā
kî-ʿāpār ʾattâ wěʾel-ʿāpār tāšûb

---

55. Burnett 2005: 217. Burnett mentions Gen 4:9, 1 Sam 26:16, Mal 2:17, and Job 35:10.

until you return to the ground, for out of it you were taken;
you are dust, and to dust you shall return.

The circle closes. Human disobedience did not make the humans "like
the gods." Man is made from dust and ends as dust.

A motif that has a central role in the plot and pervades the text as a
whole is the motif of the divine commandment. Once the trees were
planted, the LORD God 'commanded' (*wayṣaw*) the man: "You may
freely eat of every tree of the garden, but of the tree of the knowledge
of good and evil you shall not eat, for if you eat of it you shall certainly
die" (2:16–17, my trans.). The verb in question is from the same root
as *miṣwâ* 'commandment'. Later on, both 3:11 and 3:17 contain reverberations of this when God refers to "the tree about which I commanded you." Moreover, the whole central passage, 3:1–7, revolves
around the divine commandment, although neither the noun nor the
verb from the root *ṣwh* appears. I will return to this in §3.2.2 (p. 49).

In the overall plot, the resolution is reached in 3:20–24. If knowledge and life (immortality) stand out as divine prerogatives, the man
has already appropriated one by eating of the forbidden fruit. An anacoluthic *pen* clause, "lest he reach out his hand and take also from the
tree of life, and eat and live forever—," stresses that what must now be
precluded is for man also to lay hold of the other divine prerogative.
By eating of the forbidden fruit, the man has already acquired a position halfway between animals and deity.

By failing the divine test, the humans forfeited potential access to
the tree of life. This is what is expressed in the expulsion scene. The
way to the tree of life is barred and guarded by the cherubim with the
flaming sword. But God grants the human couple a "consolation
prize": "vicarious immortality,"[56] that is, procreation. Man names the
woman *ḥawwâ* 'Eve'. As Scott C. Layton argued, this is a *qaṭṭāl* formation from the root **ḥwy* 'to make alive'. This type of noun formation
in Hebrew (with a doubling of the middle radical and a long vowel in
the last syllable) is used for agent nouns denoting members of a pro-
fession or persons who habitually carry out an action, such as *ṭabbāḥ*
'butcher', *qaššāt* 'archer', or *gannāb* 'thief'.[57] The name in question,
ḥawwâ, has the meaning 'Life-Giver'.[58] Thus, at this point in the plot,
the woman receives a symbolic name, connected with procreation.

---

56. I found the expression in Gordis 1957: 130.
57. See *IBHS* §5.4a.
58. This interpretation was worked out independently by Layton (1997: esp.
pp. 30–32), but, as Layton pointed out (p. 31 n. 44), had already been suggested by

One other aspect of the plot should be mentioned, an aspect that is typical of a number of biblical narratives. The two main characters go through a drama of discovery, moving from ignorance to knowledge.[59] They do not end as unenlightened as they began. To Meir Sternberg, this passage from ignorance to knowledge that so often takes place in biblical narratives is "one of the great archetypes of literature," constituting "another Hebraic innovation, for which the Greeks got all the credit."[60]

Summary and Conclusions about the Plot

(a) My overall conclusion is that the plot is focused on a divine test of the first two humans: Will they obey the divine commandment or not? The divine test is the subject of the narrative and belongs to the world of fiction.

(b) The serpent and God agree on at least one specific point: eating from the tree of knowledge would make the humans "like the gods" (3:5, 22). The issue at stake here is ultimately whether the two humans will respect the line of demarcation between themselves and the divine world. Wisdom (knowledge) and immortality are divine prerogatives.

(c) Instead of listening to the voice of Yнwн, the man listens to the voice of the woman. The disobedience leads to a conflict between the first human couple and God. Other suggestions, such as a conflict between Life and Knowledge, seem less probable. When defining the conflict as being between man and God, we should not overlook the role of the serpent as instigator. This hints at a subliminal conflict between the serpent and God.

(d) The consequences of the first human couple's disobedience are fatal. The failure of the test means that the circle closes: the humans must return to the dust from which they were taken.

(e) Plots may be unified or episodic. What we have in the Eden Narrative is a unified plot, not an episodic one: all parts of the narrative

---

some previous scholars, to whom should be added Dijkstra and de Moor (1975: 188–89).

59. For other cases in the Hebrew Bible, see Sternberg (1987: 176–79), who uses the term *anagnorisis*. I hesitate to adopt his term as leading to the dénouement, because the original Greek term denotes 'recognition' as leading to the dénouement. Sternberg seems to be using the term in a more general sense about the move from ignorance to knowledge in a slightly more extended process. On *anagnorisis*, see Prince 2003: 82, under "Recognition."

60. Sternberg 1987: 176.

have a necessary function.[61] This also pertains to the scene of the creation of the woman: the narrator wants to tell how it came to pass that all humanity, man and woman alike, came under the spell of death. Both man and woman failed the test at the tree.

(f) The plot contains both suspense and surprise. The suspense grows first out of the prohibition and then out of the ensuing act of disobedience. The surprise occurs in the peak scene, when the woman "mistakes" the tree of knowledge for the tree "in the midst of the garden."

In his work *Reading for the Plot* (1992), Peter Brooks suggests that plot in general is a combination of the two codes that Roland Barthes termed the *proairetic code*, the code of actions; and the *hermeneutic code*, the code of enigmas and answers.[62] These two are the poles of narrative language. The preceding analysis demonstrates that this also holds true for the plot found in the Eden Narrative.

On the basis of our plot analysis, then, we may redescribe the scenes as follows, with the act of disobedience constituting the central element:

1. God creates man out of the dust of the earth (2:5–7).
2. God plants the garden, including two special trees, locates the human being there, and arranges a test. He prohibits eating from the tree of knowledge (2:8–17).
3. God creates animals and the woman (2:18–24).
4. *God arranged a test: the human couple disobey the prohibition (2:25–3:7) and thus fail the test.*
5. God conducts a hearing (3:8–13).
6. God issues sentences. Man must return to dust (3:14–19).
7. Man renames the woman: Eve. God expels the couple from the garden and the tree of life (3:20–24).

---

61. A possible exception would be the passage about the rivers of paradise (2:10–14), but White (1991: 120) suggests that it has the function of creating the distinction inside–outside, anticipating human life outside the garden. I am rather inclined to take the passage as a residue of the notion of the garden of Eden as a mountain (see Ezekiel 28, and see below, chap. 5).

62. Brooks (1992: 18), probably referring to Barthes 1970: section XI, pp. 25–27. The term "code" here denotes "the system of norms, rules, and constraints in terms of which the message signifies" (Prince 2003: 14). See also Kearns 2005a, with bibliography.

2.4. Characters

There are four characters in the Eden Narrative: the man, the woman, the serpent, and God. Direct characterization by means of describing physical appearance, character traits, or mental states is a rare phenomenon in biblical literature. Characterization is mostly indirect: the reader must draw his or her own conclusions on the basis of the acts and words of the characters.[63] This is what happens in the present case.[64]

As we saw, the plot is centered on the radical choice of the first human couple: to obey or not to obey the divine commandment. It is therefore natural to look closely at the two human protagonists when we comment on the characters in the Eden Narrative.

However, a few remarks about God and the serpent should be made first. Like the two humans, God also is a literary character who acts and reacts on the level of discourse in our narrative. Various metaphors are used to achieve the characterization of God in this text. Though none of the Hebrew words for 'clay' is used here (*ḥōmer* or *ṭîṭ*) but instead *'āpār* 'dust', I believe that the metaphor here is of God as the artisan who molds the human form by hand. The process is quite similar to creation descriptions in other Semitic literature.[65] Later on, in the creation of the woman, a verb for building is used (2:22).[66] Throughout chap. 2, God appears as the supreme provider who cares for his creation.

A particularly important role of his in the plot is closely related to the test: God as the law-maker and supreme judge. He is the one who gives his commandment, who expects obedience, and who acts upon disobedience.

Then there is the serpent. The serpent is "more crafty than any other wild animal that the LORD God had made" (3:1). Note that he is expressly said to be created by God. His notorious craftiness, however, stands in contrast to the divine prerogative connected with the tree of knowledge. Further, he is a liar who contorts the divine commandment

---

63. On characterization, see, e.g., Chatman 1980: 107–38; Berlin 1983: 23–42; Sternberg 1987: 321–64; Bar-Efrat 1989: 47–92; and Rimmon-Kenan 2005: 59–71.

64. For a previous study of the characters of Genesis 2–3, see Stordalen 2000: 233–40.

65. See Greenstein 2002: 220–29, esp. pp. 221–24. As Greenstein points out (p. 221), the metaphor is not necessarily a potter at his wheel (known from Jeremiah 18).

66. On Hebrew verbs for creation, see McCarthy 1967.

(3:1); besides, he is a creature completely disloyal to his Creator insofar as he suggests divine envy as the reason that God did not want the human couple to eat from the tree of knowledge (3:5). The function of the serpent is difficult to assess. Is his role in the plot merely as an agent functioning to bring about the change from obedience to disobedience?[67] Or is the choice of the serpent for the role of instigator somehow connected with the role of the serpent as the chaos dragon (Isa 27:1–3)? The latter is a possibility that we will come back to in §4.4 (p. 80).

Now let us turn to the two who play the leading parts: the man and the woman. The very naming of these two is an important factor here. In fiction, names are never neutral. Even after the recognition of the arbitrariness of signs in modern linguistics, we must accept that names may be given intentionally, carrying a specific semantic load. The symbolism of names is a well-known phenomenon in the Hebrew Bible, and the capacity of the Hebrew language to produce "root-meanings" is an often exploited resource.[68] The narrator in our text uses designations that are puns, not to be mistaken for etymologies in the proper linguistic sense. From the very beginning, the man is called ʾādām, a designation that connects him with ʾădāmâ 'earth'. The woman twice receives a designation from the man. First she is denoted ʾiššâ 'woman', as a means of characterizing her close association with the man, ʾîš. At the end of the narrative, the man gives her the name ḥawwâ (Eve), "because she was the mother of all living," an opaque name with the sense of 'Life-Giver' (see above, under Plot, p. 26).

It should be noted that the designation for the man is not a proper name, Adam with a capital A.[69] Throughout Genesis 2–3, ʾādām is an appellative. The three cases in which the MT does not have the definite article should be corrected to include it. Thus in 2:20b; 3:17, and 21 we should read wĕlāʾādām. The proper name Adam is found in genealogies: Gen 4:25; 5:1a, 3–5; 1 Chr 1:1; and Sir 49:16. For the sake of convenience, I shall use "Adam" in quotation marks in later chapters of this book.

---

67. On various types of characters, see Forster 1927: 93–106. Forster introduced the categories (a) round (full-fledged) characters and (b) flat characters (types). To this Berlin (1983: 23–24) added (c) the agent (mere functionary).

68. On the symbolism of names, see Barr 1969, and on root-meanings, see Sawyer 1967. On the question whether names can have a linguistic sense, see Mettinger 1988: 11–13 with bibliography. Note also Sternberg 1987: 328–41. On names as genre markers, see below, §4.1.1 (p. 66).

69. For the following, see Hess 1990: esp. p. 3.

These designations contribute to characterizing the man in his very nature as an earth creature and the woman in her basic roles as marriage partner and "mother of all living." I am not persuaded by Phyllis Trible that the first earth creature (2:7) should be not a male but a sexually undifferentiated being.[70] She also has a hard time convincing me that the woman should be less of an earth creature than the man because she is not said to have been created out of dust.[71] If man is dust and woman is created out of man, then she is dust as well. Humanity at large, represented by the man and the woman in the Eden Narrative, shares the human condition of transience and death.

Though created from dust, man has the breath of life (*nĕšāmâ*) breathed into his nostrils by God (2:7). This is what first turns the piece of clay from mere matter into a living being in the hands of God, "the breath of life." When it pleases God to take it back, the human returns to dust (Ps 104:29).[72]

Klaus Koch's interpretation of the breath of life proceeds in a specific direction. On the basis of comparative material and a semantic analysis of *nĕšāmâ*, he takes up the tradition from the Targums, arguing that the ability of humans to give names, and hence to *speak,* distinguishes them from the animals in 2:18–20. Speech requires breath, and the key word in Gen 2:7 may be associated with speech and spiritual ability.[73]

However we choose to understand Gen 2:7, it is clear that the wording does not imply eternal life, immortality. This is only to be obtained by eating from the tree of life. Failing the divine test, the humans forfeited this possibility and therefore must return to dust.

The human revolt against the divine commandment has effects along both the vertical and the horizontal axes. The rebellion entails the dissolution of the basic solidarity between the humans and God and also between man and woman. The man puts the blame on God, who gave him the woman, who misled him into disobeying (3:12). Even so, both he and the woman confess the act of disobedience. Furthermore, their rebellion affects relations between man and the rest of the creation: when God makes garments of skin for the man and his

---

70. Trible 1985: 80. For a critique of this idea, see Kawashima 2006: esp. pp. 46–53.

71. Trible 1985: 102.

72. The psalm has *rûaḥ,* but the concept is the same.

73. Koch 1989. Stordalen (2000: 235–36) follows Koch. Koch even speaks of *Sprachgeist.* See most recently Koch 2007: 332–38.

wife, we presuppose the killing of animals for the sake of humans (3:21). The consequences described in the divine sentencing contain a description of the hardships of human life: pain in childbearing, strenuous work, ultimate death. This progression may be illustrated in the following graph:

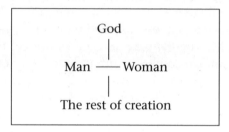

Fig. 3. The revolt and disobedience have effects on the three basic dimensions of human life: one's relation to God, one's relation to fellow human beings, and one's relation to the rest of creation.

2.5. Focalization (Point of View) and Voice

Two questions that may be considered in any piece of narrative fiction are: who sees? and who narrates? Early studies of "point of view" by scholars of literary theory tended to blur the distinction between these two related but different questions. Gérard Genette insisted that they be kept apart and suggested dealing with "who sees?" under the heading "focalization," and "who narrates?" under the heading "voice."[74]

Let us first turn to focalization or point of view.[75] This entails a relation "between subject and object, perceiving mind and perceived reality."[76] With Rimmon-Kenan, I prefer to see two categories here: when things are seen through the eyes of the narrator, we have a narrator-focalizer (external focalization); and when things are seen through the eyes of a character, we have a character-focalizer (internal focaliza-

---

74. Genette 1980: 185–94; see also Culler's "foreword" to Genette (Genette 1980: 7–14, esp. pp. 10–11).

75. On focalization, see especially Rimmon-Kenan 2005: 72–86; Jahn 2005 with bibliography. See also Chatman 1980: 151–61; 1990: 139–60, esp. p. 143; Sternberg 1987: 129–85, passim, and the index; Berlin 1983: 43–82; and Prince 2003: 31–32, 75–77.

76. Sternberg 1987: 129.

tion).[77] This has to do with the position of the perceiver relative to the story. External focalization is close to the narrating agent. Its vehicle is therefore termed the narrator-focalizer. Internal focalization takes place inside the events narrated; the perceiver is then usually one of the acting characters, the character-focalizer.

If we apply this terminology to the Eden Narrative, it is easy to see that we are dealing with a narrator-focalizer. The story is told "from outside." The representation is objective, detached.

However, as Genette pointed out, "the commitment as to focalization is not necessarily steady over the whole length of a narrative."[78] One type of focalization may not suffice to describe an entire work. Taking a closer look at our Genesis narrative, we notice that in some cases we may be faced with an internal or character-focalizer. This may be the case in the dialogue between the serpent and the woman in 3:1–7, in which the acting and speaking characters are the characters who perceive what is being narrated. God's questioning of the couple may also involve a character-focalizer (3:8–13): the man saw that he was naked.

So much for the matter of focalization. Before we leave this aspect of the narrative, however, a brief remark on the ideological element is in order. The narrative presents a system of norms, a world view, in accordance with which the characters and their actions are evaluated: the divine commandment and the obedience that the Creator expects. In the present text, this basic norm is presented through the perspective of a narrator-focalizer. The ideology of the narrator is taken as authoritative in Genesis 2–3. The narrator himself subscribes to the norms of his narrative.

Now let us proceed to the question "who tells?"—that is, to the phenomenon of "voice" and the type of narrator with which we are concerned here.[79] Flaubert says in one of his letters that the author should be in his work like God in his universe: everywhere present but

---

77. Rimmon-Kenan 2005: 75–78. Genette (1980: 186–91) suggested three categories: (a) non-focalization or zero-focalization, (b) internal focalization, and (c) external focalization. Rimmon-Kenan here builds on Bal's critique of Genette (Bal 1977: 28–29); see also Jahn 2005: 174b. Bal and Rimmon-Kenan retain Genette's category (a) but call it external or narrator-focalizer and his category (b), which they call internal or character-focalizer. These two categories relate to the position of the *perceiver*. Genette's third category (c) relates to the *perceived object* (the narrative is focused *on* a character, not *through* him) and should not be discussed under focalization. See Rimmon-Kenan 2005: 156 n. 6.

78. Genette 1980: 191.

79. On voice, see esp. Rimmon-Kenan 2005: 87–106.

nowhere apparent.[80] To put it briefly, the narrator in Genesis 2–3 may be described as "extradiegetic": he tells the events from "above"; he is superior to the story he narrates. He is not a character in the story. This will become apparent as we take the next step in our investigation.

2.6. Narrator and Characters: Omniscience and Restricted Knowledge

We now come to a highly important but neglected aspect of the Eden Narrative: the knowledge of the narrator and of his characters, respectively. First, let us have a look at an illuminating example—the story of the divine annunciation to Abraham and Sarah (Gen 18:9–15). The divine visitor, "the LORD," says to Abraham that he will come back "in due season" and that Sarah will then have a son. Abraham and Sarah are both advanced in age, and "it had ceased to be with Sarah after the manner of women":

> So Sarah laughed to herself, saying, "After I have grown old, and my husband is old, shall I have pleasure?" The LORD said to Abraham, "Why did Sarah laugh, and say, 'Shall I indeed bear a child, now that I am old?' Is anything too wonderful for the LORD? At the set time I will return to you, in due season, and Sarah shall have a son." (Gen 18:12–14)

Sternberg correctly notes that this scene operates on two levels of awareness. There is an upper level, inhabited by the narrator, the divine visitor ("the LORD"), and the reader, all three of whom know everything: the identity and old age of the main characters, the destined birth of Isaac, and Sarah's skepticism. There is, however, also a lower level: Sarah's restricted viewpoint. The story "vindicates human blindness to the glory of divine omniscience."[81]

The biblical narrator is generally omniscient. He has free access to the minds and hearts of the *dramatis personae*, even to the thoughts of God himself. He enjoys free movement in time (commuting between narrative past, present, and future is no problem) and free movement in space (he is able to follow secret conversations and to move between heaven and earth).[82]

Turning to our narrative in Genesis 2–3: it is a truism that we must distinguish between the level of knowledge of the narrator and the

---

80. Flaubert, according to Sternberg 1987: 118.
81. Sternberg 1987: 91.
82. Sternberg 1987: 84. Note Alter 1981: 155–77 on narration and knowledge.

level of knowledge of his characters—a truism, but an important one. The ensuing analysis may help us to come to grips with one of the more serious problems that modern scholars have found in this text.

To begin, there are a number of indications that *the narrator* is omniscient. He knows about the conditions on earth before the creation of the first human couple. He knows about God's planting a garden and about the two special trees. He knows the geography of the four rivers flowing out of Eden. He knows the divine techniques for the creation of man (out of dust) and woman (from the rib). He knows what the man said at that moment of marvel—when he first saw the woman. He knows the details of the clandestine conversation between the serpent and the woman. He knows about the woman's inner appreciation of the forbidden fruit. He knows about the evening walks of God himself. He knows about God's interrogation of the human couple and about the sentences pronounced by him. He knows about the "consolation prize" of procreation ("Eve"!), now that death has become the inevitable fate of everything human. And he knows what God said in the heavenly assembly, representing this in reported speech: "like one of us."

There can thus be no doubt that the narrator is omniscient.[83] Scholars who deny this tend to overlook the possibility that the narrator may be omniscient but not necessarily omnicommunicative[84] and that the characters may know considerably less than the narrator.

Then, *what about God*? It has been suggested that in biblical narrative the narrator tends to merge with God.[85] I find it difficult to agree wholeheartedly with this view. At least in our Eden Narrative, it seems to me that God is "narrated"; he is one of the characters in the narrative.[86] In saying this, I limit my perspective to the narratological aspects of the text, refraining from adopting any metaphysical perspective on matters—a perspective that may, of course, be slightly different. On the narratological level, the narrator is the master of the tale.

Whether "God"—the narrated character—is omniscient or not is a question that may invite various answers. It could be observed, for instance, that the animals did not become the help for man that God

---

83. On this I agree with van Wolde 1989: 214, 216, contra Stordalen 2000: 216–17.

84. This important distinction was made explicit by Sternberg (1987: 190).

85. Sternberg 1987: 131: The Bible "introduces a new perspective by dissociating God from the characters and aligning him with the narrator."

86. I am most grateful to my colleague Anders Palm (Lund) for helping me clarify my views on this intriguing issue.

had expected. Furthermore, God arranges an interrogation of the man and the woman, a circumstance that might be taken to indicate that he did not know.

However, it seems to me that the Eden Narrative presents us with an "upper level" of the story, a level inhabited by the narrator, God, and the reader. One can hardly imagine that the narrator did not understand God to be omniscient. Signs indicating otherwise should be understood as features necessary for the development of the narrative. So much for the "upper level" of the story.

There is, however, also a "lower level" inhabited by *the two human characters*, and it is now time to turn to this level. To the best of my knowledge, the question has so far never been raised—still less discussed—whether there is a difference between the omniscience of the narrator and the extent of the knowledge of the characters, the first human couple. To anticipate the results of my analysis: one might say that (the narrator's and God's) omniscience is placed in contrast to human ignorance.

To begin with, previous research has found a number of signs of the supposedly composite character of the text, "the problem of the one tree/two trees being only the most obvious."[87] The text seems to oscillate between a one-tree narrative and a two-tree version.

We found above that 2:9—with "in the midst of the garden" placed between the two objects, the two trees that God planted—is a case of "split coordination" (A. Michel), both trees being understood to share the position in the middle of the garden. We could stop here. But we can also go on to make some additional observations, and we will then find two points worth noticing:

1. The narrator first links the phrase "in the midst" with the tree of life while God is doing the planting (2:9). He later uses the utterance of the woman to connect the same phrase with the tree of knowledge, the forbidden fruit of which she was soon to eat (3:3).
2. The tree of life disappears from the story after 2:9 to reappear only at the very end (3:22, 24). The main body of the text seems to revolve around a single tree, the tree of knowledge.

Narratological analysis helps us make sense of these two observations. When confronted with an unevenness in a text, one can choose one

---

87. See above, chap. 1. The quotation is from Greenstein 2002: 233; Greenstein does not, however, commit himself to a specific theory of textual development behind the present narrative.

of two ways: either to go ahead and eliminate it, which is the way of textual "surgery," or to try to illuminate it and see it as being due to conscious literary art.[88] I propose that we opt for the latter here. We need not discuss Meir Sternberg's contention that "the narrator's all-knowing rules out by definition the thought of any informational lapse or shortage" (Sternberg goes on to say that, "[t]he narrator's omniscience once postulated . . . the consequences for the interpretation of dissonance logically follow").[89]

When we turn the searchlight on the characters, we soon find that the narrator's omniscience is in stark contrast to the restricted knowledge of the humans (and the serpent). There is nothing to indicate that the man had any idea that there were *two* trees being planted when he was apprised of the divine prohibition against eating from *one* tree, the tree of knowledge (2:16–17). Moreover, there is nothing to indicate that the woman had any knowledge of the two trees when she spoke to the serpent about the tree of knowledge as being prohibited for humans (3:3, cf. vv. 4–6). The reader shares the privileged knowledge of God and the narrator—knowledge that is denied to the main characters, the first humans: there is also a tree of life (2:9).

In his literary strategy, the narrator has God plant two trees and arrange a test—a test of obedience. God denies one tree to the humans. The reader may infer that the outcome of this test somehow decides the humans' access to the other tree—the tree of life. It is then interesting to note that *there is no sign that the man and the woman knew anything about the existence of a tree of life*. And apparently *they did not know that they were passing a test and that obedience to the commandment would be rewarded with the gift of eating from the tree of life*.

So far, this is a conclusion based on silence. I will return to my contention in the next chapter, looking for evidence for and against it.

At this point, I would like to introduce the following interpretation as a tentative suggestion. On the surface level of the text, the phrase "in the midst of the garden" in 2:9 is valid for both trees; the woman makes no real "mistake" in 3:3. On a deeper level, however, the poet subtly plays on the variation between 2:9 (tree of life in the midst) and 3:3 (tree of knowledge in the midst). When the woman uses the

---

88. I have borrowed the contrast elimination – illumination from Trible 1985: 72.

89. Sternberg 1987: 182–83. Sternberg does not discuss Genesis 2–3. However, in my opinion, allowance must be made for the possibility of dissonance that was not introduced by the author/narrator and thus should not be seen as conscious literary art; it may instead be due to the process that produced the particular text.

expression "in the midst of the garden" (3:3), she creates a *double entendre*. The linguistic *referent* in her crucial statement is the tree of knowledge; this is clear from what immediately follows. At the same time, she inadvertently *alludes* to the tree of life, which we find at the beginning and end of the text. Or, to be more exact: the narrator makes this important allusion. The tree of life was, as the reader recalls—and as both God and the narrator know—planted "in the midst of the garden" (2:9).

The somewhat ambiguous use of "in the midst of the garden" makes perfect sense on the level of narration. By means of this literary subtlety, which is by no means due to any composite character of the text, the narrator reminds the reader that the human couple undergoes a divine test without being aware that by eating from the fruit of one tree they will be denied the fruit of the other. The humans miss the point that, beyond the prohibition (the test) in the present, there may be blessings in the future.

Moreover, the subtle construction may even contain a note of irony. In rhetoric, irony consists of saying the opposite of what one means, or of making a statement that invites an interpretation different from the surface meaning of the words. A special kind of irony is situational or dramatic irony, "[w]hen the reader is made aware of a disparity between the facts of a situation and the characters' understanding of it," to quote David Lodge.[90] Situational irony may obtain when the audience or the reader sees a meaning unintended by the speaker.

What we have in the woman's words is, in fact, a case of situational irony:

> The woman said to the serpent, "We may eat of the fruit of the trees in the garden; but God said, 'You shall not eat of the fruit of the tree that is in the middle of the garden, nor shall you touch it, or you shall die.'" (Gen 3:2–3)

The woman refers to the tree of knowledge, which was in fact the forbidden tree. But the way she expresses herself invites the reader to understand the utterance as a tacit allusion to the tree of life. This understanding is unintended by the woman, but is probably intended by the narrator. What we have here illustrates Roland Barthes's thesis that the code of irony is a code of quotations in which the text, in a deceitful manner, deletes the quotation marks that should frame a

---

90. Lodge 1992: 179. On irony, see the article by Harris 1992: 178–83 with bibliography.

quotation.[91] Although Hebrew texts do not use this way of identifying quotations, it is fair to say that the woman so to speak uses the expression "in the midst of the garden" from 2:9 "without quotation marks." Only the reader, not the woman herself, identifies it as a quotation.

On the basis of our observations on the extent of the characters' knowledge, we are now in a position to return to the drama of discovery (from ignorance to knowledge) referred to in the preceding analysis of the plot. Seen in the light of what has been said, this process now stands out as profound irony. In their illicit desire for the fruit of the forbidden tree of knowledge, the human couple is led by their fundamental ignorance—about the existence of the tree of life and about its potential gift of immortality. At the very end of the narrative, the humans find the cherubim guarding the way to this tree.

I referred above to what I called "situational or dramatic irony." One might, indeed, consider introducing a distinction: situational irony is restricted to a specific situation—in our text, to the situation of the woman in 3:3; and dramatic irony as characterizing a larger textual unit. In relation to this distinction, we might say that our narrative as a whole is marked by dramatic irony.[92]

In previous research, there have been speculations about the humans' having had free access to the tree of life before the act of disobedience. According to Engnell, this is simply "to be taken for granted."[93] Most recently, Stordalen considers this to be a story "where the human party first had less knowledge but free admission to the Tree of Life."[94] And Hallo has the God of the Eden Narrative wanting them to eat from all of the trees (except the one forbidden), including the tree of life. The humans thus consciously chose death before life.[95]

However, if my analysis above is broadly correct, the tree of life was there from the beginning but was *unknown* to the human couple. It was to be the prize for obeying the divine commandment. That nothing is said of eating from the tree of life is therefore completely comprehensible, because, presumably, eating is a conscious act. We may conclude that they did not eat from that tree, neither before nor after

---

91. Barthes 1970: section XXI, pp. 51–52.

92. My thanks to my colleague Anders Palm (Lund) who suggested this distinction to me.

93. Engnell 1955: 116.

94. Stordalen 2000: 241–42. Note, however, the softer formulation on p. 231: "Whether or not they have by 3:22 eaten from the Tree of Life is impossible to detect."

95. Hallo 2004: 272.

the act of disobedience. Besides—and this is important—3:22 shows that they had not in fact eaten from the tree of life.

Finally, a note on the history of research on the Eden Narrative. In the above analysis, observations on the knowledge of the narrator and the knowledge of the characters have been of fundamental importance. Two previous scholars stand out as having had an inkling about what was going on at this level, but they worked long before the development of modern narratological tools and were thus unable to open up this perspective on the issues involved. Paul Humbert wrote about the "hidden tree of life," as we remember from our survey of research in chap. 1 (p. 9). Half a century earlier, Franz Delitzsch had said in his commentary on Genesis: "As a matter of fact, the narrative affirms the existence of the tree of life from the beginning, but nothing is said to the humans about this. Only one tree, the tree of knowledge, is brought to the foreground of their knowledge. The tree of life is not present to their knowledge and is, so to speak, unmasked only after the fall."[96]

It is interesting to see that this observation has not, as far as I am aware, elicited any response in more than a century of research. Delitzsch and Humbert may hence be said to have anticipated the results of a narratological analysis of the Eden Narrative.

*   *   *

At the end of chap. 1, I formulated three questions to be kept in mind during our narratological explorations. We are now in a position to answer them.

The first was this: why are there two trees but only one prohibition? And notably, why is the tree of life not forbidden? The answer is: the plot is about a divine test of the first humans. Not to eat of the forbidden tree is the test case: to obey the prohibition or not? The fruit of the other tree, the tree of life, is the prize if the test is passed. It is also clear why the human protagonists do not eat of the tree of life: they simply do not know of its existence. The second question was why the body of the narrative only deals with the tree of knowledge. The answer is that the plot is focused on a test, and the whole body of the text is about this test, in which the tree of knowledge is foregrounded. The third question was: what are the implications of the seeming "mistake" of the woman when she refers to the tree of knowledge as being "in the midst of the garden"? The answer is that this is a conscious ele-

---

96. Franz Delitzsch 1887: 81, my translation. I have had access to the 5th edition and have not checked the previous editions.

ment in the narrator's literary strategy, a subtlety that opens the eyes of the reader to the irony of the situation.

Summary and Conclusions

1. The Eden Narrative stands out as a well-structured, unified whole, in which all the different elements make excellent sense as part of the literary strategy of a conscious literary artist.

2. The plot is about a divine test of obedience to God by the first human couple. Will they respect the line of demarcation between the human world and the divine? In the test, the tree of knowledge is the test case (to obey or not?); the tree of life is the potential reward (for obedience). The divine test is the subject of our narrative. This test develops into a conflict between God and his human creation. Below the surface, however, there is also a conflict between the serpent and God. I submit that, if there is a conflict between "life" and "knowledge" at all, this is not the main, basic conflict in the text. This seems apparent from the fact that there is no "balance" between the two trees. On the contrary: one tree is a test; the other is a reward.

3. The consequences of the disobedience regarding the tree affect the two humans in their very existence: transience and death are now their inescapable fate.

4. The above analysis of focalization and voice directed special attention to the different positions of the narrator (as omniscient) and the human characters (as ignorant). The narrator, God, and the reader all know that both the tree of life and the tree of knowledge were planted in the garden from the beginning. But the human characters only know of one tree that was forbidden, the tree of knowledge.

5. The human protagonists are thus ignorant about the most essential fact: the existence of the tree of life and its fruit as a potential reward for obedience to the divine will.

6. The narrative seems to be marked by profound irony. This was tentatively argued on the basis of the play on words between 2:9 and 3:3, with "in the midst of the garden" being related to different trees on the sentence level. In saying this, I am conscious of A. Michel's demonstration that, on the surface level of meaning, 2:9 allows for the central position of both trees.

7. It seems natural to conclude that a narrative in which the details are so neatly integrated should not be made the object of textual surgery.

Chapter 3

The Theme of the Eden Narrative

From our analysis of the plot and the narratological properties of the Eden Narrative, we now move on to a treatment of its theme. First, I will briefly present what we may learn from the discussion of the notion of *theme* among philosophers and scholars of literary theory.[1] Then I will go on to a discussion of theme in Genesis 2–3.

3.1. "Theme" in Literary Theory

Monroe Beardsley, in his thorough reflection on theme, distinguishes between three steps of literary analysis: explication, elucidation, and interpretation. *Explication* is Beardsley's term for the discovery of meaning in a text—denotative or connotative. *Elucidation* is more global. Here we deal with plot, characters, and motifs. So far we are moving entirely within the fictive world of the work. The process of defining the theme or themes of the text, the process of *interpretation*, takes us to a much more abstract level which relates the work's overall content to the real world.[2]

When we read the parables in the New Testament, it is clear that their theme is not sheep-breeding, fishing, or banking. While all these may belong to the subject level of the parables, their "real content," their theme, is on a different level. Correspondingly, the novel *Moby Dick* deals with a white whale, and we read a great deal of information about the whale's anatomical details. However, the author's ultimate interest, what he really wants to communicate, is on a level above and beyond all this.[3]

---

1. Among biblical scholars who have dealt with theme, I would single out Clines 1976: 484–87; and Block 1997: 107–19 for special mention. Among philosophers and literary theoreticians, note Beardsley 1958: 400–411; Chatman 1983; Sollors 1993; Prince 1992: esp. pp. 1–13; Brinker 1993; Bremond 1993; Trommler 1995; and A. Pettersson 2000: 146–81.

2. Beardsley 1958: 401–11. See also Chatman 1983. Chatman's study is in all essentials a clear endorsement of Beardsley's position on theme.

3. I have borrowed the examples of the parables and *Moby Dick* from Block 1997: 110–11.

Beardsley distinguishes between subject, on the one hand, and theme and thesis, on the other. The *subject* belongs to the world of the fiction of the work in question, and we may refer to it by some concrete noun or nominative construction—a war, a love affair, a white whale, the first human couple, and so on. To say that a poem has a certain *theme* or a certain *thesis* "is to affirm again that the poem does not merely construct its own world but refers to the real world," says Beardsley.[4] In dealing with the theme and thesis, we are moving on the level of interpretation. A narrative theme is an abstract concept, and it is a concept of a high degree of generality. Though often not expressly formulated, it is usually extractable from the work of fiction. What distinguishes theme from thesis is, as noted by Seymour Chatman, that theme is not a proposition. "Pride" is a theme, but "man is proud" is a thesis.[5] A thesis may thus be true or false, a distinction that does not apply to a theme. This becomes especially evident if a piece of literature was composed for propagandistic purposes.[6]

A central aspect of the notion of theme is that the theme of a narrative has an integrating function. The discrete components of the text are interrelated; they work together, and together they manifest the theme. Correspondingly, "the various interpretative statements must work towards a unified view of the text, a 'theme' to which the components of the text can be seen to make a relevant contribution," says Torsten Pettersson.[7]

As was pointed out above, the theme of a narrative need not be expressly stated. The problem in such a case is that it is only the discourse of the work that is immediately accessible to observation. The theme, however, is obviously an entity that is somehow situated above the level of sheer discourse. Mere retelling is not enough to ascertain what the theme is. Ascending from the plot to the theme of a work essentially requires an intuitive leap on the reader's part. There is a degree of subjectivity involved. The text is a "pliable entity," as Torsten Pettersson says.[8] We shall see below, however, that even so, the work may contain indications to help us identify the theme.

When discussing theme as a concept in literary theory, I find it useful to set it off against the following aspects of the work being studied:

---

4. Beardsley 1958: 403.

5. Chatman 1983: 164, drawing on Beardsley 1958: 409–11.

6. For an exegetical study of a text with a thesis, see my rhetorical analysis of 2 Samuel 7 (Mettinger 2005).

7. T. Pettersson 1988: 26–27.

8. T. Pettersson 2002.

- subject
- plot
- motifs

The difference between theme and *subject* was already touched on above. As for theme and *plot*, many scholars have observed their interrelatedness. Thus David Clines notes that "'theme' tends to conceptualize plot, to focus its significance, and state its implication; it may be said (in a narrative work) to be 'plot with the emphasis on meaning.'"[9] Similarly, Jonathan Culler notes that "plot is but the temporal projection of thematic structures."[10] In a memorable statement, Gerald Prince reminds us that "theme is to plot as meaning is to form."[11] Consequently, plot may be a most helpful indicator of the theme or thesis of a literary work.

The two terms *theme* and *motif* have often been used without clear differentiation. It seems wise, however, to distinguish between them, as for instance Prince does in his *Dictionary of Narratology*. By *motif*, Prince understands "a minimal thematic unit,"[12] whereas *theme* is

> a semantic macrostructural category . . . extractable from . . . distinct . . . textual elements which (are taken to) illustrate it and expressing the more general and abstract entities (ideas, thoughts, etc.) that a text or part thereof is (or may be considered to be) about.[13]

Vis-à-vis motif, theme is thus "a more abstract and more general semantic unit manifested by or reconstructed from a set of motifs."[14] Even a recurrent motif, such as expulsion in Genesis 1–11 (the first humans, Cain, the tower-builders), does not necessarily constitute a theme.[15] Nevertheless, theme and motif are of the same substance, because the theme of a pericope may become a motif of a larger work into which that piece of writing is incorporated.[16]

A number of scholars have noted that, while the subject belongs to the fictive world of the work, the theme is a bridge that connects the work with the real, extralinguistic world. As we saw, Beardsley under-

---

9. Clines 1976: 485.
10. Culler 1986: 224.
11. Prince 1992: 2.
12. Prince 2003: 55.
13. Prince 2003: 99.
14. Prince 2003: 55.
15. As was pointed out by Clines 1976: 485.
16. Clines 1976: 485.

lined this aspect of theme. In a worthwhile study, Menachem Brinker expresses the same opinion. Brinker calls our attention to the philosopher Gilbert Ryle's distinction between two different kinds of "aboutness." Ryle distinguished between what a discourse is *linguistically* about and what it is *referentially* about.[17] In the case of the Eden Narrative, we might say that when we read the text metaphorically we find out what it is referentially about, namely, immortality and knowledge (wisdom). The trees are metaphors and must be understood metaphorically.[18] This will help us to take the next step, discussing the pragmatic dimensions of the text, reading it as an utterance that is addressed to a reader and deals with the world outside the text. This pragmatic dimension will be touched on in the next chapter, in connection with the genre of the Eden Narrative.

In view of the preceding discussion, themes may be said to permit works of literary fiction to raise profound existential questions without expressly stating these questions and without permitting easy answers. The questions raised may be of a metaphysical nature, questions such as "What is the purpose of life?" or "Why does man, created by God, ultimately die?" We may then note, with Seymour Chatman, that "the greater the work, the less likely the reader is to propose a ready answer."[19] Menachem Brinker reminds us: "Poetic worlds and fictional narratives may always be open to different and incompatible thematic readings. Nonetheless they are possessed of determinacy enough to reject some thematic interpretations as unconvincing, forced, or, at least, unnatural."[20]

An observation about themes that might be helpful in a comparative study of various works, ancient or modern, is Claude Bremond's insistence on the nature of what he calls "thematic fields."[21] Bremond asks us to imagine a related set of stories *a, b, c, d,* and *e.* In story *a*, the theme is represented by characteristics A, B, C, D; in version *b*, by characteristics B, C, D, E; and so on to version *e*, with characteristics E,

---

17. Brinker 1993: 27; cf. pp. 29, 31; and Ryle 1933. A. Pettersson also stresses the "real-world" connections of theme (Pettersson 2000: 147–48).

18. Ryle's distinction between "linguistically about" and "referentially about" may be rephrased as "rhetorically about" and "referentially about" when read metaphorically, says Brinker (1993: 27), who also refers to Nelson Goodman (Goodman 1972: 245–72) in this context. I have not had access to Goodman's work.

19. Chatman 1983: 165.

20. Brinker 1993: 33. A fine study of the openness and determinacy of texts is T. Pettersson 2002 about the text as a "pliable entity."

21. Bremond 1993: 52–53.

F, G, and H. Presented in a simple graph, this results in the following pattern:

Story	*a*: characteristics	A, B, C, D
	b:	B, C, D, E
	c:	C, D, E, F
	d:	D, E, F, G
	e:	E, F, G, H

Fig. 4. Bremond's thematic fields.

It is easily seen that *b* can be considered a variation on the theme of *a*, and *c* on the theme of *b*, and so forth, but that *a* and *e* actually have no characteristics in common. If we look at them independently of the series of variations, nothing would permit us to see them as manifestations of the same theme. I have not, however, been able to make this fascinating perspective useful in the present study.

So far in our discussion, the question has been "What is a theme?" One problem that remains is "How do we find the theme in a text?" There is obviously no standard procedure for this. Moreover, we should not deny a degree of subjectivity in the project: Thematizing is certainly not something that takes place independently of the scholar who pursues it. Because of the difficulties involved, David Clines in his study "Theme in Genesis 1–11" finds that all we can do is examine likely candidates for the theme, weighing their pros and cons.[22]

Per Block, after a penetrating discussion of the nature and ontological status of theme in the wake of Monroe Beardsley, takes a slightly less pessimistic attitude. He writes that a theme is something that is extractable from indications given in a work of literature, whether or not they are explicit.[23]

We may thus expect that the theme is somehow marked as central to the text, that it has recurrent manifestations, and that it appears in prominent elements of the text. Redundancy and prominence may thus be important hints. As Block notes, the very structure of the text may give us helpful clues. It is worthwhile paying attention to symmetrical arrangements, notably inclusios in the text. Recurrent symbols

22. Clines 1976: 486; and for his discussion of suggested themes, see pp. 487–507.
23. Block 1997: 107–19; on procedures for thematizing, see esp. pp. 114–19.

may be of special importance to the enterprise. Another significant phenomenon is what has been termed "poetic closure."[24]

In my opinion, the results gained from a study of theme should be checked against insights gained from a narratological study proper (notably concerning the plot of the text) *and* by placing them side by side with an assessment of the genre of the text (see chap. 4). Also to be kept in mind is that the theme chosen by an author may be expected to leave its imprint on the material he has appropriated from previous tradition (see chap. 5).

3.2. The Theme of the Eden Narrative

In discussing the theme of our specific text, the Eden Narrative, I will take the following steps: (1) On the basis of a number of textual markers, I will first discuss death versus immortality. (2) On the basis of previous observations about the plot, I will deal with the divine test as a central aspect of the text and argue that disobedience and its consequences are the central theme. (3) Finally, I will comment on theodicy as an important thematic aspect of the text. At the end of this chapter, I shall also deal with the symbolism of the two trees, especially the tree of knowledge.

1. Death versus Immortality

There are some important inclusios in the text. Thus, the tree of life appears at the beginning of the passage (2:9) and also at the end (3:22, 24). One might also see the repetition of the phrase "in the midst of the garden" (2:9) as a marker of the centrality of the tree of life to the theme of the narrative.

Another inclusio is formed by references to man's creation out of the dust of the earth (2:7; 3:19, 23); the very designation ʾādām alludes to the word for ground, ʾădāmâ. And this inclusio, man created out of dust, is in stark contrast to the potentialities of the tree of life. The two inclusios together, the tree of life and creation out of dust, strike a note of human transitoriness and the possibility of immortality that was never realized.

The fact that immortality was only potential and was not to be realized is clear from the closure of the text. Poetic closure is often an important phenomenon. In our text, we actually find two final "peaks," more or less two endings—what looks like a "double closure." In 3:14–

---

24. On poetic closure, see especially Smith 1968.

19, the divine sentences passed on the serpent, the woman, and the man contain the divine punishment for the act of disobedience. In 3:22–24, the expulsion from the garden serves the same purpose. Thus, these two closures end on the same note. Gen 3:19 says of the man:

> By the sweat of your face you shall eat bread
> until you return to the ground, for out of it you were taken;
> you are dust, and to dust you shall return.

Gen 3:22–24 places the main stress on the man's expulsion from the garden and on God's barring the way to the tree of life so that man should not stretch out his hand to eat of it also and thus live forever. Here the motif of man created out of the dust of the earth reappears for the last time (3:23).

Even if the human had become like one of the divine beings in one respect (namely, knowledge) after eating from the forbidden tree (3:5, 22), it is clear that he will not be allowed to acquire the other divine prerogative, immortality. The words "you are dust" (3:19) read like a final verdict on this issue. Of the two divine prerogatives, man has robbed one but is definitely denied the other.

The mortality of the human, the earth-being created out of dust, is certainly very close to the core of the Eden Narrative. It is obvious to anyone that the text ends with a *fermata* that stresses the tragic fact that the human being missed the chance to gain immortality.

As a corollary, there has been a protracted discussion among scholars whether the first human couple is presented as mortal from the beginning or not. Paul Humbert surveyed the debate up to 1940, the year of his monograph's publication. Mapping out the lay of the land, Humbert found two extreme positions and one intermediary:

- The humans were mortal from the beginning, created out of dust. In this, moreover, they were just like the animals, which are certainly not thought of as immortal (2:19).
- The humans were immortal, having access to the tree of life from the outset, but they lost this sort of nourishment through the fall.
- The intermediary position: the humans were created mortal but were destined for immortality.[25]

This issue, of course, is linked to the issue of the tree of life: whether or not it was present in the garden and whether or not it was acces-

---

25. Humbert 1940: 125–26 with bibliography.

sible. Humbert summarizes scholars' various positions on the tree of life as follows:

- absent from the garden, sacrificed by some scholars as being a redactional element;
- present and visible but inaccessible to the humans;
- present and inaccessible because hidden from the humans (Humbert's own position);
- present and inaccessible because prohibited, just as the tree of knowledge is explicitly said to be;
- present, visible, and accessible but not consumed before the fall;
- present, visible, accessible, and consumed by the humans before the fall.[26]

One of the results of the present investigation is that uprooting the tree of life from the garden of Eden because it is presumed to be a redactional addition is unwarranted (see above, chap. 2). This tree was supposed to be there, just like the tree of knowledge (2:9): unknown to the humans but known to the narrator and to God.

Whether the humans were thought to be mortal or immortal from the beginning and whether the text purports to describe prelapsarian conditions before the "fall" are two questions we shall turn to below (§3.2.3, p. 59).

In any case, the issue of death versus immortality is essential in our text, but *it is not per se the central theme* of the Eden Narrative as I understand it. This will become apparent in the following part of our investigation.

2. The Test of Obedience:
Disobedience and Its Consequences

My plot analysis in chap. 2 demonstrated the central position of the divine test. According to the Eden Narrative, death is only the consequence of the human failure to obey the divine commandment. It is here, in the disobedience of the first human couple, that we have the main theme of our narrative. I will now try to demonstrate what leads to this conclusion.

1. Deuteronomistic Affinities. There is one perspective on the Eden Narrative that was broached by a couple of scholars but that has not so far played a decisive role in current research. In 1965, Norbert Lohfink suggested that the covenant tradition lies behind the story of the

---

26. Humbert 1940: 126–27 with bibliography.

"fall."[27] Yhwh found Israel outside Canaan, brought them into the wonderful land (compare with "garden"), gave them his commandments, and exiled them (compare with expulsion from garden) because of their disobedience. Covenant theology is the key to the narrative sequence in Genesis 2–3, says Lohfink. However, because the covenant was for the people of Israel and Israel does not appear in history until Sinai, the word "covenant" does not appear in the Eden story. Lohfink especially points out the role of the commandments as covenant conditions. Obedience to the commandments leads to blessings and "life," disobedience to curses and "death." Lohfink's work should be seen against the background of the covenant discussion in the 1950s and 1960s, with an early dating for both the covenant and the Eden Narrative.

John Van Seters made another important observation, namely, concerning the relative date of the Eden Narrative: "If one views the covenant theology as largely the creation of the Deuteronomic tradition, then the Yahwist must be understood as subsequent and indebted to this theological tradition. It would appear that he has given this national covenant theology a universal dimension."[28]

A further step was taken by Eckart Otto. In his study of Genesis 2–3 as a post-Priestly didactic narrative, Otto comments on its vocabulary and finds traces both of wisdom and of Deuteronomistic covenant theology.[29] The ensuing discussion of the Deuteronomistic affinities to the Eden Narrative builds on these three scholars, especially on Otto's essay, but tries to make the matter fruitful with regard to defining the theme of the narrative.

---

27. Lohfink 1965: 90–95, esp. pp. 91–92.

28. J. Van Seters 1992: 127–29, quotation from p. 128. Note that, to Van Seters, the Yahwist is the author of the Eden Narrative. For my views on the covenant tradition, see Mettinger 1990: 399–400. My thanks to Göran Eidevall (private communication), who called my attention to Van Seters 1992, which in turn led me to Lohfink 1965.

29. Otto 1996: 175–83, especially pp. 178–83. Otto does not seem to be aware of Lohfink and Van Seters. On a few points, Otto goes beyond the evidence. This is the case when he reads Gen 2:15 as alluding to the Deuteronomistic notion of "rest" and translates *wayyanniḥēhû* 'und liess ihn Ruhe finden' (p. 180). As is well known, the verb *nûaḥ* has two different Hiphil forms, and Otto's understanding presupposes the other form, *hēnîaḥ*, not the form actually used here, *hinnîaḥ*. I am also not convinced by his suggestion to read Deut 13:5 'wie ein Vokabular für Gen 2–3' (p. 181). The uses of the crucial words in this passage and in the Eden Narrative are quite different. Nevertheless, I am convinced of the Deuteronomistic affinities of Genesis 2–3.

In our preceding discussion of the plot, we observed a motif that has a central role and pervades the text as a whole—the motif of the divine commandment. Having planted the trees, the LORD God 'commanded' (*wayṣaw*) the man: "You may freely eat of every tree of the garden, but of the tree of the knowledge of good and evil you shall not eat, for if you eat of it you shall certainly die" (2:16–17, my trans.). The verb in question, *ṣwh* in the Piel, is from the same root as *miṣwâ* 'commandment'. The rest of the narrative contains reverberations of this when God refers to "the tree about which I commanded you" (3:11, 17). As Otto points out, the verb *ṣwh* (Piel) is the classical lexeme for the promulgation of the law, especially in Deuteronomy and in the Priestly Code.[30] The whole central passage, 3:1–7, turns on the divine commandment, although neither the noun nor the verb from the root *ṣwh* occurs in this passage.

Another Deuteronomistic phrase is 'to listen to the voice of YWHW' (*šāmaʿ bĕqôl yhwh*).[31] With this in mind I am inclined, with Otto, to ascribe special significance to a statement found in our Eden Narrative:

Because you have listened to the voice of your wife (*kî šāmaʿtā lĕqôl ʾištekā*),
and have eaten of the tree about which I commanded you (*ṣiwwîtîkā*)
"You shall not eat of it,"
cursed is the ground because of you. (3:17)[32]

Instead of listening to what God commanded, the man listened to the voice of his wife. A further point of contact with Deuteronomistic

---

30. Otto 1996: 181. Stordalen (2000: 226) notes that the syntax in 2:16 is *ṣwh ʾl*, "which typically denotes a provisional instruction from a ruler (or father) concerning his subordinates," while *ṣwh ʾl* is "the technical term for YHWH's issuing laws." This difference should be noted, but the Deuteronomistic affinities pointed out by Otto and me make it clear that the author behind the narrative has a background in Deuteronomistic theology.

31. Note especially the constructions that parallel "YHWH's voice" and his "covenant" (Exod 19:5, Judg 2:20, 2 Kgs 18:12). For similar associations of "to hearken/obey my (your) voice" (*šāmaʿ bĕqôl*), see Deut 8:20; 13:19; 15:5; 26:14, 17, 27:10; 28:1, 2, 15, 45, 62; 30:8, 10; Jer 3:25; 7:28; 40:3, etc. See the list of appearances in Bright 1951: 35 no. 46. Bright notes, "ca. 50 in Dtr (of which a number in old narratives)," 18× in Jeremiah prose and 0× in P. Note also the importance of this formula as a key statement for Aurelius in his analysis of the redactional development of the Deuteronomistic History, especially its appearances in Exod 19:5; 2 Kgs 18:12. See Aurelius 2003: especially p. 3.

32. Otto 1996: 181. Admittedly, the preposition used here is *lĕ-*: *šāmaʿ lĕqôl*. Otto does not comment on this. Note, however, the same preposition used in the phrase in Exod 15:25 (Dtr).

language is found in the curses on the serpent and on the ground in
3:14–19.[33]

The Eden Narrative speaks of a radical choice, a choice between
obedience and disobedience to the divine commandment. This reminds us of passages in Deuteronomy, such as the following:

> See, I am setting before you today a blessing and a curse: the
> blessing, *if you obey* the commandments of the LORD your God that
> I am commanding you today; and the curse, *if you do not obey* the
> commandments of the LORD your God but turn from the way that I
> am commanding you today to follow other gods that you have not
> known. (Deut 11:26–28; my emphasis)

> See, I have set before you today life and prosperity, death and ad-
> versity. *If you obey* the commandments of the LORD your God that I
> am commanding you today, by loving the LORD your God, walking
> in his ways, and observing his commandments, decrees, and ordi-
> nances, then you shall live and become numerous, and the LORD
> your God will bless you in the land that you are entering to possess.
> But *if your heart turns away and you do not hear*, but are led astray
> to bow down to other gods and serve them, I declare to you today
> that you shall perish; you shall not live long in the land that you
> are crossing the Jordan to enter and possess.
> I call heaven and earth to witness against you today that I have
> set before you life and death, blessings and curses. Choose life so
> that you and your descendants may live loving the LORD your God,
> *obeying him*, and holding fast to him, for that means life to you and
> length of days, so that you may live in the land that the LORD
> swore to give to your ancestors, to Abraham, to Isaac, and to Jacob.
> (Deut 30:15–20; my emphasis)

When the humans transgress the divine prohibition, they are expelled from the garden and its blessings.[34]

2. The Divine Test.   Lohfink, Van Seters, and Otto paved the way
for a better understanding of the Eden Narrative. They did not, however, discuss the theme of the narrative in this light.[35] Notably, they

---

33. Otto 1996: 183.

34. Ricoeur (1969: 233) was on the right track when he said that "the Deuteronomic idea of a radical choice imposed by the prophetic summons portends the
evolution of the Adamic myth." Of course, he never noticed that the Eden Narrative has *linguistic* features that reveal its close ties with *Deuteronomistic* theology.

35. Lohfink was mainly interested in the sequence of the narrative and Van
Seters in its late date. Otto, in turn, obviously saw theodicy as the main theme
(Otto 1996: 189–92).

overlooked the fact that there is another Deuteronomistic concept that plays a prominent role in Genesis 2–3: God testing humans. This is true even though the actual term (*nsh*, Piel) does not appear in the Eden Narrative. The attestations for this use of *nsh* for God's testing of humans hardly can be prior to the Deuteronomistic movement. [36] One of the most striking examples is found in Deuteronomy 8:

> This entire commandment (*miṣwâ*) that I command you today you must diligently observe, so that you may live and increase, and go in and occupy the land that the LORD promised on oath to your ancestors. Remember the long way that the LORD your God has led you these forty years in the wilderness, in order to humble you, *testing you* (*nsh*, Piel) *to know what was in your heart, whether or not you would keep his commandments.* He humbled you by letting you hunger, then by feeding you with manna, with which neither you nor your ancestors were acquainted, in order to make you understand that one does not live by bread alone, but by every word that comes from the mouth of the LORD. (Deut 8:1–3; my emphasis)

There is an immediate connection between obedience to the divine commandment and life (vv. 1, 3). The divine test was arranged in order for God to "know what was in your heart, whether or not you would keep his commandments" (v. 2). Unsurprisingly, we find at the end of chap. 8 a reference to divine punishment, "because you would not obey the voice of the Lord your God" (v. 20), with the expression *šāmaʿ bĕqôl yhwh*.

Deut 8:3 contains a reference to the manna episode. As a corollary of this, we find the following statement in Exodus 16: "In that way [that is, by giving them the manna] I will *test* them, *whether they will follow my instruction or not*" (v. 4, my emphasis). The term for testing is the same (*nsh*), although the word for the divine will here is *tôrâ*.

Exodus 15 is also worth considering in the present context. Again we hear of God's testing Israel to determine whether they would listen to his voice:

> There [at Marah] the Lord made for them a statute and an ordinance and there *he put them to the test.* He said, "*If you will listen carefully to the voice of the Lord your God*, and do what is right in his sight, and *give heed to his commandments* and *keep all his statutes*, . . ." (Exod 15:25–26; my emphasis)

---

36. See Blum 1984: 329; and Veijola 1988: 150–51. On Genesis 22, see Norin 2002.

We recognize the Deuteronomistic phrase for obedience to the law, "listening to the voice of the LORD," and we also note the variation in the preposition, *šāmaʿ lĕqôl yhwh*, with exactly the same preposition as in Gen 3:17.

In line with this Deuteronomistic wording (*nsh*, Piel) with reference to God's testing of Israel, there are cases in which God tests individuals.[37] The best known is, of course, Genesis 22, where God tests Abraham.[38] The first verse of this narrative contains the formulation that is used to explain what happens as being a divine test (using the verb *nsh*, in the Piel). It should be noted that this knowledge is not communicated to Abraham himself. This piece of information is found in the rubric of the narrative and is thus disclosed only to the reader.[39] The test is carried out in order to establish whether Abraham fears God or not (v. 12). After the test, the divine angel in his second speech tells Abraham about the blessings to come "because you have obeyed my voice" (v. 18), thus using the well-known formula. It is natural to view Genesis 22 from the perspective opened up by Deuteronomy 8 (see above).[40]

As has been pointed out by both Blum and Veijola, there are interesting signs of an intertextual connection between Genesis 22 and the prologue of the book of Job.[41] In both cases, a test is carried out to ascertain whether the human being who undergoes the test fears God or not (Gen 22:12, Job 1:8–9). Neither Abraham nor Job knows that what he experiences is a divine test. In Genesis 22, the central term appears, though only in the rubric (v. 1). In Job, the term does not appear at all, but the events are nevertheless understood as a divine test (note Job 1:9). And both Abraham and Job perform well under the circumstances of the test.

Now let us return to the Eden Narrative. We do not find the term for testing in this text (*nsh*, Piel). Nevertheless, the narrative is about a divine test to determine whether the first human couple will obey the divine commandment or not (Gen 2:16–17). One specific feature of the text becomes especially interesting in this perspective. We found in our narratological analysis (chap. 2 above) that the narrative refers to two trees (not just one), planted by God (2:9). However, the corpus

---

37. Gen 22:1, 2 Chr 32:31, Ps 26:2.
38. On Genesis 22, see especially Blum 1984: 320–31; Veijola 1988; 2002.
39. As was pointed out by Veijola 2002: 139.
40. Veijola 2002: 137.
41. Blum 1984: 329 and Veijola 2002. Veijola argues for direct dependency, so that the Job prologue presupposes both Ezek 14:12–23 and Genesis 22.

of the text only deals with one of the trees, the forbidden tree of knowledge. The human protagonists are not informed about the existence of the tree of life. They do not know that they are undergoing a divine test; they are only confronted with the "naked" commandment of God with no "paragraph" about a reward appended. It seems clear to the reader, however, that some reward is presupposed if they pass the test: the tree of life will be revealed to the humans and become accessible to them.

A comparison with the book of Job seems natural at this point. Here, too, we have a divine test but without the proper terminology. Here the Satan persuades God to test pious Job. The purpose of this test is to ascertain whether Job's piety is disinterested, unselfish piety or not: "Does Job fear God for nothing?" (Job 1:9). The key word is *ḥinnām* 'for nothing'. The Eden Narrative tells about an analogous case. Not knowing about the potential reward—being allowed to eat from the tree of life—the two humans are asked for obedience, obedience that is not contingent on reward. They are asked for what will ultimately be disinterested piety—just as in the case of Job.

The comparison with Abraham and Job confirms our general understanding of Genesis 2–3 as dealing with a divine test. More specifically, it bolsters our contention that the tree of life was unknown to the two humans when they underwent the test.

3. Disobedience and Hubris. There are other aspects of the act of human disobedience in the garden. The two trees obviously stand for immortality and for knowledge. Here we touch on two divine prerogatives that we will have reason to return to in greater detail in two subsequent chapters (chaps. 5 and 6). Immortality is a prerogative of the deity. This is clear from 3:22–24. To the same degree, it is obvious in 3:5 and 22 that, from the perspective adopted in the text, knowledge is similar in character. The serpent thus says about the tree of knowledge: 'when you eat of it your eyes will be opened, and you will be like the gods, knowing good and evil' *kēʾlōhîm yōdʿê ṭôb wārāʿ* (3:5, my translation). And when the humans have eaten, the LORD Elohim says in his heavenly assembly that now man has become "like one of us, knowing good and evil" (3:22).[42]

There is hence a border, a line of demarcation between the divine and human spheres. Human disobedience in the Eden Narrative is

---

42. With Garr (2003: 17–92), I take the expressions here and in Gen 1:26, 6:1–4 and 11:7 to refer to a plurality in the divine world.

seen to consist not only of not doing the will of God but also of deliberately doing what is contrary to his will, perpetrating an act of infringement on the divine realm.

This means it is correct to say that the attitude of the first human couple is marked by hubris. Gerhard von Rad captures this well in the following lines:

> What the serpent's insinuation means is the possibility of an extension of human existence beyond the limits set for it by God at creation, an increase of life not only in the sense of pure intellectual enrichment but also of familiarity with, and power over, mysteries that lie beyond man. That the narrative sees man's fall, his actual separation from God, occurring again and again in *this* area (and not, for example, as a plunge into moral evil, into the subhuman!), i.e. what we call Titanism, man's *hubris*—this is truly one of its most significant affirmations.[43]

The hubris motif is also present in another important narrative in the primeval history, the story of the Tower of Babel in Gen 11:1–9. Further, we find it in a tradition that is prior to the Eden Narrative. This is clear in Ezekiel 28 (see vv. 2, 5, 6, 17); compare with Job 15:7–8. In the latter passage, primeval man is believed to have appropriated—without due authorization—wisdom in the heavenly assembly (*sôd 'ĕlôah*). We will return to this in chap. 5. In spite of statements to the contrary, the primeval history of Genesis very clearly comprehends the notion of human aspiration to divine status.[44]

In the Eden Narrative, man endeavored to go beyond human limitations in order to be equal to the gods. But all this came to nothing: 'You are dust, and to dust you shall return' *kî-'āpār 'attâ wĕ'el-'āpār tāšûb*, Gen 3:19. Correspondingly, the verdict in Ezekiel is: '[y]ou are but a mortal, and no god' *wĕ'attâ 'ādām wĕlō'-'ēl* (Ezek 28:9).

Summary and Conclusions about the Divine Test. I have called attention to Lohfink's, Van Seters', and Otto's findings with regard to traces of Deuteronomistic language in Genesis 2–3 (*ṣwh*, Piel; *šāma' lĕqôl* [*yhwh*]; and the curses). Taking a new, decisive step, I have introduced

---

43. Von Rad 1961: 87, emphasis in the original. Von Rad here writes in the vein of Wellhausen, who noted: "This is what transcends, in the writer's view, the limits of our nature; prying out the secret of things, the secret of the world, and overlooking, as it were, God's hand to see how He goes to work in His living activity, so as, perhaps, to learn His secret and imitate Him" (Wellhausen 1961: 302, German original 1895: 306).

44. See below, §7.2.1 (p. 126).

the Deuteronomistic notion of God's testing his people, using the word *nsh*, Piel, as the main term. A paradigmatic case appears in Deuteronomy 8, where God tests Israel to ascertain what is in their hearts: obedience or disobedience. Further, I argued that Genesis 2–3 is a text that moves in the theological neighborhood of late, postexilic compositions such as Genesis 22 and the Job prologue. A graph may illustrate the main features of these three texts:

	Genesis 22	Job	Genesis 2–3
Test	+	+	+
Purpose: to ascertain obedience/fear of God	+	+	+
Human ignorance about the test	+	+	+
The term *nsh*	+	0	0

Fig. 5. The main elements of the three texts dealing with divine tests of individuals.

The subject of the Eden Narrative is the divine test, and this subject is an aspect of the world of fiction within the work. What then about the theme? Death versus immortality is an important theme in the Eden Narrative, but it is not the main theme. Death occurs as the result of disobedience to the divine commandment. *The central theme is disobedience and its consequences.* The author communicates this in the sharpened form of a *thesis*, and this thesis runs as follows: *Obedience to the commandment leads to life, disobedience to death. All evil—death and the human condition at large—is seen as being due to this ultimate sin, disobedience against the divine commandment. The Deuteronomistic notion of law is here repristinated to the divine commandment, addressed* in illo tempore *to the first human couple in the garden of Eden.* None of the Deuteronomistic terms for the law is used. I believe that this has to do with a universalizing tendency. The law is for Israel; the commandment in the primeval garden is for humanity.[45] This universalizing tendency could explain why the divine designation used in the narrative is YHWH Elohim. Of the two combined elements, the first refers to God

---

45. As was pointed out by Moberly 1988: 26.

as Israel's covenant partner and the second to God as the universal Creator.[46]

In our theoretical discussion of theme, we saw that the plot of a narrative may be a valuable guide to the scholar. It is thus worth noticing that our conclusions about plot (chap. 2) and about theme (chap. 3) interlock perfectly.

3. Theodicy

Theodicy is an essential aspect of the theme of the Eden Narrative. Edenic bliss is obviously not what prevails in the world of the narrator. This real world is marked by hardships, suffering, and death. The question is unavoidable: who is to be blamed for this state of affairs? The Eden Narrative speaks of a divine test that the human couple failed. They did not obey the divine commandment. The blame thus falls on the human part of the God-human relationship. The text makes it clear that the state of affairs in the real world of the author is not willed and authored by the Creator. Man's actual lot is a perversion of what it was meant to be.

I believe that we should view this aspect of the narrative in the perspective of Deuteronomistic theology, with its emphasis on the connection between acts and consequences, between human actions and divine retribution—the term *retribution* being taken in both its negative and positive senses.[47] The radical choice between obedience and disobedience in Deuteronomistic theology is the choice between life and death (Deut 11:26–28, 30:15–20). The Deuteronomistic History is a work that begins with the apostasy of Israel in the desert and in the land of fulfilled promises and that ends with the Exile, the expulsion from that same country. It constitutes one great etiology of the loss of the land.[48] Disobedience to the law, notably the first commandment, led to the expulsion from the promised land.

I am inclined to view the Eden Narrative as a corollary to this history: the Eden Narrative displays a close connection between disobedience to God's very first commandment and the expulsion from the

---

46. See L'Hour 1974: especially p. 555; Wenham 1987: 57. For more details with regard to this designation, see below, §7.2.3, at the end (p. 132).

47. For a classic study of retribution in the Hebrew Bible, see Rankin 1936. There is a vast literature on the topic; note esp. Boström (1990: 90–140) and Janowski (1994).

48. Manfred Weippert stressed this aspect of the Deuteronomistic History (Weippert 1973: esp. pp. 435, 441).

Garden of Bliss. The story produces a paradigmatic case. The disobedience of Israel in the Deuteronomistic History is here transformed into the disobedience of the first human couple. The consequences of this primeval act of disobedience by the first humans are understood to affect all human life. Having missed the chance to attain immortality, the first man and woman succumb to the fate of having to die. In this, they are representative of the whole human race. Thus, *while the DH supplies an etiology for the loss of the land, the Eden Narrative serves as an etiology for the loss of the Garden of Bliss.*

So far, we have focused on the Eden Narrative as a self-contained unit. However, we must also widen our scope and include the preceding text in our perspective. This entails viewing the Eden Narrative as a response to the Priestly account of creation in Genesis 1.

Based on the thorough discussion of the matter by Terje Stordalen and Eckart Otto, we should now regard Gen 2:4 as a literary unit inserted by a redactor to function as a bridge between the P-account of creation and the Eden Narrative.[49] Otto reads Genesis 2–3 as an answer to Genesis 1. The Priestly Code speaks of the corruption of creation and the increase of violence (Gen 6:11–13). It does not, however, explain the origin of this corruption. Otto therefore understands the Eden Narrative as an etiology for the corruption of creation, which was altogether good from the outset.[50] Note God's repeated, favorable evaluation of the creation in Genesis 1, concluding with the final verdict: "God saw everything that he had made, and indeed, it was very good" (Gen 1:31). We will look at more aspects of theodicy in the following chapters (§4.4, p. 80, and §7.4, p. 132).

We now return to some questions raised above, namely, whether the first humans were thought to be immortal from the beginning and whether the text purports to describe a prelapsarian state, a situation before "the fall" (§3.2.1, p. 47). It should be clear by now (based on the premise of our narrative) that whether the first humans were to be mortal or immortal was an open issue until they failed the test. It seems clear that immortality was never granted. It was only a possible reward that never materialized. Without the divine gift of immortality,

---

49. Stordalen 1992 and Otto 1996: 185–89. See above, §1.2 near the end (p. 10).

50. Otto 1996: 189–92. Without discussing theodicy, Sawyer (1992: 64–66) also pointed to connections between the two entities and suggested that the Eden Narrative is "an expansion of the 'image of God' story in ch. 1" (p. 64). Schüle (2005) evinces an interesting reading of Genesis 2–3 as a response to Genesis 1. A moot point in his argument, however, is his comparison of Genesis 2–3 with the Babylonian *mis pi* ritual (the ritual for the dedication of divine statues).

the first humans remained beings created out of dust who must return to dust.

As has repeatedly been pointed out by others, the author hardly intended to describe a prelapsarian state (that is, before the fall). The narrative is constructed from the perspective of the "now" of the author, providing an etiology for the present state of things with the subordinate position of woman and the general fate of all: suffering and death.[51] What the narrative does say, however, is that this was not God's intention.

4. The Two Trees

Before leaving the question of theme in Genesis 2–3, we must comment on the two trees—trees that produced not only such palatable fruit as knowledge and immortality but also an amazing quantity of secondary literature. The two trees are symbols. Among the many definitions of "symbol," I choose Clifford Geertz's: "any physical, social, or cultural act or object that serves as a vehicle for a conception."[52] In any discussion of the two trees, the following two points should be kept in mind.

First, the two trees produce wisdom and immortality, and these are the two main divine prerogatives. For the tree of life, this goes without saying; immortality is not for humans. The end of the narrative stresses the fact that the Creator found it necessary to prevent the humans from gaining access to this prerogative of the deity. God expelled them from the garden and put the cherub there with a flaming sword to bar the way to the tree of life. The same applies to the tree of knowledge. The knowledge concerned is divine knowledge. This is clear from the words of the serpent in 3:5 and of God in 3:22. It is also clear from Job 15:7–8, where the first man (*ri'šôn 'ādām*) is interrogated about acquiring wisdom in the heavenly council (*sôd*).

Second, the two trees served different functions in the divine test of the two humans. The tree of knowledge served as the test case; the tree of life was the potential reward if the humans passed the test. The accent is slightly different: to attain divine knowledge by an illicit act, or to receive immortality as a gift.

The tree of life seems to have been an entity that the author of the Eden Narrative found in previous works, notably in the Wisdom litera-

---

51. See especially Westermann 1976: esp. pp. 356–57, English trans. 1984: 262–63.
52. Geertz 1993: 208 n. 19.

ture. In the Hebrew Bible, the tree of life appears only in Prov 3:18, 11:30, 13:12, and 15:4; and additionally, in the LXX of Isa 65:22. From these passages, we can see that the tree of life was an established metaphor but not a metaphor for immortality. It was the Eden author who provided the metaphor with this meaning. The tree of life appears to have been a creation of the Israelite wisdom circles. Contrary to what one might expect, it is not found in Sumerian or Akkadian literature.[53]

The tree of knowledge, on the other hand, was probably a metaphor created ad hoc by the author of the Eden Narrative. It appears nowhere else in the Hebrew Bible. There may be cases in the iconography, although this remains unclear.[54] Two different questions are connected with the tree of knowledge: the linguistic issue of how to understand the grammatical construction and the question of the symbolism of the tree of knowledge (what sort of "knowledge"?).

First, then, the linguistic question. The expression *ʿēṣ hadda'at ṭôb wārā'* ('the tree of the knowledge of good and evil', Gen 2:9, 17) has been considered by some to be linguistically problematic, but this is not a correct assessment of the evidence. If *hadda'at* is taken to be a noun in the absolute state in a genitive relation with the preceding word, then the problem is how to understand the function of the following *ṭôb wārā'*. If we take *ṭôb wārā'* to be part of a construct chain with *hadda'at*, then the problem is the definite article on the second word of the four. Dohmen notes that what one expects is *ʿēṣ hadda'at [da'at] ṭôb wārā'*.[55] Now, verbal nouns used as full nouns may take an object. Gesenius lists both Gen 2:9 and Jer 22:16 as cases in point of nominalized infinitives taking an object.[56] In the Jeremiah passage, the construction is *hadda'at 'ōtî*—that is, the same verbal noun takes both an article and an object. I believe, with Ellen van Wolde, that the Genesis construction is a case in which *da'at* does "double duty" as both a noun (in a genitive relationship with the preceding word) and a verb (that takes an object).[57] We may illustrate this in the following way:

---

53. On the situation in Sumerian literature, see Sjöberg 1984: 219, and on the situation in Akkadian literature, see Watanabe 1994: 579–80. For a discussion of the "tree of life" in the iconography, see Winter 1986.

54. See Edelman 2006: seals with two figures flanking and stretching their arms towards a tree. The problem is how to know that the tree represents wisdom.

55. Dohmen 1996: 55.

56. GKC §115d. Wallace (1985: 115–16) called attention to this.

57. Van Wolde 1994: 36.

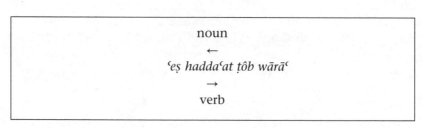

Fig. 6. The much-discussed phrase in Gen 2:9: does hadda'at *belong to what precedes or to what follows?*

Thus the grammar here, though not exactly common, is completely possible and certainly does not require literary-critical surgery.[58]

Let us proceed to the sort of knowledge that the tree was supposed to provide. On the basis of the fine discussions by Claus Westermann and Howard N. Wallace, we can single out the following as the main interpretations:[59]

1. *The acquisition of human qualities.* This interpretation takes a number of forms. Some scholars have stressed the aspect of a development from childlike innocence to adult maturity.[60] Others have stressed human independence and self-determination.[61]

2. *Sexual consciousness.* This interpretation is especially associated with Ivan Engnell and Robert Gordis.[62] Engnell speaks of the capacity of procreation. The tree of life implied eternal life. That the first humans should have both eternal life and a capacity for procreation was out of the question for YHWH and the other "gods" (p. 116). Gordis, in the same vein, speaks of the two trees as representing two roads to eternal life: personal immortality by eating from the tree of life and "vicarious immortality" by means of the procreation of children (p. 130).

3. *Ethical knowledge.* Eckart Otto chose this approach, as did James Barr.[63] However, Otto noted the paradox in this way of reasoning: the

---

58. Contrary to von Rad (1961: 77), who takes *ṭôb wārāʿ* to be a later insertion.

59. For a survey and critique, see Westermann 1976: 328–33, English trans. 1984: 242–45; Wallace 1985: 115–32, both with ample references to earlier literature.

60. See van Wolde 1989: 216–19 and Bechtel 1995.

61. Thus especially Steck 1970: 35 n. 43 and pp. 124–25.

62. Engnell 1955: 115–16; Gordis 1957: esp. pp. 130–34. Note also D. Michel 1997.

63. Otto 1996: 191; 1999: esp. pp. 228–29; and Barr 1993: 62. Barr speaks of "the power of rational and especially ethical discrimination."

humans would possess moral discernment by means of disobedience to the divine will.[64] Earlier Julius Wellhausen had decided against this position: "The knowledge spoken of cannot be moral knowledge. What could the assertion mean that God would have no one but Himself know the difference between good and evil, and would deny to man this knowledge?"[65]

4. *Universal knowledge.* This interpretation, which now seems to be the most widely accepted,[66] takes its cue from the well-known phenomenon of *merismus* in Biblical Hebrew, that is, a means of referring to a totality by mentioning the two ultimate points of a spectrum, thereby implicitly referring to the whole spectrum.[67] Thus, sea // dry land in Ps 95:5 refers to the whole earth, young // aged in Job 29:8 refers to everybody, and the sole of the foot // the crown of the head in Isa 1:6 refers to the whole body. According to this interpretation, the two main Hebrew words should not be understood as "good and evil" (which unduly limits the scope to ethical insight) but "good and bad"—what promotes and what does harm.[68] The expression covers everything that is between these two extremes as well.

Summary and Conclusions

1. I have consulted modern literary theory to come to grips with the notion of *theme*. The theme of a narrative should be distinguished from the subject, plot, and motifs. With Gerald Prince, I understand motifs to be minimal thematic units and theme to be a macrostructural concept. In order to establish a theme, observations about the structural properties of a text may be helpful. Conclusions about the theme may be tested against conclusions about the plot and genre of a narrative.

2. Structural characteristics point up the importance of the motif of death versus immortality in the Eden Narrative. This, however, is not the basic theme of the narrative.

---

64. Otto 1996: 178; cf. p. 191.

65. Wellhausen 1961: 301, German original 1895: 306.

66. See Wellhausen 1961: 301–3, German original 1895: 305–8; P. Humbert 1940: 113; von Rad 1961: 79; Westermann 1976: 331, English trans. 1984: 243, and others.

67. On merismus, see Krašovec 1977: esp. pp. 102–3, no. 99; Watson 1986: 321–24.

68. See Westermann 1976: 331, English trans. 1984: 243.

3. I define the subject as the divine test of obedience to the commandment and the theme as disobedience and its consequences. The discrete components of the text work together to manifest this theme, which thus has an integrating function in the text. The author communicates this theme in the form of a concise thesis: obedience to the commandment leads to life, disobedience to death. Death is seen as the consequence of disobedience to the commandment. The theme and thesis of the Eden Narrative should be seen as being inspired by Deuteronomistic theology.

4. Important Deuteronomistic texts speak of divine tests, the purpose of which was to ascertain whether Israel was obedient in the desert. The central term used is *nsh* in the Piel, 'to try', 'to test' (Deuteronomy 8; Exod 15:25–26, 16:4). The testing of Abraham in Genesis 22 should be seen as an instance of this "theology of testing." The testing of Job (note Job 1:9) is also relevant here. Interestingly, in the cases of Job and the first human couple, the specific term for testing is not used. One salient point that stands out in certain texts is human ignorance about being tested. This was true of Abraham, Job, and the first human couple.

5. The consequences of the test in the Eden Narrative should be seen in the light of the Deuteronomistic theology of retribution. Disobedience vis-à-vis the word of God is followed by divine curses. Note that the punishment of death in Deuteronomistic theology becomes the forfeiture of immortality in the Eden Narrrative.

6. The divine commandment to Israel in the Deuteronomistic History is repristinated and retrojected into primeval times and transformed into the divine commandment to the first human couple. The consequences of their primeval act of disobedience affects all human life and is presented as the ultimate explanation of the human condition at large, in which suffering and death are inescapable. While the Deuteronomistic History provides an etiology for the loss of the land, the Eden Narrative supplies an etiology for the loss of the Garden of Bliss.

7. The two trees represent the two divine prerogatives of wisdom (knowledge) and immortality. The grammatical construction of the phrase "the tree of the knowledge of good and evil" is not a major difficulty (see Jer 22:16). Regarding the type of knowledge implied, we found that universal knowledge best suits the quality of the knowledge that is a divine prerogative.

8. The observations made on the plot and on the theme interlock: the divine test has a central function.

Chapter 4

The Genre and Function
of the Eden Narrative

In analyzing narratives, one must give due attention to the *conflict* going on and to the *values* that are at stake.[1] In the plot analysis, I clarified the conflict that is taking place: the conflict between the first human couple and YHWH Elohim, instigated by the serpent. As we proceed to a discussion of the *genre* of the text and an analysis of the *functions* that the Narrative of Eden may have fulfilled, we will find that looking at these factors yields a possible answer to the question of *the values at stake* in this piece of literature. We will then be proceeding on the level of what the narrative was intended to perform, exploring its pragmatic dimension. From the fictive world of the narrative discussed in the plot analysis, we moved on to the real-world dimensions of the text in our discussion of its theme. In the present chapter, dealing with the genre and function of the Eden Narrative, we will proceed in the same direction. When discussing the functions of the text, we will be dealing with both its validating and its explanatory aspects.

Asking about the function of the text and identifying the values at stake entail examining the intention of the author. Umberto Eco once said that there is only one thing written for its own sake, and that is a shopping list; everything else we write in order to say something to somebody.[2] Frank Kermode, a literary scholar who cannot be accused of being unduly conservative, says that "in talking about 'signals' I have allowed the inference that they are emitted from an identifiable source, namely the author; and the further inference that their emission is under conscious control."[3]

---

1. Dr. Greger Andersson (Örebro) brought this feature to my attention (personal communication).

2. Eco 2002: 358: "Ogni altra cosa che scrivi, la scrivi per dire qualcosa a qualcuno."

3. Kermode 1983: 23.

Contrary to what many literary scholars have regarded as gospel truth for decades, I contend that asking about authorial intention is a justified and meaningful enterprise.[4]

4.1. The Genre of the Eden Narrative

1. The Genre: Myth

Scholars of literary theory have called attention to the implications of various generic signals or markers. Owing to their specific evocative power, names often have a special place in literature; they may even have a specifically generic function, connecting a certain piece of literature to a specific genre. In pastoral poetry, for example, there is a group of names that appear again and again from Theocritus on, such as Amaryllis, Amyntas, Daphnis, Galatea, and so on. Correspondingly, the setting of a poem may be an Arcadia (the Greek region of mythological fame). We may say, with Alastair Fowler, that these names serve as generic signals.[5]

We have already defined the designations for the man and the woman in the Eden Narrative as symbolic names (above, §2.4, p. 30). When we read in Genesis 4 that Cain, having murdered his brother, fled "to the land of Nod, east of Eden" (v. 16), we quickly recognize in "Nod" ('wandering') a similarly symbolic name. We do not ask for the

---

4. The issue of authorial intention is a minefield. There is a vast amount of literature on the subject. For an anthology with representatives of various positions, see recently Krausz 2002. One of the best studies of the intention issue in my opinion is Vanhoozer 1998. Vanhoozer stresses the fact that texts can be seen as acts of communication. This work deserves the special attention of all scholars who work with texts. I would also like to call attention to Torsten Pettersson, "The Literary Work as a Pliable Entity: Combining Realism and Pluralism" (Pettersson 2002). As the title indicates, Pettersson argues against monistic positions, assuming one "right" interpretation, including the subtype of intentionalist monism. The alternative, however, constructivism in the sense that literary works are not accounts of their objects but projections from critical stances and sets of values (p. 217), is also untenable to him. His own alternative is "pluralistic realism" (pp. 219–30). Thereby he hopes to do justice to the "combination of flexibility and resistance" of the literary work. He is thus skeptical about global monistic interpretations but still does not hold that "anything goes." The literary work is "pliable" in the sense that it may be open to different interpretations but still be resistant to arbitrary suggestions. Vanhoozer writes in the tradition of Hirsch 1967. The most "right wing" of the intentionalists is Juhl (1980); for a critique, see Hirsch (1983: 201–20). On intention in pictorial art, see Panofsky (1955: 1–25, especially pp. 11–14) and Baxandall (1985).

5. Fowler 1982: 75–87.

location of Nod on the map of the ancient Near East, nor should we ask for a definite location for the garden of Eden.[6] (Understood according to its etymology, the name *Eden* had the connotations of 'luxuriance', 'bliss'.[7]) Neither do we look upon the Eden Narrative as reflecting a one-time, historical event. Because of the restricted occurrence of "names" such as Eden, Adam, and Eve, we cannot interpret them as genre markers in the truest sense of the word, that is, connecting the Eden Narrative to one specific genre. In order for them to be genre markers, we would need examples of their appearance in other texts of the same type. But names of this sort certainly do point to the symbolic nature of the text in which they occur.

When reading a text, we should reflect on its relationship to extra-linguistic reality. As Torsten Pettersson reminded us in his worthwhile essay, a text may have a *referential ambition* in the sense that it purports to tell the truth about an extralinguistic reality.[8] We sometimes read about specific events in space and time. For instance, if a work of history states that "Gaius Julius Caesar was murdered on March 15th, 44 B.C.E.," then its referential ambition is manifested by the fact that a person who was in the relevant place at that particular time would have been able to watch that very event. On the other hand, certain texts, notably works of fiction, have a different kind of relation to reality: they may possess *representativity*, that is, a validity that is greater than the individual case. A text of this sort lacks referential ambition in the above-mentioned sense, and this is normally clear to both author and audience.[9]

In reading the Eden Narrative, we see a text that relates to reality not by referential ambition but by representativity—that is, universal applicability. We do not ask about the *factuality*, the historicity of the event narrated, but about the *relevance* of the narrative. How can it contribute to our understanding of what it means to be a human being? When we discover this symbolic function of the myth, to quote Ricoeur,

> we should not say, "The story of the 'fall' is *only* a myth"—that is to say, something less than history—but, "The story of the fall has the

---

6. On time and location, see above, §2.2 (p. 14).
7. See Millard 1984; Stordalen 2000: 257–61.
8. For the following, see T. Pettersson 2005.
9. This, as Pettersson points out (2005: 221 n. 3), distinguishes a work of fiction from a lie; a lie is intended to be received as having referential ambition.

greatness of myth"—that is to say, has more meaning than a true history.[10]

Living after Immanuel Kant, we must accept that the apparatus of our human senses is competent to perceive the empirical reality of this world, neither more nor less. We must accept the fact that, where transcendental reality is concerned, we can express ourselves only in metaphors. "Man only has two possibilities: Either he keeps eternal silence, or he talks about God in human words, a choice between agnosticism and anthropomorphism," according to a Dutch professor of systematic theology, Herman Bavinck.[11] Analogous constraints apply to our dealings with existential dimensions of reality such as evil and death.

The narrative in Genesis 2–3 moves on the level of metaphors and symbols. If we were to find a text of the same type as the Eden Narrative in any other culture, we would certainly designate it a myth. There is no reason to avoid this label when we discuss the Eden Narrative. It is a myth.[12] It is true that Odil Hannes Steck suggested reading Genesis 2–3 as an etiological narrative.[13] Understanding the text in light of its final section (3:20–24), as Steck suggests, is an illuminating exercise.[14] Identifying the text in question as an etiological narrative is certainly not wrong, but it is insufficient as a genre designation. As we will see, the etiological aspects of the text, stressed by various authors, will be quite comprehensible from the perspective of its function as myth.

Rather than attempting the virtually impossible task of working out one, all-encompassing definition of myth,[15] I will list a number of aspects of myth that are essential to my understanding of the phenomenon.[16]

1. *Form.* Myth is narrative in form. Consequently, the study of myth is instructed by the modern discipline of narratology. The Eden

---

10. Ricoeur 1969: 236.

11. Quoted in Korpel 1990: 10.

12. For Gunkel's vacillation between this and other definitions of the genre of the Eden Narrative, see Rogerson 1974: 57–65.

13. Steck 1970: 66–73, esp. p. 69.

14. Steck suggests understanding the text from the standpoint of its ending: "[G]leichsam von hinten her will sie auch gelesen sein, wenn ihr konstitutiver Gegenwartsbezug mit im Blick bleiben soll" (Steck 1970: 68).

15. A multidefinitional approach commends itself, as Rogerson notes (1974: 166). For brief, compact syntheses on myth and the interpretation of myths, see Childs 1968; Rogerson 1974; Otzen, Gottlieb, and Jeppesen 1980; Doty 1997; Assmann and Assmann 1998; Segal 2004 and 2005, all with bibliographies.

16. For the following, see Stordalen 1998: 284–87; Mettinger 2001: 46–53, esp. pp. 50–52; Segal 2004: 4–6, all with bibliographies.

Narrative is a well-wrought piece of narrative art, and we have already subjected it to narratological analysis.

2. *Content*. Myths deal with one or several gods and/or supernatural beings. In my view, myth does not necessarily presuppose a polytheistic outlook. The time of the narrative is often the distant past (*in illo tempore*). For example, in Akkadian cosmogonic narratives adopted from Sumerian, the phrase *ina ūmī ullûti* 'in those [distant] days'[17] is characteristic. One could ask, with H.-P. Müller, whether the formula "in the day that the LORD God made the earth and the heavens" (Gen 2:4b) might be understood as a genre marker of this sort. Müller points out that the beginning of *Adapa* has a similar formula: "In those days, in those years."[18] However, because Gen 2:4 in its entirety is a redactional bridge,[19] we should remind ourselves that the "not-yet-passage" of Gen 2:5 also has a corollary in the introduction of the Babylonian creation epic, *Enuma Elish*.[20]

3. *Function*. Myth accomplishes something. It may have one of the following functions:

a. To provide *entertainment*.
b. To serve as a *paradigm for the present*:
    as *validation* (legitimation) for institutions and values;
    as an *explanation* for the burdens of human existence.
c. To offer a *counter-present* that relativizes the deficiencies of the prevailing situation.[21]

In its paradigmatic function, a myth offers a sort of "historical analysis" or etiology. It provides an "explanation of a presently observed condition by appeal to an imaginary one-time event in the past," thus using the "punctual" to explain the "durative."[22]

4. *Context*. It was formerly often believed that the Sitz im Leben of myth was ritual, but this is no longer so.[23] It is now widely recognized that some myths may be ritual myths, while others serve in contexts outside the cult.

My *conclusion* so far is that the Eden Narrative meets the requirements for defining its genre as myth. The fact that two human beings

---

17. See Dietrich 1995.
18. *Adapa* A 5. See Müller 1991a: 127 with n. 45. See also Müller 1983–84: 80.
19. See Stordalen 1992 and note also Otto 1996: 185–89.
20. See Gunkel 1910: 5; Stordalen 1992: 168.
21. On the last point, see Assmann 2002: 78–83, esp. p. 79.
22. I am here using the words of Hallo 2004: 267.
23. Fontenrose (1966) demonstrated that it is not essential to link myth and rite.

are important in this story along with a deity hardly suffices to counter this conclusion.

2. A Sociofunctionalist Interpretation of the Eden Narrative

Because I am interested in the pragmatic aspects of the Eden Narrative—what values it seeks to impart to the reader—I have chosen to adopt a functionalist approach to the myth. I cannot quite sympathize with Mircea Eliade's ahistoric interpretation of myths that tends to decontextualize the material he is dealing with; it would rob our narrative of its sociocontextual meaning.[24] Another option, the structuralist approach, is hardly more attractive: it disregards the important clues for further investigation that the plot has given us (see the excursus on structuralist interpretations of the Eden Narrative, below).

The functionalist paradigm for the interpretation of myths harks back to Bronislaw Malinowski. The function of myth, says Malinowski,

> is to strengthen tradition and endow it with a greater value and prestige by tracing it back to a higher, better, and more supernatural reality of initial events.[25]

To Malinowski, myth is action. His later stance, as a mature writer and as presented in *Myth in Primitive Psychology* (1926), was pragmatic functionalism.[26] Myth, as a statement of primeval reality, provides "justification by precedent [and] supplies a retrospective pattern of moral values."[27] Or, to quote Joseph Campbell, myth serves to "validate, support, and imprint the norms of a given, specific moral order" and to authorize its moral code "as a construct beyond criticism and human emendation."[28] Myth serves the purpose of "supporting cultural and social values by grounding them in a transcendent realm, by projecting them outside the culture."[29]

Edmund Leach made the interesting observation that scholars studying myth have only found this functionalist perspective fruitful

---

24. On the antireductionist (Eliade) versus reductionist (Segal) debate, see Allen (2002: 3–63 with bibliography) and the essays in Idinopoulos and Yonan 1994. On Eliade, note also Strenski 1987: 70–103 with bibliography.

25. Malinowski 1926: 125. Malinowski was influenced by Durkheim, as was noted by, for example, Strenski 1987: 50–55 and Doty 1997: 43–44.

26. On Malinowski's development, see Strenski 1987: 42–69.

27. Malinowski 1926: 124.

28. Campbell, as cited by Doty 1997: 54. Doty does not give exact references.

29. Doty 1997: 43–44.

in dealing with Genesis 1, which may be seen as a mythical charter for the seven-day week, whereas the Eden Narrative seems to have "no obvious implications for the functionalists."[30] I believe the following examination will show that this narrative—contrary to received wisdom—is a text well worth reviewing precisely from a sociofunctionalist perspective.

What insights, then, do we gain from an analysis of this sort? In the first place, the Eden Narrative may be seen as serving the function of supporting a specific system of norms. This function of *validating social values* is apparent at the very center of the narrative, in the demand for obedience to the divine commandment. Disobedience to the commandment, to the law, stands out not only as an aspect of negative conduct in general but, indeed, as leading to death: the first human couple missed the chance to attain immortality. It was the act of disobedience that barred the way to the tree of life and brought about the expulsion from Eden.

Is it possible for us to anchor this specific ethos in a specific social milieu? I believe that it is. During the last few decades, it has become normal to view the Eden Narrative as a very late piece, to be placed not before the Exile but rather in the Persian era. The text most likely presupposes the Creation Narrative of P in Genesis 1, and other features point to a late date as well.[31]

Moreover, we found above that the text has certain affinities with wisdom and Deuteronomistic covenant theology. Most importantly, we studied the divine test of the human couple in Genesis 2–3 as an illustrative instance in a series of divine tests undertaken to ascertain whether there was obedience to the divine commandment. We compared the Eden Narrative with God's testing of Israel (Deuteronomy 8), with the testing of Abraham (Genesis 22), and with the case of Job.

These observations point in a specific direction when we seek to determine the social milieu behind the Eden Narrative. Certain characteristics of this narrative reflect an ethos similar to the world view of circles close to or at least inspired by the Deuteronomistic theologians. The stress on human obedience to God's commandment as a matter of vital importance (the radical choice being foundationally a choice

---

30. Leach 1970: 53–54, quotation from p. 54.
31. For the insight that the text presupposes Genesis 1, see Sawyer (1992: 64–66), Otto (1996), and Schüle (2005). Note also Stordalen's discussion of the date (2000: 206–13).

between life and death) can be read as an attempt to validate the place held by the Deuteronomistic law in postexilic Judah.[32]

Validation of social values may also be involved in the motif of the woman as created from the rib of the man. Though 2:23–24, in which a man must leave his father and mother and cling to his wife, hardly reflects established marriage customs in Israel,[33] one should not disregard the possibility that these verses with the formula "bones of my bones and flesh of my flesh" may nevertheless validate marriage as a fundamental social institution.[34] If this is going too far, the formula may be seen to serve as a primeval explanation for the force that draws the sexes together.[35]

Here we touch on the explanatory, etiological function of the myth.[36] Proceeding in the same direction, we should remember (with Ricoeur and others) that the myth has ontological implications: it points to the relation between "the essential being of man and his historical existence."[37] And the historical existence of humankind is marked by suffering and hardships. Two passages from the Eden Narrative are especially noteworthy in this context: the divine sentencing (3:14–19) and the expulsion of the human couple from Eden (3:22–24).

First and foremost among the hardships of human life to be explained in the Eden Narrative is, of course, the fact that life, created by YHWH and animated by his divine breath, ends up in demise and dissolution: death. The Eden Narrative relates a story of human disobedience and seduction by the serpent. Immortality was a possibility—if they had obeyed—but it was forfeited. Man is dust: he is taken out of dust, and to dust he shall return (3:19). The cherubim were placed to the east of the garden of Eden "to guard the way to the tree of life" (3:24). Death is thus "accounted for" as being due to primordial discord between humankind and God, caused by the disobedience at the tree. Death, indeed, runs counter to the original intentions of the Creator.

---

32. On the Deuteronomistic History with its stress on the law, see recently Albertz 2003: 271–302.

33. This circumstance was stressed by Westermann (1976: 315–18, English trans. 1984: 231–34), who is skeptical about finding here the validation for marriage as a social institution.

34. On this formula, the *Verwandtschaftsformel*, see Reiser 1960. For other relevant passages, see Gen 29:14; Judg 9:2–3; 2 Sam 5:1; 19:13–14.

35. Von Rad 1961: 82–83.

36. The etiological aspects have often been noticed, but as far as I know they have not been discussed in a functionalist interpretation of the Eden Narrative as myth. On etiologies in general, note Long 1968; Van Dyk 1990.

37. Ricoeur 1969: 163.

When, in turn, we study the divine sentences (3:14–19), we should note that they contain curses. These, however, are not directly addressed to the human couple but primarily concern the serpent and the ground. The divine sentence on woman and man strikes at the two culprits' gender roles. In the case of the woman, it speaks to the pain of child-bearing and subordination to the man: 'Your desire shall be for your husband, and he shall rule over you' (*wĕʾel-ʾîšēk tĕšûqātēk*, . . .).[38] The man is told, "By the sweat of your face you shall eat bread" (3:19). The ground he worked was placed under a curse (3:17).

In the case of the woman, we may read the statement about subordination as illustrating the function of myths to legitimate social order, to explain socially prevailing inequalities. At the same time, it is clear that this position of the woman is not something that was originally willed and authored by the Creator.

The functionalist perspective on myth is in line with the general approach to the phenomenon of religion found in the sociology of knowledge.[39] This branch of sociology offers an understanding of symbolic universes as "social products with a history,"[40] a stress on the close relationship between human thought and the social context within which it arises. There is "a high degree of continuity between social and cosmic order."[41] Symbolic universes operate on the "nomic," ordering level and serve to legitimate institutional order. Mythology is thus a form of "universe-maintenance."[42] An approach to myth informed by the sociology of knowledge inspires historical awareness: We realize "the inevitable historicity of human thought," its "situational determination."[43] We realize that "[w]e cannot emigrate from our historical moment"—nor could the ancients.[44]

My *conclusion* is that the Eden Narrative meets the criteria for the genre designation "myth." Contrary to what some have believed, it is a worthwhile enterprise to undertake a functionalist analysis. The narrative serves the function of validating and explaining. It validates the

38. Incidentally, the Song of Songs in an allusion to this expression hints at love as a force that is able to overcome this hierarchy when the woman says: 'I am my beloved's, and his desire is for me' (*wĕʿālay tĕšûqātô*, Song 7:11[10]).

39. For the following, see Berger and Luckmann (1985: esp. pp. 110–46) for their discussion of symbolic universes.

40. Berger and Luckmann 1985: 115.

41. Berger and Luckmann 1985: 128.

42. Berger and Luckmann 1985: 128. On the terms "nomos," "nomic," and "anomic," see Berger 1969: 189 n. 23, 190 n. 26.

43. Berger and Luckmann 1985: 19.

44. Quotation from Kermode 1979: viii.

ideal of obedience to the law, of submission to the will of God. In addition, it explains the hardships of human life: suffering and death.

4.2. Excursus:
Structuralist Approaches

The preceding interpretation of the Eden Narrative was carried out with the tools of the sociofunctionalist approach to myth. Before I leave this part of our investigation, I would like to refer to some interpreters who have adopted a structuralist approach instead.[45]

As a matter of fact, there are a number of different structuralist approaches, some germane to the Lévi-Strauss tradition in anthropology, some more related to what goes on in literary studies, the Propp-Greimas tradition. Typical of the Lévi-Strauss approach is finding binary oppositions that the myth serves to resolve (nature versus culture, etc.) and searching for elements such as times, plants, social roles, and so on. The process of interpretation is one of decomposition and recomposition: the task of the analysis is to decompose the symbolic network into its constituents and then study them as codes that constitute deep structures. The various elements receive their meaning from their place in the structure. The analysis programmatically disregards the narrative line, the plot, in the myths studied, focusing on the structures instead. This is one feature that distinguishes the structuralist study of myth from all other methodologies.[46]

One of the studies of Genesis 2–3 from a structuralist perspective, the book by Hans Jörgen Lundager Jensen, deserves special mention.[47] His writing is marked by a penetrating treatment of the Hebrew text, by balanced comparisons with other ancient Near Eastern material, and by the working out of a number of oppositions and structural lines. He singles out the alimentary (nutritional) code as the most important element in the Eden narrative, noting the place held by the plants and the bread and also the frequency of the root *ʾ-k-l* 'eat' in Genesis 2–3; with its 23 occurrences, it is second only to "Elohim" and "Adam" (both 24×).[48] One should note that the importance of the act of eating supports our above-mentioned plot analysis, in which this act marks the peripeteia of the narrative (§2.3.3, p. 23).

---

45. On structuralist approaches to myth, see the survey in Doty (1997: 192–213) and Segal (2004: 113–25).

46. For presentations and discussion of the Lévi-Strauss approach: see Lévi-Strauss's programmatic article 1955; the excellent presentation by Jensen 2004: 21–38; note also Rogerson 1974: 101–27.

47. Jensen 2004: 69–142. Among other studies, I would especially like to mention Edmund Leach 1970.

48. Jensen 2004: 124–35; for the statistics, see p. 129.

Other studies of our text are more marked by a connection with the Propp-Greimas tradition. Again one finds stress on binary oppositions, such as good – bad, male – female, human – animal, life – death. Further, there are a number of deficiencies and deficiencies filled, such as no water, no herbs, no man to till the ground, no suitable mate for the man. Some scholars also apply Greimas's actantial model (sender – object – receiver; helper – subject – opponent), sometimes complemented by the Proppian model of a hero and villain.

There is no doubt that these studies have helped us perceive important features in the text.[49] Jobling's stress on the notions of inside and outside the garden and also on the need for someone to till the earth is certainly valid. Susan Niditch has offered a worthwhile suggestion, too: she sees two major thematic chains in Genesis 1–11—one involving the passage from an initial state of chaos to an ideal cosmos, the other involving the passage from this ideal state to reality. In her overall structure, Genesis 2–3 expresses the passage from an ideal state to the reality marked by social hierarchies and sexual and procreative roles.[50] Individual suggestions, however, such as Jobling's idea of seeing Yhwh Elohim as the villain,[51] seem to me slightly counterintuitive.

Some scholars maintain the structuralist-semiotic tradition. One example is Ole Davidsen, who has a clear eye for the loss of eternal life as the potential focus of the text.[52] A most impressive study along these lines was written by Ellen van Wolde in *A Semiotic Analysis of Genesis 2–3* (1989).[53] In this step-by-step analysis, characterized by methodological awareness and intellectual rigor, van Wolde works out her semiotic approach to narrative texts, a combination of the perspectives of Greimas and Peirce.

In her application of this model to the Eden Narrative, van Wolde first develops a "narrative analysis," focusing on the characters who appear as subjects of the actions and on the actions themselves. She concludes that there was a main narrative programme with man as the tiller of the garden

---

49. Note the collections of essays edited by Patte (Patte ed. 1980; 1998), the first containing a number of structural readings of Genesis 2–3 and the second some semiotic studies of these chapters. Note Patte's valuable introductory essay to the first volume (Patte 1980) and Croatto's critical response to the Eden essays in the second volume (Croatto 1998: 187–210). Note also Jobling 1986 and Slivniak 2003.

50. Niditch 1985. The trajectory from chaos to order is found in Gen 1:1–2:4a, 2:4b–25, 6:5–9:19; from ideal order to reality in Gen 3:1–24, 6:1–4, 11:1–9. It may be a problem that she thus divides Genesis 2–3 and dissolves its unity. On pp. 30–35, however, she discusses Genesis 2–3 as a narrative of its own.

51. Jobling 1986: 24–26. Jobling regards this as the "keystone of the entire analysis" (p. 25).

52. Davidsen 1982.

53. She returns to Genesis 2–3 in a number of later works; see, e.g., van Wolde 1994: 3–47.

(pp. 115–16). In her "semantic analysis," she lays bare a number of "isotopies" or lines of meaning. A "careful reading of Genesis 2–3" (p. 132) yields five distinct lines of meaning, constituted by certain relationships in the text: God and man, man and earth, man and animal, man and woman, and life and death. All are subjected to thorough analysis (pp. 133–209). The final step is taken in the "discursive analysis." Here van Wolde studies the strategies of the narrator. She finds "an omniscient narrator who is not present in the text" (p. 214). Her ideas about maturation as the theme of the Eden Narrative have been presented above (§1.1, p. 4).

Looking back at these contributions by scholars in the structuralist tradition, one must be grateful for a host of worthwhile individual observations. Certainly, these studies have helped us perceive a number of important textual features and see them in a new light. In one respect, however, I must confess to having a major objection: myths are narratives, and a most important feature of a narrative is its plot. This feature is grossly neglected in structuralist approaches. Everything revolves around structures. Even a scholar who himself works with a modified structuralist approach, G. S. Kirk, wisely remarks: "It seems to me . . . that the 'meaning' of the myth is to be found, not in any algebra of structural relationships, but quite explicitly in its *contents*, seen in terms, no doubt, of certain significant relationships that have analogies at different levels."[54] The stress on structures at the price of neglecting the plot is basically due to overstretching the linguistic analogy. Kirk aptly remarks: "The function of the language is to convey content, not to convey its own grammatical and syntactical rules—its own structure, that is. . . . If the myth-language analogy is valid, then myths, like language, will convey messages distinct from their own structure."[55]

Consequently, for the purposes of the present project, I find it more fruitful to proceed from a sociofunctionalist approach. However valuable we may find van Wolde's carefully worked-out "isotopies" (narrative lines), or Jobling's observations about the inside-outside of the garden and about the importance of a man to till the earth, or Jensen's "alimentary code," I feel that the narrative focus on the divine commandment and test, worked out above in our narratological analysis, is unduly neglected in all these studies (see fig. 7).

4.3. The Nature of Genre and How Genre Works

In our discussion of the genre of our text, we arrived at the conclusion that the Eden Narrative is a myth. We thus group it with other narratives that contain large-scale interpretations of the shared human

---

54. Kirk 1973: 71, emphasis his. For Kirk's critical assessment of the structuralist approach, see 1973: 42–83. Note also Doty 1997: 204–5, with bibliography.
55. Kirk 1973: 43.

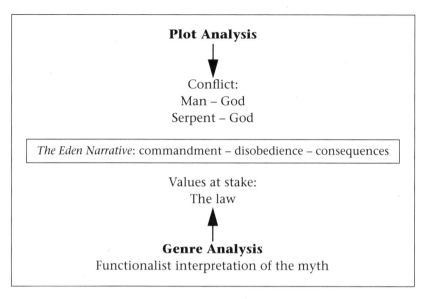

Plot Analysis

Conflict:
Man – God
Serpent – God

The Eden Narrative: commandment – disobedience – consequences

Values at stake:
The law

Genre Analysis
Functionalist interpretation of the myth

Fig. 7. Various methodological perspectives help us see different aspects of the Eden Narrative. Plot analysis reveals the conflict(s) going on, and genre analysis makes us aware of the values at stake.

experience of real-life conditions.[56] So far, so good. A question one would have liked to have an answer to is this: was there in the ancient Near East a "myth" genre that was recognizable to the ancients and that served as a norm or an ideal for the production of new works of the same kind, a genre that was recognized and shared by the Eden author?

The answer to this question is not as simple as one might think. Indeed, it may be impossible to find an answer. This is due partly to the chances of preservation in ancient Near Eastern archaeology and partly to the much-debated nature of genre in general. There is intense discussion about genre in the field of literary theory today.[57] A good

---

56. I have seen this formulation as a description of the nature of myth, but I cannot recall where.

57. On the phenomenon of genre see, for a first orientation, Kearns 2005b. I find the following contributions from the last few decades especially worthwhile: Hempfer 1973; Fowler 1982; the anthologies edited by Haettner Aurelius and Götselius 1997 and by Duff 2000, both of which contain a number of classic essays by Bakhtin, Genette, Jauss, and Todorov. Note the magisterial surveys of the whole problem with specific awareness of the philosophical and linguistic aspects involved by

definition of *genre* has been proposed by David Duff in his collection of theory-of-genre essays as a "recurring type or category of text, as defined by structural, thematic and/or functional criteria."[58]

This debate concerns the nature of genre, revealing radical dissent over what sort of existence a genre actually has and how a genre works vis-à-vis the reading/listening audience of a work and vis-à-vis the author who produces a piece of literature.

First, some remarks on the ontological status of genre: What sort of existence does "genre" have? Does genre have the status resulting from logical classification, carried out *post rem*? Or does it have independent existence prior to the production of a particular literary work, as a norm or an ideal—that is, *ante rem*? Foundationally, this problem is linked to the philosophical controversy over the ontological status of universals, such as "horse," "man," "woman," and "genre," as different from individual designations such as "the author of the present work." In this continuous philosophical debate, realists and nominalists assume the extreme positions at either end of a wide range of attitudes.

Viewing the problem from this perspective, Hans Robert Jauss notes that "[t]he theory of literary genres is at the point of seeking a path between the Scylla of nominalist skepticism that allows for only a posteriori classifications, and the Charybdis of regression into timeless typologies, a path along which the historicization of genre poetics and the concept of form are upheld."[59] Jauss is inclined to view the different genres not as genera (classes) in the logical sense but, rather, as a group of historical families, thus alluding to what Wittgenstein termed "family resemblances."[60] This perspective was developed by Alastair Fowler.[61] Seen in this light, a genre appears as a tradition that forms a historical continuum, recognizable to the members of a given culture but also changeable over time.

Haettner Aurelius (2003) and A. Pettersson (2006). The monograph by Fishelov (1993) is highly illuminating. Fishelov investigates the metaphors and analogies used by scholars in their studies of genre: genres as biological species, as families, as social institutions, and as speech acts.

58. Duff 2000: xiii.

59. Jauss 1982: 78. Other scholars who have made important contributions on the issue of the nature of the genres are Hempfer (1973: chap. 3; note Hempfer's "constructivist synthesis" between a nominalistic and a realistic stance, pp. 122–27), Fowler (1982), and A. Pettersson (2006).

60. Jauss 1982: 79–80.

61. Fowler 1982: 37–44.

The next question is how genre works vis-à-vis the audience and vis-à-vis the author. The reader-response aspect of the phenomenon of genre is a natural place to start. E. D. Hirsch, in his *Validity in Interpretation* (1967), subjects genre to a penetrating analysis from the point of view of the reading process (chap. 3). Hirsch argues that "an interpreter's preliminary generic conception of a text is constitutive of everything that he subsequently understands, and . . . this remains the case unless and until that generic conception is altered" (p. 74). Hirsch goes on to note that "[a]ll understanding of verbal meaning is necessarily genre-bound" (p. 76). This sense of the genre-bound character of understanding is, of course, a version of the hermeneutical circle: the reading expectations pull the reader into a process of preliminarily identifying the genre and subsequently correcting this identification.

An important step forward in this discussion was taken by Jonathan Culler in his *Structuralist Poetics*.[62] On the basis of his linguistic analogy, Culler coins the term "literary competence": just as there is linguistic competence, there is what may be termed *literary competence*. The reader who possesses competence of this sort has internalized the "grammar" of literature.

Against this background, we understand why John Barton in his book on method in biblical study devotes his very first chapter to "'literary competence' and genre recognition," as the chapter heading reads. Barton wisely understands literary competence "as *the ability to recognize genre*."[63]

Now it is time to consider the way that genre works vis-à-vis the author. All literature shares the intertextual nature of any verbal construct. No author moves in a literary vacuum. There is a prior body of discourse that the new writer "implicitly or explicitly takes up, prolongs, cites, refutes, transforms."[64] The genres work as points of contact with which a new piece of literature engages, in dialogue with other parts of the literary universe. The author who knows the conventions at work is thereby able to engage with a literary tradition. His or her activity as a writer is made possible by the existence of the genre, "which the author can write against, certainly, whose conventions he may attempt to subvert, but which is nevertheless the context within which his activity takes place."[65] Whether or not the new

---

62. Culler 1986: 113–30, originally published in 1975.
63. Barton 1984: 8–19; quotation from p. 16, emphasis his.
64. Culler 1992: 101.
65. Culler 1986: 116.

writer is plagued by the anxiety of influence, he/she seldom or never works from a completely new starting point. He or she stands on the shoulders of others.

Let us now return to our introductory question: Was there in the ancient Near East a "myth" genre that was recognized and shared by the author of the Eden Narrative? In modern times, Malinowski was able to distinguish three different types of narratives cultivated by the Melanesians he studied. One of these types was myths, and this third class was referred to by the natives as *liliu*; thus, the natives' own classification system manifested a special term. [66] The Masai in Africa also have a special designation for myth: *enk-iteru-n-oto,* a word that means 'beginning'. [67] The scholarly, etic designation (*myth*) may thus have a counterpart in an emic designation. As far as I know, however, no such term has been preserved from the ancient Near East. But this does not necessarily mean that there was no awareness of a special type of narrative.

We know that there were genres such as various types of hymns: the imperative hymn so well known from the Psalms and the participial hymn known from the book of Job. It seems clear that the Hebrew writers had an awareness of the demands that a genre could make on an author. The fixed structure and fixed grammatical characteristics exerted their inexorable governing power in these cases. With a genre such as myth, the situation is slightly different. Our classification is mainly based on various aspects of the content of these texts (see above). Consequently, I am much less certain that we can demonstrate a generic awareness on the part of the "myth-makers."

Nevertheless, it is interesting to note that there are indications that our Eden Narrative was indeed in dialogue with a prior mythological tradition, although it is impossible to speak of an intertextual relationship with a specific text. We now turn our attention to this matter.

4.4. The Eden Narrative versus the Chaos Battle Drama of Creation

It is clear that the serpent acts as the agent that instigated the human insurgence against God. There is thus, at a deeper level, a conflict between the serpent and Yʜwʜ Elohim. In a work unduly neglected

---

66. Malinowski 1926: 35.
67. See Olsson 1977. I am grateful to Tord Olsson for calling my attention to this designation (personal communication).

by biblical scholars, *The Symbolism of Evil*, Paul Ricoeur evinces a typology for myths that are about the beginning of evil that is quite significant with regard to the ancient Near East, including Israel.[68] Two of his types are relevant to the present discussion.

1. *The myth of chaos or the drama of creation* implies that the origin of evil is coextensive with the origin of things. *The creative act of the deity here works upon chaos.* As a corollary, salvation is seen as identical with the act of creation itself. "The act that founds the world is at the same time the liberating act."[69] "The identity of evil and 'chaos,' and the identity of salvation with 'creation,' have seemed to us to constitute the two fundamental traits of this first type," says Ricoeur.[70] No wonder that salvation history has no place in this theological concept.[71] This is a type of thinking that seems to have been fostered in circles in Israel that were marked by cult and wisdom.[72]

2. *The idea of a "fall" of man* or, as *Ricoeur prefers to call it, "the Adamic myth,"*[73] entails a change of type. Here we have an irrational event *in a creation that is already completed.* "[T]he idea of a 'fall' of man becomes fully developed only in a cosmology from which any creation-drama has been eliminated."[74] The Adamic myth—or (for specific reasons) in my terminology, the Eden Narrative[75]—has its corollary in the idea of salvation as a new peripeteia in relation to primordial creation, in salvation history.[76]

The Babylonian creation myth, *Enuma Elish*, is an example of Ricoeur's first type as are such specimens of Hebrew poetry as Pss 74:12–

---

68. Ricoeur 1969: 171–74 and 232–78.

69. Ricoeur 1969: 172.

70. Ricoeur 1969: 172.

71. Ricoeur 1969: 191.

72. Note Hermisson's observation that the wisdom traditions know of a border that protects the created world against chaos (Ps 104:9, Job 38:11, Jer 5:22), while the Jerusalemite cult tradition with the idea of an annual reenactment knows of no such protecting border (Ps 89:10–14; Psalm 93). Here the Sea remains as a threat. See Hermisson 1978.

73. Ricoeur (1969) finds the term "fall" unsatisfactory for reasons that he points out on p. 233.

74. Ricoeur 1969: 172.

75. It should be noted that I reserve the designation "Adamic myth" for the oldest recoverable story about the first man's sin and expulsion from Eden, applied by Ezekiel to the king of Tyre; see Ezekiel 28 and chap. 5, below. Ricoeur uses this label for the Eden Narrative in Genesis 2–3.

76. Ricoeur 1969: 173. It is hence interesting that Ricoeur seems to have had an inkling of the importance of the Deuteronomistic ideas of a radical choice behind the development of the Adamic myth (Ricoeur 1969: 233).

17 and 89:10–13[9–12]. In these two poems, we first find references to God's victory over the chaotic forces, represented by the Sea and various monsters such as Leviathan and Rahab, and then references to God's act of creation.[77] The last-mentioned passage runs:

> You rule the raging of the sea;
> when its waves rise, you still them.
> You crushed Rahab like a carcass;
> you scattered your enemies with your mighty arm.
> The heavens are yours, the earth is also yours;
> the world and all that is in it—you have founded them.
> The north and the south—you created them;
> Tabor and Hermon joyously praise your name.

It should be clear from our discussion in the previous chapter (§3.2.2, p. 49) that the Eden Narrative is a very late text. It is therefore interesting to see that in the Eden Narrative we find the serpent in an important role. The serpent is introduced as one of the many creatures of God (3:1). Nevertheless, in its capacity as a counter-divine force, it seems to have some "genetic" relation to the serpent of the chaos battle myth in the form known from Job and the Isaiah Apocalypse: "Leviathan the fleeing serpent (*nāḥāš bāriaḥ*)" (Job 26:13, Isa 27:1) and "Leviathan the twisting serpent (*nāḥāš ʿăqallātôn*)" (Isa 27:1). The word-pair in Isa 27:1 occurs much earlier, in the Ugaritic myth of Baal and Mot.[78]

In Genesis 3, the importance of the serpent is emphasized by his central position in the inclusio arrangement found in the passage containing the divine hearings and the divine sentences.[79] I believe that the role of the serpent in Genesis 3 as the force that sets the human couple up against the will of God should be seen against the background of its role in the chaos battle mythology.[80] The Eden Narrative thus "communicates subterraneously with the other myths of evil," to quote a felicitous statement by Paul Ricoeur.[81] The narrator of Genesis

---

77. On the chaos battle motif, see for example Mettinger 1988: 92–122, esp. pp. 98–100, with further biblical references and bibliography. Note that in Pss 74:12–17 and 89:10–13, the chaos battle and description of creation are linked together by means of a phrase that characterizes God's ownership of the created world. See also Pss 24:1–2 and 95:5. On this, see Metzger 1983a.

78. *CAT* 1.5.I: 1–2, 28–29.

79. Note: man – woman – serpent – serpent – woman – man; see §2.3.3 (p. 25).

80. I thus disagree with Rogerson (1974: 141–42). Note that van Wolde is, for all her structuralist-semiotic interests, open to the prehistory of the serpent; see van Wolde 1989: 111, 119, and cf. pp. 163–68.

81. Ricoeur 1969: 234.

2–3 thus retains the antidivine character of the serpent arising from the chaos battle myth, pointing at a conflict between the Creator and the serpent, but also affirms that the serpent was a mere creature under God's power. "The tension created in the language of this broken myth reflected, although inadequately, the incomprehensibility of a reality denied existence in the creation, yet which was active and demonic in its effects on creation," says Brevard Childs in an attempt to express the paradox of the serpent in Genesis 3.[82]

There is thus some sort of "intertextual" relation between the Eden Narrative and the tradition of the chaos battle drama of creation. I put the word "intertextual" within quotation marks here, because intertextuality proper is a relation between texts.[83] Nevertheless, it is worth noticing that the Eden Narrative seems to be in dialogue with a prior mythological tradition, whether or not this indicates some kind of generic awareness on the part of the author.

So much for the Eden Narrative and the chaos battle myth. A question we have not raised so far is whether the Eden Poet had access to an older version of an Eden myth, comprising the first man, sin, and expulsion, and if so, what the Eden Poet did with this material. The next chapter addresses these questions.

Summary and Conclusions

1. Various cultures have narratives in which the conditions of real life in the present are seen, in a validating and explanatory perspective, as being founded on events between god(s) and man in primordial time. In the modern study of religion, a narrative of this sort acquires the genre label *myth*. The Eden Narrative belongs to this genre.

2. Mythological narratives relate to reality but not in the sense that they refer to individual events in space and time; they do not have a referential ambition. Rather, their relation to reality manifests itself in their representativity. They have universal applicability and thus make an implicit claim to relevance.

---

82. Childs 1968: 49. It is clear from what has been said that I find it difficult to agree with van Wolde when she says that "[t]he serpent does not represent chaos, . . . , for chaos is discontinuity. The serpent represents the opposite of chaos: complete continuity" (van Wolde 1994: 10; cf. 1989: 168 n. 57). What leads van Wolde to this opinion is that the serpent tries to minimize the distance between God and the humans.

83. On intertextuality, see Mettinger 1993 with ample bibliographical references. For a recent survey of issues involved, see Orr 2003.

3. The structuralist approach has been applied to the Eden Narrative in a number of studies. The most serious weakness of this approach is, in my opinion, its neglect of the narrative line, the plot. Looking for an approach that pays serious attention to this most basic characteristic of a narrative and that wrestles with the question of what purpose an individual myth is designed to fulfill, I opted for a functionalist interpretation of the Eden Narrative.

4. The Eden Narrative functions to validate and to explain. It validates the loyal observance of the divine commandment as the very foundation of the value system. It also explains the hardships of the human condition: suffering, vicissitudes, and death.

5. We asked about the genre awareness of the artist behind the Eden Narrative. Was the author aware of a "myth" genre that could serve as an ideal or a norm? A discussion of the nature of genre made us aware of the difficulties involved in trying to answer this question.

6. However, the role of the serpent in the Eden Narrative can be traced to a dialogue between the author and the preceding tradition of the chaos battle myth, in which the serpent is the antidivine power.

7. What we said in a previous chapter about the theme's being human disobedience and its consequences is neither falsified nor proved by our genre discussion. It is clear, however, that this theme makes excellent sense when we subject the myth to a functionalist interpretation.

Chapter 5

Traces of a Tradition:
The Adamic Myth in Ezekiel 28

There are two passages that reveal the existence of an "Adamic myth" prior to and different from the Eden Narrative, Job 15:7–8 and Ezekiel 28. In this chapter, I shall concentrate on the Ezekiel text, dealing with Job 15 at a specific point in my discussion.

Ezekiel 28 contains two oracles against the king of Tyre (vv. 1–10 and 11–19).[1] The two oracles belong to different genres, the first being an oracle of judgment comprising a reproach and a threat, and the second being a funeral dirge (a *qînâ*, v. 12). The two oracles nevertheless belong together, and together they contribute to a meaningful reconstruction of the Eden myth used by the prophet. The king of Tyre is here portrayed on a screen that presents a story about the garden of Eden, a primeval human being, his sin, and his expulsion from the garden. There are obvious similarities to what we have found in the Eden Narrative of Genesis. Three questions arise that I would like to answer in the present chapter:

1. It seems that Ezekiel used an already existing myth about primordial events in Eden, which he applied ad hoc as an attack on the king of Tyre. What, then, were the basic constituents of this myth? Can it be retrieved from Ezekiel 28?
2. In particular, are there any traces of the thematic construct "wisdom and immortality" in the Adamic myth in Ezekiel 28?
3. If we assume that the Eden Poet of Genesis knew and used an already existing myth closely resembling the myth used by Ezekiel, what innovations did the Eden Poet make and for what purpose?

---

1. On Ezekiel 28, see Gunkel 1910: 34–35; Pope 1955: 97–102; Habel 1967; Zimmerli 1969: 661–89, and note his introduction to the oracles on Tyre, pp. 600–606; Gowan 1975; Mettinger 1976: 268–75; Wilson 1987; Van Seters 1989; Jeppesen 1991; Barr 1992; Van Seters 1992: 119–22; Stordalen 2000: 332–56, 478–79; Callender 2000: 87–136, 179–90. That there is a tradition behind Genesis 2–3 that is visible in Job 15:7–8 and Ezekiel 28 has long been known: see Gunkel 1910: 33–35; Westermann 1976: 334–37, English trans. 1984: 245–48.

I shall begin by citing most of this chapter of Ezekiel (NRSV):

1 The word of the LORD came to me:
2 Mortal, say to the prince of Tyre, Thus says the Lord GOD:
Because your heart is proud and you have said, "I am a god;
I sit in the seat of the gods/god, in the heart of the seas,"
yet you are but a mortal, and no god, though you compare your mind
  with the mind of a god.
3 You are indeed wiser than Daniel; no secret is hidden from you;
4 by your wisdom and your understanding you have amassed wealth
  for yourself,
and have gathered gold and silver into your treasuries.
5 By your great wisdom in trade you have increased your wealth and
  your heart has become proud in your wealth.
6 Therefore thus says the Lord GOD:
Because you compare your mind with the mind of a god,
7 therefore, I will bring strangers against you, the most terrible of the
  nations;
they shall draw their swords against the beauty of your wisdom and
  defile your splendor.
8 They shall thrust you down to the Pit, and you shall die a violent
  death in the heart of the seas.
9 Will you still say, "I am a god," in the presence of those who kill
  you,
though you are but a mortal, and no god, in the hands of those who
  wound you?
10 You shall die the death of the uncircumcised by the hand of
  foreigners;
for I have spoken, says the Lord GOD.

11 Moreover the word of the LORD came to me:
12 Mortal, raise a lamentation over the king of Tyre, and say to him,
  Thus says the Lord GOD:
You were the signet of perfection, full of wisdom and perfect in
  beauty.
13 You were in Eden, the garden of God; every precious stone was
  your covering,
carnelian, chrysolite, and moonstone, beryl, onyx, and jasper,
  sapphire, turquoise, and emerald;
and worked in gold were your settings and your engravings.
On the day that you were created they were prepared.
14 You were the anointed cherub, shadowing widely, and I installed
  you; you were on the holy mountain of God/the gods;
you walked among the stones of fire.
15 You were blameless in your ways from the day that you were
  created, until iniquity was found in you.

16 In the abundance of your trade you were filled with violence, and
you sinned;
so I cast you as a profane thing from the mountain of God/the gods,
and I drove you out, you shadowing cherub,
from among the stones of fire.

What I have reproduced above is the translation of the NRSV, except
for vv. 14 and 16, in which I offer my own rendering. In these two
verses, the NRSV has followed the LXX, which has two beings in the
garden—namely, the king and the cherub—and which has the cherub
as the acting subject driving out the king in v. 16. For reasons that I
shall not repeat here, I prefer to follow the MT, which identifies the
king and the cherub.[2]

5.1. The Contents of the Adamic Myth

Is it possible to get behind the remarkable text of Ezekiel 28 and retrieve the myth used by the prophet? The subject of the chapter is the
king of Tyre. I shall now work on the basis of the hypothesis that there
was a prior myth that Ezekiel applied ad hoc to the king of Tyre in order to denounce his arrogance.[3] I shall call the myth thus retrieved the
"Adamic myth" in order to distinguish it from the Eden Narrative in
Genesis (see p. 81 n. 75).

On the basis of this assumption, I find it reasonable to adopt a process of simple subtraction: the features that are due to the historical
situation, the specific application to this king, may be disregarded as
not belonging to the original myth.

---

2. See Mettinger 1976: 270–72 with bibliography; and, more recently, Barr 1992.
This may still be a minority position, but I find no convincing reason to deviate
from it. The "problematic" *'att* at the opening of v. 14 is the personal pronoun being used for second masculine (otherwise *'attâ*). The Masora refers to three instances of this form in the Bible. Bauer and Leander (1965: 248e) list another five.
The verb *wā'abbedkā* in v. 16 is to be taken as a Piel imperfect form of *'ābad* in
which the *'alep* of the prefix has assimilated to the *'alep* of the root (BDB 2a).
3. In some controversial publications Van Seters (1989 and 1992: 119–22) has
argued (a) that behind Ezek 28:2–10 lies a myth of the fallen god El, as argued by
Pope (1955: 97–103); and (b) that Ezek 28:12–19 deals with the primeval and therefore prototypical king. He argues the latter point on the basis of a Neo-Babylonian
text that deals with the creation of humankind and of a king (published in Mayer
1987). His suggestions have attracted little following. For critical remarks, see Otto
1996: 177–78; Jensen 2004: 64–65. As will become apparent in what follows, I find
it easier to argue that the royal features of the figure in Ezekiel 28 are due to the
special application of a prior myth to the king of Tyre.

Whether this myth was polytheistic in outlook or was already an Israelite composition is hard for us to know. One should note that the application in Ezekiel 28 is to a foreign king. In order to make a comparison with the Eden Narrative easier, I shall consider a number of separate points in order.

1. *Time and Location.* The myth used by the prophet deals with the first man. Note the verb 'to create' (*bārā'*), used twice (vv. 13, 15). The king of Tyre is a contemporary of the prophet, but the myth that the prophet uses takes place in the most distant past, *in illo tempore*, as myths often do. With regard to the setting in space—the statement "I sit in the seat of the gods/god (*môšab 'ĕlōhîm*) in the heart of the seas" is the first clue to its identity (v. 2). The words "in the heart of the seas" (recurring in v. 8) are probably due to the comparison with Tyre, with its well-known position on an island. This also seems to hold for "the seat of the gods/god (*môšab 'ĕlōhîm*)," which probably refers to the throne carved in a piece of rock that stood in the Temple of Melqart in Tyre.[4]

A bit further down in the text, however, the location is described as "the holy mountain of God/the gods (*har qōdeš 'ĕlōhîm*)" (v. 14), or simply "the mountain of God/the gods (*har 'ĕlōhîm*)" (v. 16). In my opinion, this may derive from the preexisting material used by the prophet. The idea of an elevated position for the garden is reflected in the notion of four rivers streaming forth from Eden in Gen 2:10–14. Note also the "mount of assembly" in Isa 14:13.

Of still greater interest for a comparison with Genesis 2–3 is the description of the location as "Eden, the garden of God" (28:13). This setting also appears in another relevant text in Ezekiel (31:8–9, 16, 18). A remarkable formulation is the temple allusion in 28:18. This allusion may be due to the fact that Tyre was the center of worship for the god Melqart, with an important sanctuary for his cult. We should not forget, however, that holiness has also been claimed for the garden of Eden in Genesis.[5]

2. *Characters.* Apart from God, our Ezekiel 28 passage deals with one individual only, the male figure in the garden. This figure is depicted as the first human, though the word *'ādām* is not used;[6] as we noticed, the verb 'to create' (*bārā'*) appears twice (vv. 13, 15). The jewels listed in v. 13 are known from the "breastpiece of judgment" of

---

4. See Bonnet 1988: 61.
5. See Wright 1996.
6. This word does appear in Job 15:7.

the high priest in Exod 28:17–20 and are thus sometimes taken to indicate the priestly character of the figure in the Ezekiel 28 garden. On the other hand, if an Adamic myth is secondarily being applied to a royal figure, the king of Tyre, then an alternative interpretation is perhaps more attractive—that is, comparing the jewelry to the pectorals of the Phoenician kings.

3. *Plot.* The first of the two oracles puts special stress on the hubris of the figure in the garden. Note the expressions *ʾēl ʾānî* and *ʾĕlōhîm ʾānî* 'I am a god' (Ezek 28:2, 9). In line with this, we hear of him that his "heart is proud (*gābāh*)" (vv. 2, 5). The figure in the garden thus expresses a claim to divinity. Now, we have reason to believe that the king of Tyre was deified in the cult of Melqart.[7] We should not, however, be overhasty in writing off this notion of divine aspirations as being due to the myth's special application to the king of Tyre. This feature may well be an element of the myth used by the prophet. We also know that primeval man (*ʾādām*) appears in the heavenly council in a form of the Adamic myth that is attested in Job 15:7–8 (see below, §5.2, p. 92).

The national god of Israel is obviously disturbed by the arrogance of the king in the garden. The "sin" committed in Ezekiel's garden of Eden is nothing less than hubris. The wording is clear. The being in the garden was blameless until iniquity (*ʿawlâ*) was found in him (Ezek 28:15). "You were filled with violence (*ḥāmās*), and you sinned (*ḥāṭāʾ*)" (v. 16). Verse 18 continues in this vein. The sin is thus hubris.

The plot then moves on to the expulsion from the garden. The verb used for this in our Ezekiel text is *ʾābad* in Piel (v. 16), a strong expression often meaning 'cause to perish', 'destroy', 'kill'; here used in the sense 'to cause to stray', 'to drive away', as in Jer 23:1 and Qoh 3:6. Interestingly, in 28:16 we also find the verb *ḥālal* in Piel, used to express God's banishing the sinner as a profane thing from the mountain. The corollary of this notion is the holiness of the garden.[8] Note v. 18, where the MT reading *miqdāšêkā* ('your [sing.] sanctuaries [pl.]') in the plural perhaps should not be altered; it can be understood in the light of Jer 51:51 (*miqdĕšê bêt yhwh*). The verb *gāraš* ('drive out'), found in Gen 3:24, does not appear in our text. This very verb, however, appears in a related text about sin and expulsion from the garden of Eden (Ezek 31:11).

---

7. See Bonnet 1988: 45.
8. Again, see Wright 1996 on this.

On the basis of the above observations, I assume that the prophet
used an Adamic myth known to him containing the above-mentioned
constituents: a primeval male human being, a garden of Eden, sin, and
expulsion. I shall return below to a comparison with the Eden Narrative in Genesis 2–3. For the present, I simply note that the similarities
between the two versions are obvious.

5.2. *Wisdom and Immortality*
in the Adamic Myth

We have now reached the point at which it is natural to recall the
symbolism of the two trees in the Eden Narrative. It is obvious that we
would look in vain for the two special trees in Ezekiel 28. But we must
ask: do we find their symbolic content, knowledge and immortality?

Let us first turn to knowledge, or wisdom. One whole section of our
text expressly refers to the wisdom of the figure in the garden:

3 You are indeed wiser than Daniel; no secret is hidden from you;
4 by your wisdom and your understanding you have amassed wealth
    for yourself,
and have gathered gold and silver into your treasuries.
5 By your great wisdom in trade you have increased your wealth,
and your heart has become proud in your wealth. (Ezek 28:3–5)

There is an established exegetical tradition to the effect that vv. 3–5
should be regarded as a later insertion, a position that "[a]lmost all
critical scholars agree on."[9] The verses seem to be unrelated to the sur-
rounding material. In his interesting discussion of Ezek 28:1–19, R. R.
Wilson comes to the conclusion that "[i]n this unit there is only one
indisputable editorial addition, the comments on wisdom in vv 3–
5."[10] The same position is taken in Walther Zimmerli's classic commentary on Ezekiel.[11]

Let us assume for a moment, however, that "almost all critical scholars" who have expressed an opinion on this issue are wrong—that the
primeval human being in the garden actually possesses extraordinary
wisdom.

---

9. Wilson 1987: 212 n. 5, with bibliography. Habel (1967: 519) is one of the
few who disagree.
10. Wilson 1987: 216.
11. Zimmerli 1969: 663, 664, 671, 677. Zimmerli of course takes the wisdom reference in Ezek 28:7 as secondary (p. 663) but forgets (?) the other reference, in v. 17
(p. 672).

Then the first thing to be noted is that the wisdom passage (vv. 3–5) is framed by the specific Hebrew expression *wattittēn libběkā kělēb ʾělō-hîm* (v. 2; slightly varied in v. 6), literally, 'you made your heart like the heart of a god'. What does this expression mean?

Modern Westerners tend to locate intellectual capacities in the brain and emotions in the heart. At the risk of oversimplifying, I would say that in the Hebrew Bible people think with the heart and feel with the viscera. Certain words in the semantic field of 'compassion', for example, are etymologically related to the word used for 'womb' (*rehem*): *lěrahēm* 'to have compassion', and *rahǎmîm* 'compassion'. The 'heart' (*lēb, lēbāb*), however, is the organ where the ancient Hebrews often placed their intellectual capacities. Let me cite some passages:

> *Hos 4:11* (text emend.): Wine and new wine take away the understanding (*lēb*).
>
> *Job 11:12*: But a stupid person will get understanding (*yillābēb*) when a wild ass is born human (which amounts to "never"; the verb used is, of course, a Niphal denominative from *lēb* 'heart').
>
> *Job 34:10*: you who have sense (the Hebrew has *ʾanǎšê lēbāb* 'men who have a heart').
>
> *Song 4:9*: You have ravished my heart (*libbabtinî*; with a privative Piel form of the same verb as in Job 11:12).
>
> *Sir 17:6*: [A] mind (καρδία) for thinking he gave them.

Against this background, the two statements that surround the wisdom passage in vv. 3–5 may be taken to refer to the wisdom of the figure in the garden. The figure in the garden considers himself as wise as an *elohim* being, as one of the gods. The RSV got it right when it translated *wattittēn libběkā kělēb ʾělōhîm* 'though you consider yourself as wise as a god'.[12] This is, of course, an expression of his hubris. Compare the wording in Isa 14:14: "I will make myself like *ʿelyôn*."

Moreover, the second of these two statements that surround the wisdom passage, the one in v. 6, leads to an announcement of judgment, introduced by *lākēn* 'therefore', in v. 7: "[T]herefore, I will bring strangers against you, the most terrible of the nations; they shall draw their swords against the beauty of your wisdom." Thus, the punishment is for the "wisdom" of the sinner. Indeed, wisdom appears again in the second oracle of our chapter (28:12, 17).

There is thus a reasonable degree of probability that the wisdom passage (vv. 3–5) was in fact an original part of Ezekiel 28 and, moreover,

---

12. The NRSV translates 'though you compare your mind with the mind of a god', which may have the same correct understanding.

that wisdom was a feature of the myth used by the prophet for his purposes. That this wisdom mainly manifested itself in the mercantile suc-
cess of the figure depicted seems to be due to its application to the king
of Tyre.

A passage that supports this interpretation is Job 15:7–8. Eliphaz
tells Job that there is no question of Job's having a monopoly on
knowledge. Job was not the first human. Eliphaz here refers to a myth
about the first man's having gained wisdom in the heavenly council:

$$\text{הֲרִאישׁוֹן אָדָם תִּוָּלֵד וְלִפְנֵי גְבָעוֹת חוֹלָלְתָּ:}$$
$$\text{הַבְסוֹד אֱלוֹהַ תִּשְׁמָע וְתִגְרַע אֵלֶיךָ חָכְמָה:}$$

hări'šôn 'ādām tiwwālēd wĕlipnê gĕbā'ôt ḥôlālĕtā
habsôd 'ĕlôah tišmā' wĕtigra' 'ēlêkā ḥokmâ

Were you [Job] born the first human (*ri'šôn 'ādām*)?
Were you brought forth before the hills?
Did you listen in the council of God (*bĕsôd 'ĕlôah*)?
And did you grab (*gāra'*) wisdom (*ḥokmâ*) for yourself?

The verb used here, *gāra'*, has the basic sense of 'to cut off' and can be
used of grooming the beard (Jer 48:37, Isa 15:2). Other meanings are
'diminish', 'shorten' (Exod 5:8, 11, 19), and 'take away' (Deut 4:2, 13:1).
In our passage, it means 'snatch, seize, grab [for oneself]'.[13] I am inclined to see an almost illicit act of appropriation here.

In this context, the wisdom of the first human being is the quality
that was seized by the first man in the divine council. The situation is
not one of eavesdropping. Rather, the first man supposedly had access
to the divine assembly. There is an affinity between the first human
being and the angelic beings of the divine council. (Is this affinity reflected in Ezekiel in the notion of the first man as a cherub, Ezek 28:14,
16?) Having access to divine wisdom should follow as a natural consequence of having access to the divine council.[14] What we find in the
Job passage, however, is the development of the notion of the god-
granted wisdom of the first man into the notion that this wisdom was
attained without divine authorization.[15] This development is important for our understanding of Genesis 2–3.

---

13. On the verb discussed, see Ringgren 1977. On Job 15:7–8, note also the discussion by Callender 2000: 137–53.

14. Does this idea figure into Sir 24:1–2? Note also Num 24:15–16 and Prov
30:3.

15. On wisdom as granted by the gods, see the following chapter on *Adapa* and
Gilgamesh.

The first man of our reconstructed Adamic myth lays claim to wisdom that transcends normal human capacity. The presupposition here is the established role of wisdom as part of the divine equipment possessed by "the firstborn of the human race" (Job 15:7).

If this is correct, we may take a further step. We should remember that wisdom (knowledge) *and* immortality are two basic constituents in the Eden Narrative of Genesis. We must therefore ask whether we find the notion of immortality in the myth used in Ezekiel 28.

On the level of express statements, we find nothing. The king of Tyre never says that he will "live forever." There is, however, a feature that I must call attention to precisely in this context: the contrast between the alleged claims of the king in the garden to be a god and God's repeated statements that he is only a mortal.

> 2 Mortal (*ben 'ādām*), say to the prince of Tyre, Thus says the Lord
> GOD:
> Because your heart is proud and you have said, "I am a god (*'ēl
> 'ānî*); . . . ,"
> yet you are but a mortal (*'ādām*), and no god, though you compare
> your mind with the mind of a god.
>
> 9 Will you still say, "I am a god (*'ĕlōhîm 'ānî*)," in the presence of
> those who kill you,
> though you are but a mortal (*ādām*), and no god, in the hands of
> those who wound you?
> 10 You shall die the death of the uncircumcised. (Ezek 28:2, 9–10)

My point is not that the Bible translators chose to render the word for 'human' as 'mortal'. Rather, the key statement is found in v. 9, in which the claim to be a god comes to nothing "in the presence of those who kill you" and "in the hands of those who wound you" (v. 9). The fact that the king of Tyre dies is the final proof that he was not a god. Indeed, the second oracle of Ezekiel 28 finishes on this very note: "you have come to a dreadful end and shall be no more forever (*wĕ'ênkâ 'ad 'ôlām*)" (v. 19). Logically, immortality is the ultimate difference between gods and humans. The claim to be a god is thus implicitly a claim to be immortal.

The fact that these statements are found precisely in the first oracle, where wisdom also figures, makes me inclined to conclude that wisdom and immortality are constituents of the Adamic myth that were known to the prophet.

5.3. The Innovations of the
Eden Poet (Genesis 2–3)

It should be clear by now that the Eden Poet used a myth about primeval man in Eden that was broadly similar to the myth we have retrieved from Ezekiel 28.[16] However, the Eden Poet was not a passive recipient of a tradition; he left his own stamp on it in important ways. Noticing the innovations thus introduced may help us toward a clearer appreciation of the deepest concerns of the Eden Poet. Our questions are, therefore:

1. What did the Eden Poet do with the material at his disposal?
2. For what purpose were the innovations made?

Let us begin with a brief comparison of the two, the Adamic myth as retrieved from Ezekiel 28 and the Eden Narrative in Genesis 2–3.

1. *Time and Location.*   Both compositions deal with primeval man and the events taking place in the garden of Eden immediately after the creation of the world, *in illo tempore.* The notion of the garden as a mountain in Ezekiel (see also Isa 14:13, where "the mount of assembly" interchanges with "heaven") only vaguely figures in the passage of the four rivers flowing out of Eden (Gen 2:10–14).[17] In contrast to the Ezekiel version of the myth, the two special trees form a striking new feature of the work of the Eden Poet.

2. *Characters.*   Apart from God, the Ezekiel version only has one individual appearing in the garden: the king/first man. The Genesis version has a human couple, the animals, and the serpent. The Ezekiel version has its main person appearing in royal attire—a feature probably due to the myth's being applied to the king of Tyre—while the humans of the Genesis version enjoy each other's company in nakedness. Denoting the first humans as "earth-being" and "mother of all living" ("Adam" and "Eve") affords maximal universality in the Eden Narrative.

Wisdom and immortality are important features of both versions but with strikingly different functions. The Adamic myth has a first human who owns wisdom from the outset but who makes unsubstan-

---

16. Note that we cannot decide whether the Eden Poet knew precisely the manifestation of the myth that appears in Ezekiel 28. The important thing is that there was a tradition prior to Genesis 2–3 and that the Eden Poet transformed this tradition.

17. On Eden and the mountain of the gods, see Day 2000: 29–34. As Gary Anderson has noted (Anderson 1988), the idea of Eden as the cosmic mountain was stressed by interpreters in early Syriac Christianity.

tiated claims to being divine and, thus, immortal. The Eden Narrative has a human couple that seizes wisdom and knowledge through an illicit act of acquisition and who thereby forfeit the possibility of immortality, which would otherwise have been granted as a reward for obedience.

3. *Plot.* In both versions, the salient points of the plot are sin and its consequences, but there are important differences. Both versions stress the sin as being hubris. The Adamic myth speaks of the claim of the figure in the garden to be divine (self-deification); the Genesis version speaks of the ambition of the first human couple to become "like the gods." A new, decisive feature of the Genesis version is the notion of sin as disobedience. Here the divine commandment is central—a feature completely absent from the Ezekiel version.

The fact that express terminology for "sin" (present in Ezek 28:15, 16, 18) does not appear in the Eden Narrative should not lead to premature conclusions. The behavior of the first two humans in the Genesis version was certainly as displeasing to God as was the behavior of the first man in the Adamic myth.

In both versions, the events of the plot lead up to the expulsion of the sinner(s) from the garden. In the Genesis version, the poet takes a profound interest in the consequences of disobedience. The series of curses, with the hardship and death of the humans, refers back to the introductory description of the creation of the humans out of dust. In the Ezekiel version, the creation allusions use the verb *bārāʾ* 'to create', otherwise known from the Priestly creation account of Genesis 1, whereas, the Genesis version of the Eden myth has man formed by being molded (*yāṣar*). The Genesis version thus stresses the motif "from dust to dust."

After this short comparison, let us proceed to ask about the nature of the innovations introduced by the Eden Poet. As is easily seen from our comparison above, the Eden Poet has provided the Eden myth with a new focus: everything now revolves around the question of obedience or disobedience to the divine commandment. The myth is now a narrative about a situation marked by a radical choice. This aspect of the narrative has been given special emphasis by means of the symbolism of the two trees.

Where the Eden Narrative has the two trees, the Adamic myth has wisdom and immortality "in the abstract." The two trees are "symbolical materializations" of these two entities. As was already indicated

above, the Eden Poet may have found the tree of life in wisdom traditions (§3.2.4, p. 60). The tree of knowledge, however, seems to be his
own creation.

The setup in Genesis 2–3 has an almost emblematic character: the
Eden Poet planted the two trees in the garden of Eden and—to use a
figure of speech—placed the divine commandment in the middle.

The Eden Poet transformed the Eden myth into a narrative that
serves to teach a lesson about the vital importance of the divine commandment—the word "vital" taken in its most basic sense. Moreover,
the myth was thereby transformed into a narrative that provides an ultimate etiology for the dire conditions of all human life—life created
by God but now destined for death. The series of sentences, not found
in the version used by Ezekiel, was added by the Eden Poet. Interestingly, this explains the double closure of the Eden Narrative: the prior
tradition had a simple expulsion; the Eden Poet gives additional emphasis to the consequences of sin by means of the sentencing.

By providing this myth about the lone first man in the garden with
the woman who was to become "the mother of all living," the Eden
Poet introduced the first primeval couple into the myth—an innovation that grants universality to the narrative.

I have worked on the basis of the theory that there was an already
existing Adamic myth that Ezekiel used secondarily for his denuncia-
tion of the king of Tyre. Both the first man and the king of Tyre were
figures of peculiar arrogance. My reasoning implies that Ezekiel and
the Eden Poet used an Adamic myth that existed prior to both compositions. The whole argument remains a hypothesis; but in my view it is
a hypothesis that works extremely well.

The Eden Poet stands in a line of tradition; he appropriated the
Adamic myth. We are used to thinking of tradition in terms of X's in-
fluencing Y and of Y as a passive recipient, not an agent. The case of
the Eden Narrative should teach us that things may be different. It
shows us a literary genius appropriating a tradition and at the same
time enriching it in a way that leaves his own indelible fingerprints on
it, creating something profoundly new.[18]

It has not been possible to draw any conclusions about the original
date and milieu of the Adamic myth. It is prior to Ezekiel 28, but how
much older we cannot say. Ezekiel was deported to Mesopotamia.[19]

---

18. For this perspective on tradition in general—for Y rather than X as the
agent—see Baxandall 1985: 58–59 and Orr 2003: 83–93, esp. pp. 83–84.

19. This was stressed by Chrostowski (1996: 181–278; see Lipiński 2001), who
argues that Genesis 1–11 was composed during the Assyrian Exile, in the seventh

However, because the study of Mesopotamian remains has not as yet yielded any story with a similar outline, there is no reason to assume a Mesopotamian origin for the Adamic myth of the Hebrew Bible.

We should note—and I think this is most important—that where the Eden Poet has the striking symbols of the two trees, the Adamic myth has wisdom and immortality, as it were, "in the abstract." This observation leads me to ask another question: Might this combination of wisdom and immortality—at hand already in the Adamic myth and so beautifully worked out in the Eden Narrative—perhaps have existed prior to the Adamic myth? Because I have not found any Hebrew or other West Semitic text in which this is the case, I shall turn to two outstanding pieces of Mesopotamian literature in chap. 6.

Summary and Conclusions

1. We studied Ezek 28:1–19 with the aim of retrieving the myth used by the prophet. By subtracting features that may be due to the ad hoc application to the king of Tyre, we retrieved an original myth comprising the following elements: a primeval first man, a garden of Eden, sin, and expulsion.

2. This myth also contained the elements of wisdom and immortality. Contrary to what has been maintained in previous research, the wisdom of the figure in the garden was an integrated element in the myth used by the prophet. This interpretation is supported by Job 15:7–8. The myth used by the prophet also contained the notion of immortality. The primeval first man possessed wisdom from the outset and made unsubstantiated claims to possess immortality.

3. The Eden Poet who produced the narrative known in Genesis 2–3 made a number of important innovations. Above all, the myth now received a new focus: everything revolves around the divine commandment and the issue of obedience versus disobedience. Now the story acquires the curses in Deuteronomistic spirit. Where the Adamic myth had wisdom and immortality "in the abstract," the Eden Poet planted the two trees and placed the divine commandment in between. The lone first man of the Adamic myth was now provided with a wife. The fate of the first human couple is paradigmatic for all of humanity. If not before, the story is now profoundly etiological. We also noted that the serpent has been introduced by the Eden Poet.

---

century, and that the Eden motif of Ezekiel came into existence in Babylonia, in the early sixth century, independently of Genesis 1–11.

4. My analysis of the innovations introduced by the Eden Poet confirms the previous definition of the theme as disobedience and its consequences, a theme with Deuteronomistic affinities.

5. What we have found is a case of tradition and elaboration. The Eden Narrative stands out as a piece of highly conscious literary art.

6. No detailed conclusions were reached about the original date and milieu of the Adamic myth. It existed prior to Ezekiel's oracle against the king of Tyre. In spite of Ezekiel's Babylonian exile, nothing indicates a Mesopotamian origin for the myth.

Chapter 6

Wisdom and Immortality in Adapa *and* Gilgamesh

The Eden Narrative is an innovative piece of literary art. The myth about the first humans and the two trees in the garden of Eden reflects in a sophisticated way on the ultimate human condition. Man acquired wisdom but was denied immortality. So far, research has not been able to point to any literary composition from the ancient Near East outside Palestine that might have been a pattern for the Hebrew poet based on extended similarities of plot structure. However, I shall argue that there was in Mesopotamian literature a traditional line of demarcation between gods and humans: wisdom and immortality are divine prerogatives. Humans have wisdom but not immortality. Only gods have both. This concept may belong to the common stock of ideas in the Mesopotamian and West-Semitic world.

Half a century ago, Johannes Pedersen took an important step in this direction. Pedersen studied notions of human kinship with the gods: in Egypt, this idea was expressed by man's creation in the image of a deity. In Mesopotamia, the corresponding notion was found in man's creation from the blood of a (rebellious) god. In his wisdom, man approximates the gods; immortality would make the kinship of man and gods complete. Pedersen referred to *Gilgamesh* and *Adapa* as important texts for the combined motifs of wisdom and immortality, and he suggested contemplating Genesis 2–3 from this perspective.[1] His study, however, drowned in the flood of publications on the primeval history of Genesis. After Pedersen, though without express reference to him, similar lines of thought were formulated by Shlomo Izre'el in his edition of the Adapa myth.[2]

---

1. Pedersen 1955b: esp. pp. 240–45; see also 1955a: 164–66. Pedersen concludes: "Thus these myths are expressive of the flickering relation between God and man. Man is related to the gods, a relation which appears in his wisdom. . . . The kinship would be complete if man were also given immortality. He has been close to immortality, but still, he did not obtain it, and if he did so, he would no longer be human" (Pedersen 1955b: 244).

2. Izre'el 2001: 120–30.

In the ensuing discussion of the Mesopotamian material, I will begin
with *Adapa*, because it provides an especially clear case of the connection between wisdom and immortality. I will then go on to deal with
Gilgamesh. Because the Eden Narrative is a late, postexilic text, I find it
appropriate to focus on *Adapa* and *Gilgamesh* in their developed form,
known from the libraries of Ashurbanipal. I will comment on their earlier literary stages only in connection with specific points.

6.1. *The Myth of* Adapa and the South Wind

S. A. Picchioni's edition (1981) marked a new stage in the study of
the Adapa myth. It has recently been complemented by Shlomo Izre'el's edition (2001), which contains extensive commentary. I will follow Izre'el's line numbering and quote from his edition and translation, but his readings will of course be compared with the readings of
other scholars.[3]
 There are now six major fragments of the myth.[4] The earliest was
found at Amarna (Fragment B). The others were found in Ashurbanipal's libraries at Nineveh. There is also a Sumerian version of the myth
from the Old Babylonian period, reported to be similar to the Akkadian version.[5] Though the textual material for the myth itself is limited to these fragments from Amarna and Nineveh, other material
shows that the literary figure of Adapa was well known, as apparent in
the comprehensive compilation of references to Adapa in Mesopotamian literature brought together by Picchioni.[6]
 The largest and most important fragment of *Adapa and the South
Wind* was found at Amarna, which supplies an ante quem about 1350
B.C.E. (Fragment B). The Adapa myth is considered to have been a one-
tablet work at this stage of its literary history.[7] The relationship between Fragment B and the later Fragment A from the libraries of Ashur-

---

 3. In addition, the Amarna version (Frag. B) was transliterated and translated by
M. Dietrich 1991: 127–32 and Kämmerer 1998: 254–59. For translations, see also
Foster 1993: 1.429–34 and Dalley 1991: 182–88. Note also E. A. Speiser, "Adapa,"
ANET 101–3. The research prior to 1981 is well documented by Picchioni 1981: 31–
77. The research from 1973 to 2003 is surveyed by Hallo 2004: 275–77. Comprehensive bibliographies are found in Picchioni 1981 and Izre'el 2001.
 4. On the fragments, see Izre'el 2001: 5–8.
 5. See Cavigneaux and Al-Rawi 1993: 92.
 6. Picchioni 1981: 82–101. Some of the more interesting references are dealt
with by Wilcke 1991: 263–69.
 7. See Dietrich 1991: esp. p. 122, with reference to a previous study by Kienast.

banipal in Nineveh is not completely clear. Either this later fragment (A) was composed to serve as a sophisticated introduction to the story with the purpose of making the message clear to the reader from the beginning (thus Shlomo Izre'el),[8] or it was an independent piece—a piece that never belonged to B (thus Manfried Dietrich).[9] But even if the latter theory is true, I am inclined to believe that A tells us something about the understanding of the Adapa myth in the first millennium B.C.E. I am thus reading B in the light of A.

For our purposes—because of the late date of the Eden Narrative in the Bible—it is this late understanding of Adapa, based on Fragments A and B, that is of interest. The other fragments can be disregarded in the present context; they are quite small and in some cases badly damaged.

The opening of Fragment A is of immediate interest to us. After some broken lines, there are three catch phrases in which the poet presents his theme:

> He [Ea] perfected him [Adapa] with great intelligence (*uzna rapašta*)
> to give instruction about the ordinance of the earth (*uṣurāt māti*).
> To him he gave wisdom (*nēmeqa*), he did not give him eternal life
> (*napišta darīta*). (*Adapa* A 3–4)

This is a keynote formulation of the thematic duo wisdom and immortality. That Ea is the acting subject who bestows wisdom is clear from the context (see also B 57–59). Ea gave Adapa wisdom but not eternal life. This statement whets the reader's curiosity. It creates suspense by presenting a deficiency that may or may not be filled. What is the poet going to tell us about immortality? The statement anticipates the central scene of the poem, in which Adapa misses the possibility of eternal life by a narrow margin.

The *plot* may be summarized as follows. Fragment A contains background information about Adapa as a sage and native of Eridu. Adapa was a priest in the service of Ea's Temple, which we know the Babylonians considered one of the oldest in Mesopotamia, a temple that was foremost in wisdom.[10] Adapa prepared food for the daily temple service and caught fish for this purpose. Fragment B opens with a fishing expedition during which the South Wind has just plunged Adapa into the sea. On the verge of death, Adapa pronounces a curse that breaks

---

8. Izre'el 2001: 111–19, esp. pp. 111 and 114 with table 3.

9. Manfried Dietrich, personal communication. Dietrich understands A and C as two completely different interpretations of the myth from the first millennium.

10. On Eridu and wisdom, see Foster 1974: 346 n. 9 with bibliography.

the South Wind's wing. This places the cosmic order in disarray (causing drought[11]) and is an insult to Anu, the god overseeing the cosmic
order. Summoned to account to Anu in heaven for this crime, Adapa
receives advice on protocol from his god, Ea: he should appear dressed
in a mourning garment and with his hair strewn with ashes, thus ex-
pressing grief for the vegetation gods who are now absent from the
earth. Moreover, he must not accept any food or drink offered to him
in heaven, because this would be "the food of death" and "the water of
death."

Adapa ascends to heaven and finds Dumuzi and Gizzida (= Nin-
gishzida), the vegetation gods, at the gate. Seeing Adapa in mourning,
the two gods decide to intercede for the culprit. Anu commands that
Adapa be brought "the food of life." Adapa, however, refuses both "the
food of life" and "the water of life," thus provoking Anu's surprised reaction and resulting in Adapa's summons back to earth. Fragment D
seems to contain a different version, in which Anu takes Adapa into
his service (lines 9–10).

1. *Adapa: Wisdom, the Gift of Ea*

Though "wisdom" is somewhat of a misnomer as applied to Babylonian literature,[12] I shall continue to use it, in accordance with established scholarly convention.[13] Adapa is a priest of Ea (A 6–15), the god
of wisdom:[14]

> In those days, in those years, the sage, a native of Eridu,
> Ea made him (his) follower[15] among people.
> The sage's speech—no one repudiates;
> Skilled, foremost in understanding, of the Anunnaki is he.[16]
> (*Adapa* A 5–8; Izre'el 2001: 9–10)

---

11. See Roux 1961.

12. Thus, Lambert, *BWL* 1.

13. For the Sumerian and Akkadian terminology, see Wilcke 1991: 259 and Denning-Bolle 1992: 32–39. One should perhaps speak of a Mesopotamian wisdom "tradition" rather than of wisdom "literature" (Buccellati 1981; Denning-Bolle 1992: 13).

14. On Ea as the god of wisdom, see Galter 1983: 95–103; Wilcke 1991: 259–60;
Denning-Bolle 1992: 39–41.

15. See the discussion in Izre'el 2001: 12. Compare Picchioni 1981: 112–13, 127.

16. These lines may be ambiguous. Note that the Anunnaki are gods, but Adapa
is a human being. See Izre'el 2001: 12–13. Peter Machinist suggests that in the lines
just quoted (A 5–8) there is a deliberate ambiguity: these lines may refer to both Ea
and Adapa; thus, the characteristics and abilities of these two are intertwined.
This adumbrates the problem of the following narrative (Machinist, personal
communication).

Most fittingly, Adapa here carries the epithet 'foremost in understanding' *atra-ḫasīsu* (line 8). He is an *apkallu* 'sage', 'expert' (5, 7), being one of the seven antediluvian sages.[17]

A myth about the seven *apkallū* is alluded to in the third tablet of the incantation series *Bit Meseri*.[18] Of the seven listed in this passage, U_4-*Anna* (later known from Berossos as Oannes) is the first, and "*Utu-Abzu*, who ascended to heaven" appears as number seven. This name means 'born in the Abzu', Abzu being Ea's cosmic domain. This seventh entry on the list obviously refers to Adapa under a different but perfectly appropriate name.[19] The relation between Adapa and U_4-*Anna* (Oannes) is not quite clear; some scholars assume that they are identical, and others do not[20]—an issue of no specific importance to the present study. It may well be that two originally independent characters merged in the course of time.[21]

Another reference to Adapa occurs in a first-millennium catalog of texts and authors, found in Ashurbanipal's libraries at Nineveh and published by Lambert (1962). Here we find, for instance, a reference to the *Gilgamesh Epic* as being authored by Sin-leqi-unninni (VI 10). The first "author" to be listed is the god Ea (I 4). Additionally, Lambert considers Adapa, the legendary human, to be the "author" of two unidentified works (I 5–7) and of yet another work later in the text (VI 16).[22] Adapa's talent for the art of writing is also alluded to in a text in which King Ashurbanipal boasts of his own cultural literacy: "I learned the work of wise [*apkallu*] Adapa, the hidden secret of all scribal art." He goes on to say that he mastered both Sumerian and "obscure Akkadian"—supposedly referring to the hardships created for students by the cuneiform script—and read "inscriptions from before the flood."[23]

---

17. On *apkallu*, see Kvanvig 1988: 191–213; Denning-Bolle 1992: 20–22, 48–56.

18. See Reiner 1961; Borger 1974; Kvanvig 1988: 191–213; and Wilcke 1991: 263–69.

19. Note that Adapa, understood as a Sumerian name, may be interpreted as meaning 'recovered from the water'. See Hallo 2004: 272.

20. See Denning-Bolle 1992: 45.

21. Peter Machinist calls my attention to Picchioni (1981: 99, the fourth section from the top of the chart) with several first-millennium examples of names that combine the elements U-An(na) and Adapa (Machinist, personal communication).

22. However, there is a problem in I 5–7: Lambert restored the line with the broken text according to the *Persian Verse Account*, in which the text referred to is a rhetorical concoction that probably never existed; see Machinist and Tadmor 1993. My thanks to Peter Machinist for calling my attention to this problem (personal communication).

23. Text and translation in Streck 1916: 2.254–57, col. I 10–18 updated translation in Wilcke 1991: 268–69.

To summarize, wisdom is one of Adapa's most prominent characteristics. Moreover, this legendary human being bears epithets that specifically connect him with wisdom, and this wisdom he holds as a gift from the god of wisdom himself—the god Ea, his creator and divine mentor.

2. Adapa: Immortality Forfeited

In the Adapa myth, we also find profound reflections on the ultimate distinction between gods and humans: both have wisdom, but only gods have eternal life. The lot of all humanity is death. This traditional understanding of the myth has been challenged by Giorgio Buccellati. According to him, Ea is not deceiving Adapa when he orders him to refuse food and drink in heaven, because it would in fact be lethal. Ea's warning is considered sound. According to Buccellati, Anu's retort to Adapa when he refuses to eat and drink what is offered to him in heaven "does not contain any reference to the hero's acquiring eternal life."[24] If Buccellati is right, the Adapa myth is of less interest as a means of shedding light on the Eden Narrative. Therefore, we must look closely at his suggestions.

There are two problems in this context: the nature of Ea's warning (B 28–34) and the character of Anu's words after Adapa's refusal to eat (B 60–63). There are a number of interpretational options for the first issue.[25] A number of scholars have held that Ea was sincere and his warning appropriate.

- H.-P. Müller argued that the relation of trust between Ea and his priest speaks for Ea's sincerity. Besides, Adapa was too smart to be cheated.[26]
- D. O. Edzard held that Ea's warning should be understood as being conditional: "If they offer you bread of death, then do not eat [it]! If they offer you a drink of death, then do not drink [it]!" Adapa presumably understood that, if the food and drink of life were offered, he was free to accept.[27]
- Böhl suggested that heavenly food and drink are only for gods. A human who enjoys them must die: "To mortals, nectar and ambrosia are poison."[28]

---

24. Buccellati 1973: 61–66, p. 63.
25. For bibliography on this, see Buccellati 1973: 62; Picchioni 1981: 57–62.
26. H.-P. Müller 1983–84: 85–86.
27. Edzard 2002, my translation.
28. Böhl 1959: 426, my translation.

Others have assumed Ea to be ignorant about things in heaven. As a chthonic god, Ea did not know about matters in heaven.[29]

I believe that the issue must be decided on the basis of what we otherwise know of the god Ea. Ea's craftiness is legendary. He is a god who "persuades, tricks, or evades to gain his ends"; indeed, he is "the cleverest of the gods, the one who can plan and organize and think of ways out when no one else can."[30] Ea is very active in *Atrahasis*. It was Ea who came up with the idea of the creation of humans when the gods were on the verge of being overworked. When the gods decided to annihilate humanity, Ea made certain that one man survived the Flood, thus ensuring the gods' future access to a work force. He knew the method of keeping the growing number of humans in check: death.[31] "Also, in the Adapa myth he protects the gods from the effects of a premature decision; he prevents Adapa from acquiring the eternal life reserved for the gods."[32]

At this point, I would like to call attention to a perspective on the Adapa myth that has been proposed by Manfried Dietrich. He understands the Adapa myth on the basis of the tension between the Ea cult at Eridu and the Anu cult at Uruk–Nippur. In the myth under discussion, Anu tempts Ea's priest Adapa with immortality.[33]

Building on Dietrich's observation, I would like to go on to argue that Ea, the master of cunning among the gods, anticipated this move on the part of Anu. Ea had a private interest in preventing Adapa from gaining immortality: Ea had endowed Adapa with wisdom in order to promote the prosperity of Eridu and his own cult in that city.[34] By eating of the heavenly meal, Adapa would become immortal, a god, and

---

29. Hutter 2003: 649 with references. Note, however, that in B 14 Ea is someone "who knows heaven."

30. Jacobsen 1976: 116.

31. Wilcke 1991: 260. On Ea and the institution of death, see Lambert's restoration of OB Atrahasis III vi 47–50 (Lambert 1980: 57–58).

32. Wilcke 1991: 260, my translation.

33. On the tension between Eridu and Uruk–Nippur, see Dietrich 1984. In his study of *Adapa* (Dietrich 1991), Dietrich restricts his analysis to the Amarna version, frag. B, and understands this as a "one-tablet work." It should be noted that my study is based on the first-millennium understanding of the myth, evidenced by frag. A and by B read in the light of this. The introduction, A 3–4, suggests that at this stage the Babylonians understood the Adapa myth as dealing with the issue of wisdom and immortality in relation to the demarcation between gods and humans. On two points I disagree with Dietrich. I believe there was deception on Ea's part, and I believe that the issue of immortality was more important than he thinks.

34. Galter 1983: 170.

thereby be lost for Ea's service on earth. He therefore prevented Anu's plan by tricking Adapa into not accepting the offer made in heaven.

I thus *conclude* that, when Ea warns Adapa against partaking of the heavenly meal, he is being cunning Ea at his best, acting out of self-interest. He wants Adapa to remain a human being and thus tricks him into not accepting Anu's offer of the heavenly meal.

The second problem to be dealt with is the meaning of Anu's words after Adapa's refusal:

> Come, Adapa, why did you not eat or drink!
> Hence you shall not live. Alas for inferior humanity!
> (*Adapa* B 67–68; Izre'el 2001: 20–21)

If the verb *balāṭu* here only has the sense 'live', 'stay alive', there is hardly any reflection on eternal life.[35] An interpretation of this sort, however, has been justly criticized by J. D. Bing.[36] In the first place, the hermeneutical key to the whole poem is A 3–4, where we are told: "To him [Adapa] he [Ea] gave wisdom, he did not give him eternal life (*napišta darīta ul-iddiššu*)." When we read A and B together, this statement functions as the keynote to our understanding of the myth.

Once this is appreciated, one feels justified, with J. D. Bing, in understanding the sense of the word *balāṭu* in B 68 as very similar to what we have in the *Gilgamesh Epic* in the Old Babylonian Meissner-Millard tablet. At one of the stations in his search for immortality, wise Gilgamesh is told by the ale-wife that the gods assigned death to mankind but retained life, immortality (*balāṭum*), for themselves.[37] If one misses this aspect of the poem, "the simple idea of the story, how humanity lost an opportunity for immortality, is diluted to the point of disappearing."[38]

The following words spoken by Anu to Adapa are also noteworthy: "Alas for inferior humanity!"[39] This expression reveals that Adapa's

---

35. See Buccellati 1973: 63–64. Similarly, M. Dietrich: "Adapa, warum hast du nicht gegessen, nicht getrunken, willst du nicht am Leben bleiben?" (Dietrich 1991: 132). Nevertheless, Dietrich takes into account the possibility that it is a reflection on immortality (p. 126).

36. Bing (1984), who strongly disagrees with Buccellati. Izre'el also takes immortality to be the main issue in these lines (Izre'el 2001: 32).

37. The Meissner-Millard frag. iii 2–5; George 2003: 278–79.

38. Bing 1984: 53.

39. *Adapa* B 68. The line is damaged and difficult. The Akkadian as restored by Izre'el reads: *ayya niši da[llāt]i* (Izre'el 2001: 20), already suggested by him in a previous work and accepted by Kämmerer (1998: 258). For a different reading, see Dietrich (1991: 129): *da[šāt]i*, "reichspriessende (Menschheit)," a form of *dešû(m)* I 'to

refusal to partake of the offered meal will have dire consequences for humanity at large. The text deals with more than the individual case of Adapa. The issue at stake is immortality for humanity.

On this understanding of the crucial features of the Adapa myth, Izre'el's conclusion seems fully justified: its theme is "the distinction between humans and gods, viz., the divine capacity for living eternally."[40] Adapa has one of the two divine prerogatives, wisdom, but not the other one, immortality. His name also never appears with the divine determinative, a fact that is in line with the stress on his exclusively human nature.

There is another factor that Manfried Dietrich has properly stressed: when Anu offers Adapa the real food and water of life, he is offering him a place among heavenly immortals. Had Adapa accepted it, he would have obtained the same happy position as Ziusudra/Utanapishti, who was the only one to survive the Flood and who was thereby worthy of deification.[41] The god who makes the offer is Anu, who is chief deity of the divine assembly. We thus find the divine assembly figuring in a text in which immortality is at stake, just as in the Eden Narrative (Gen 3:22). We will find the same feature in *Gilgamesh*.

My *conclusion* so far is that immortality—or to be more exact, immortality forfeited—is an important aspect of the Adapa myth. This means that wisdom and immortality appear together in a stable thematic "marriage" in the myth as understood in the centuries before the Eden Narrative was composed.

3. Adapa and the Eden Narrative:
A Comparison

Ever since the discovery of the Adapa myth, biblical scholars have discussed the possibility of a connection with Genesis.[42] The *similarities* are striking. Both texts are myths that tell about early human forfeiture of the possibility of immortality. The two main characters, Adapa and "Adam," bear designations that have been believed to be

---

sprout'. For yet another reading, see Foster (1993: 1.433, line 83). Picchioni (1981: 120–21) does not commit himself to a reading and leaves the line untranslated.

40. Izre'el 2001: 123.

41. Dietrich 1991: 125.

42. Note, for example, Gunkel 1910: 38; Pedersen 1955b; Westermann 1976: 335–36, English trans. 1984: 246–47; Shea 1977; Andreasen 1981; Erikson 1990; H.-P. Müller [1982] 1991b: 68–87, esp. 81–84; 1991a: esp. pp. 122–28; Stordalen 2000: 245–47; Izre'el 2001: 126–28; Hallo 2004. For a survey of research before 1981, see Picchioni 1981: 33–37.

etymologically related.[43] In their forfeiture of immortality, these two characters stand as representatives of humanity at large. In both texts, there is a divine prohibition against consuming the critical substance(s). Neither of the two protagonists actually seeks immortality (in contrast to Gilgamesh; see below); however, both miss it. Finally, in both texts wisdom and immortality together have a thematic function as being divine prerogatives.

This being said, we must observe that the *differences* are considerable. The plot, the setting, and the characters are very different indeed. *Adapa* is a text without the garden, without the woman, without the serpent, and without the temptation found in the Eden Narrative. The vitalizing foods are of different kinds. The crime or sin is strikingly different: the sin is against a divine commandment in one, while the other text speaks of breaking the wing of the South Wind, thereby causing drought on earth. Wisdom as a divine prerogative is important in both: but in one it is freely granted by the god of wisdom to Adapa, who thereby becomes one of the seven antediluvian sages. In the other, wisdom is gained through an illicit act of human acquisition. The respective status of the two protagonists is also very different. "Adam" is certainly not presented as an ideal for human behavior; on the contrary, he is an example of the dire consequences of human disobedience to the divine commandment. Adapa, again, is a cultural hero who is rather similar to humans of legendary sagacity in the West-Semitic ambit such as Kirta (the Ugaritic texts), Daniʾilu (Ezek 28:3), and Job (also Hebrew Bible).[44] Most importantly, the perspective applied to the human condition is different: in *Adapa*, death is simply what is ordained for humanity from the beginning; in the Eden Narrative, death and vicissitudes are the consequences of human sin, not circumstances that have been willed by the deity.

Conclusion: I find it difficult to argue that the Adapa text served as a pattern for the narration in Genesis 2–3. What is important, however, is that wisdom and immortality have a thematic function as divine prerogatives in both.[45]

43. In favor of a connection: Layton 1977: 30–31; Andreasen 1981: 181–82. More hesitant: H.-P. Müller 1991a: 122–23; Erikson 1991: 123. I am not prepared to assume an etymological relation: The name Adapa, understood from Sumerian, seems to mean 'recovered from the water'. See Hallo 2004: 272.

44. For the wisdom of Ugaritic Kirta, see *CAT* 1.16.IV: 2 and for the wisdom of Daniʾilu, see Ezek 28:3. The Ezekiel passage can hardly refer to the hero of the book of Daniel; rather, it refers to the person known as Daniʾilu in Ugarit.

45. It is interesting to compare the relation between the Old Babylonian *Gilgamesh Epic* and some of the Sumerian Gilgamesh (Bilgames) compositions: the Old

*   *   *

The Adapa Myth: Conclusions.   My perusal of the Adapa myth has
led to the following insights.

1. I have focused on the Adapa myth as it was understood in the
first millennium, as evidenced by Fragment A (from Ashurbanipal's libraries) and by Fragment B (from Amarna) when read in the light of
Fragment A.

2. Based on the introduction of Fragment A, the myth is understood
to have as its theme wisdom and immortality as divine prerogatives.

3. Wisdom is granted to Adapa by his god, Ea. Immortality, however, is offered by Anu but not accepted. Immortality remains the one,
nonnegotiable distinction between gods and humans. Note, however,
that in Frag. D 9–10 Anu takes Adapa into his service and frees him
from Ea.

4. It is Anu, the head of the pantheon and chief of the divine assembly, who offers heavenly bread and water. Had Adapa accepted the
offer, he would have become a member of the divine assembly. There
is thus a clear reference to the divine assembly as being the sole authority for bestowing immortality.

5. Adapa is depicted as a representative of humanity at large. His refusal has consequences for humanity.

6. During the Late Bronze Age the Adapa myth was known in the
West-Semitic ambit, which we know because *Adapa* B was found in the
Amarna archives.

6.2. The Gilgamesh Epic

It did not take long after the publication of the *Gilgamesh Epic*, a
good one hundred years ago, before it was recognized as one of the
masterpieces of world literature. The poet Rainer Maria Rilke was almost intoxicated by the poem and described it as "das Epos der Todes-
furcht," the epic about the fear of death.[46] What we have found in our
perusal of the Adapa myth helps us see essential features of the *Gilgamesh Epic* in perspective. Gilgamesh has wisdom that derives from
antediluvian times, and he is engaged in a quest for immortality. The

---

Babylonian author developed only themes, not plots. See Tigay 1982: 53.

46. Moran 1980: quotation from p. 209. Maier 1997 contains a number of studies
both on the Mesopotamian material and on *Gilgamesh* in later, Western literature.

borderline between gods and humans is stated with inexorable clarity already in the Old Babylonian Meissner-Millard fragment, in which the ale-wife in a famous quotation says to Gilgamesh:

> You cannot find the life (*balāṭam*) that you seek:
> when the gods created mankind,
> for mankind they established death,
> life (*balāṭam*) they kept for themselves.
>   (*GE*, Meissner-Millard frag. iii 2–5; George 2003: 278–79)

Our task will now be to study wisdom and immortality in relation to the human/divine distinction in the *Gilgamesh Epic*. I will use the edition of A. R. George (2003) and follow George's line numbering.[47]

Adapa is a myth, but *Gilgamesh* is better designated an epic.[48] The mention of deities in *Gilgamesh* is not of such a nature as to justify the classification of the work as a myth.

First, a brief summary of *the plot*:[49] Gilgamesh, a great hero and king, tyrannizes the people of his city Uruk to such an extent that the gods decide to create a companion, Enkidu, to divert him. Gilgamesh and Enkidu together set out on an adventurous journey to the Cedar Forest. Here, they fell its guardian, Humbaba. The goddess Ishtar makes erotic overtures to Gilgamesh, but her love is rejected; her offer of sacred marriage is not accepted. Ishtar has her father, Anu, send the Bull of Heaven to avenge this rejection, but the two heroes kill him as well. The gods convene and decide to punish Enkidu by death. Enkidu falls sick and dies. Gilgamesh, mourning his friend deeply, sets out on a long journey to Uta-napishti in order to find life—that is, eternal life. The journey takes him along the Path of the Sun and across the Waters of Death. Finally, he reaches the realm of wise Uta-napishti, who survived the Flood. After a short version of the Flood narrative, Uta-

---

47. Note also Parpola's study edition (1997) with a useful glossary that sometimes comes close to being a concordance. I will quote from the translation by George (2003). George has also produced a translation adapted for the general reader (George 2000). For other translations, see E. A. Speiser, "Akkadian Myths and Epics," *ANET* 72–99; A. K. Grayson, "Akkadian Myths and Epics," *ANET* 503–7; Dalley 1991: 39–153; Hecker 1994: 3/4.646–744; Tournay and Shaffer 1994. There are a great many others.

48. For my understanding of "myth," see above, §4.1.1 (p. 66). *Epic* I understand with Vanstiphout (1990: 68–73) to refer to narratives with "heroic intention," which deal with human beings (admittedly extraordinary, almost superhuman), and gods partake in a secondary way (exception: Ishtar in *GE* VI). On *myth* and *epic* as labels for Mesopotamian texts, see also Hecker 1974: 1–24.

49. Note the discussion by Jacobsen (1976: 193–219), with his illuminating presentation of the plot in a graph (p. 216).

napishti tells Gilgamesh that he himself had been granted immortality by a decree of the gods in council but that this was a unique event. This way to immortality is closed; Uta-napishti instead teaches Gilgamesh about the magic "plant of heartbeat," which can make an old man young again. Gilgamesh finds the magic herb but soon loses it to a serpent. He now realizes the frailties of human life and returns home to Uruk, taking pride in his heroic feats.

The plot of this standard Babylonian version may thus be graphically represented as follows:

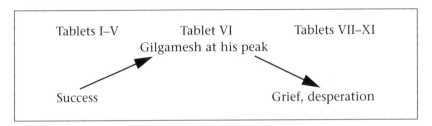

Fig. 8. The plot of the Gilgamesh Epic *has a distinct peak in Tablet VI.*

With regard to structure and theme, this is a satisfying whole.[50]

It is natural for me to concentrate on a version of the epic that belongs broadly to the same intellectual period as Genesis 2–3. Thus, although each period and region had its own version of the *Gilgamesh Epic*, as Jeffrey H. Tigay has demonstrated in his fundamental work *The Evolution of the Gilgamesh Epic* (1982), our attention will remain focused on the Standard Babylonian version (henceforth: the SB), mainly known from tablets from Nineveh.[51] According to ancient tradition, the SB is the version that can in some sense lay claim to being called *the* canonical version. This SB version is understood to have been composed by a certain Sin-leqi-unninni, who lived around 1200 B.C.E., and is referred to as the author of "the Gilgamesh series" in the list of authors and works found at Nineveh.[52] The 12th tablet is probably an addition to this composition.[53]

---

50. As George notes (2003: 48).

51. George 2003: 379–417.

52. Published by Lambert 1962: see esp. p. 66, col. VI 10.

53. Various attempts have been made, for instance by Vulpe (1994), to vindicate tablet XII as being an original part of the *Gilgamesh Epic*, but they are unconvincing; see George 2003: 47–54.

The SB *Gilgamesh Epic* has a very long prehistory, the details of which the reader will find in Tigay's monograph and in George's edition.[54] The early kernel of this Gilgamesh tradition concerned a historical king of Uruk by the name of Gilgamesh (Sumerian Bilgames), known from the Sumerian King List, who lived sometime during the Early Dynastic Period in Sumer (2700–2500 B.C.E.[55] There is a group of Sumerian poems about Gilgamesh (Bilgames), but they do not form a unified epic; they are only separate, independent texts. These Sumerian poems are currently dated to the Ur III Period (21st century B.C.E.).

The Babylonian Gilgamesh tradition goes back to Old Babylonian times. There are three tablets preserved containing portions of the Gilgamesh tradition. One of these is a tablet allegedly deriving from Sippar, the Meissner-Millard fragment of the Old Babylonian *Gilgamesh Epic* (George's OB VA + BM).[56] The central idea here is a theme that was already adumbrated in three of the Sumerian poems: Gilgamesh's concern with the problem of death and his quest for "life." The OB *Gilgamesh* should probably be understood as having been a complete composition in its own right—more than just three unrelated tablets.

The hero of the Middle Babylonian *Gilgamesh* was already an internationally known figure. Copies of the epic have been found in the Late Bronze Age cities of Emar, Ugarit, Megiddo, and Hattusa.[57] There are translations into Hittite and Hurrian.

The later, SB version is mainly known from finds in Nineveh. Some 19 centuries separate the oldest Sumerian fragment from the latest Babylonian manuscripts.[58]

It seems that the *Gilgamesh Epic* held a much more important place in the literary life of Babylonia than the Adapa myth. This is especially clear from its function in the training of scribes.[59]

1. Gilgamesh: Wisdom from the Antediluvian Age

To begin with, we must note that Gilgamesh's wisdom is a character trait that received special emphasis in the SB version. This appears in

---

54. See Tigay 1982 and George 2003: especially chaps. 1 and 5–7.

55. A. L. Oppenheim, "Babylonian and Assyrian Historical Texts," *ANET* 266; and *TUAT* 1:4: 332.

56. Now available in a new edition in George 2003: 272–86.

57. This Middle Babylonian material is now available in George 2003: 287–347. The Ugaritic material is still unpublished (George 2003: 24).

58. See George 2003: 4.

59. See George 2003: 33–39. George points out that the impression that the *Gilgamesh Epic* was not used in pedagogy is false (p. 38).

the new introduction that constitutes the first part of tablet I (lines 1–28). That this is a new introduction, specific to the SB version, is clear from a comparison of the various designations that the Babylonians themselves used to refer to the poem:

1. 'He who saw the deep' (*ša naqba īmuru*)
2. 'Surpassing all other kings' (*šūtur ēli šarrī*)
3. 'The series of Gilgamesh' (*iškār Gilgāmeš*)

The last designation is of no interest in this specific context. The other two are examples of the convention of referring to a text by citing its incipit. Aaron Shaffer made a brilliant observation based on this convention.[60] As he points out, "surpassing all other kings" is the designation in the colophon of the second tablet of the Old Babylonian version and may thus be be assumed to form the opening phrase of that series.[61] In the SB version, however, this expression is found as the beginning of I 29. The beginning of the Old Babylonian version, as we can retrieve it from the SB version, opens with triumphant praise for Gilgamesh's heroic deeds (I 29–46).

What precedes this, namely lines 1–28, is as Shaffer points out a new beginning proper to the SB version of the epic. This is a much more re-flective passage, focusing on Gilgamesh's antediluvian wisdom. This piece of sombre reflection forms a new introduction—moreover, an in-troduction that gave the *Gilgamesh Epic* the designation "He who saw the Deep."

It was probably Sin-leqi-unninni who was responsible for this new prologue. George notes that "[t]he new prologue converted the epic into autobiography in the third person, a genre of Mesopotamian belles-lettres known today as *narû*-literature."[62] A *narû* is said to have been authored by Gilgamesh in I 10. The Akkadian word *narû* is usu-ally translated 'stele', but it can also refer to an inscription.[63] The item referred to in I 10 in the prologue is thus probably identical with the lapis-lazuli tablet contained in the "tablet-box of cedar," which de-scribed "all the misfortunes that Gilgamesh went through" (I 24–28).[64]

---

60. For the following, see Shaffer apud Wiseman 1975: 158 n. 22. See also Wilcke 1977: 208–11; Walker 1981: 194; Tigay 1982: 48, 103–5, 140–66; Machinist 1986: 194; and George 2003: 28–33, especially p. 32.

61. The Pennsylvania Tablet OB II, now available in George 2003: 180–81.

62. George 2003: 32.

63. See Tigay 1982: 144 with n. 11 and *CAD* N/1 367.

64. See Longman, who views the stele and the tablet-box in *GE* I 10, 24–28 in the light of the fictional Akkadian autobiographies (the Adad-guppi autobiography, the

Gilgamesh is thus the ostensible author of the epic. We shall revert to
this "author fiction" below. The *narû* is the epic of Gilgamesh itself. In
the final analysis, the epic is a text that is talking about itself.

This new prologue (I 1–28) "changed the thrust of the entire poem,
placing emphasis on the hero's acquisition of wisdom and self-knowl-
edge"; there is now an emphasis on "the notion that wisdom is the
prize of life."[65] Wisdom in the sense of advice regarding the future is a
feature found in the earlier Gilgamesh tradition, but it acquires a high
profile in the SB version. The idea of an inscription or a stele (or what-
ever) commemorating the deeds of the hero is an old custom in the
Gilgamesh tradition.[66]

Sin-leqi-unninni not only gave the poem a new introduction, he
also created an inclusio between the beginning and end of the poem
by means of repeating the invitation to inspect the wall of Uruk, built
by Gilgamesh (I 18–21; XI 323–26). In addition, he interpolated the
abbreviated telling of the Flood myth (tablet XI).[67]

Thus, the very opening section of the SB version speaks about Gilgamesh's wisdom:

> [He who saw the Deep, the] foundation of the country,
> [who knew . . . ,] was wise in everything!
> [Gilgamesh, who] saw the Deep, the foundation of the country,
> [. . .] . . . equally [. . . ,]
> he [*learnt*] the totality of wisdom about everything.
> He saw the secret and uncovered the hidden,
> he brought back a message from the antediluvian age.

Cuthean legend of Naram-Sin, and the Sennacherib autobiography); see Longman
1991: 129 and 97–128. Tigay (1982: 144 with n. 12), on the other hand, construes
a difference between *Gilgamesh* and the *narû*-literature by supposing that the issue
of third-person narrative versus first-person story is a decisive difference. If this
were right one could at most assume a "genre allusion" in *Gilgamesh* to the *narû* literature. On this type of allusion, see Genette (1982: 7–14), where "architextualité"
is the same as what I call genre allusion. However, Peter Machinist (personal communication) points out that the lines are not as clear-cut as Tigay assumes. He
finds no basic problem with George's conclusion that the new introduction converted the epic into a specimen of *narû* genre (George 2003: 32). Note that the tablet of lapis lazuli in the tablet-box may be the foundation document of the wall of
Uruk; see Machinist 1986: 194. See also *CAD* N/1 367.

65. George 2003: 32 and 68.

66. It is a feature found in both the Sumerian *Bilgames and Huwawa A* (see George
2000: 151 and the OB Akkadian *Gilgamesh Epic* (see OB III = Yale Tablet v 188; George
2003: 202–3.

67. See Tigay 1982: 103–5; and George 2003: 32.

He came a distant road and was weary but granted rest,
[he] set down on a stele all his labours.

(GE I 1–10; George 2003: 538–39)

The phrase "He who saw the Deep" has been the subject of much discussion. The word *naqbu* can mean 'totality' or 'deep', 'underground water'. The latter sense works best here.[68] The reference to the Deep here anticipates the reference to the Apsu in the passage describing how Gilgamesh found the rejuvenating herb (XI 287–93). The Apsu is the sweet-water ocean, the cosmic domain of Ea, the god of wisdom. "In acquiring from Ea's protégé, Uta-napishti, the knowledge for which he was celebrated, Gilgamesh was initiated into Ea's realm, the source of all wisdom."[69] One could add that this association between Gilgamesh's wisdom and the wisdom of Ea is made explicit in III 104, where Gilgamesh is 'wise with Ea of the Apsu' (*itti* ^{d}*ea apsî īmeq*);[70] compare I 241–42, where "Anu, Enlil and Ea broadened his wisdom."

Gilgamesh's wisdom has the same origin as the wisdom that Adapa possessed: it derives from the god Ea. Therefore, it is all-encompassing (I 4, 6), and it is antediluvian: "he brought back a message from the antediluvian age (*ṭēma ša lām abūbi*)" (I 8).

This latter statement of course points forward to Gilgamesh's consultation with Uta-napishti in tablet XI. Uta-napishti bears the epithet *atra-ḫasīs* 'Exceeding-Wise' (XI 49; 197). He lives 'at the mouth of the rivers' (*ina pî nārāti*, XI 205), a designation that in some contexts comes close to being a by-name for Ea's cosmic domain, the Apsu.[71] To quote A. R. George: "In the epic Uta-napishti fills the role of the quintessential wise man who knows the secrets of the cosmos—as it were, the meaning of life. He and his knowledge, ancient and unique among men, are the end of Gilgamesh's long and arduous quest."[72]

Uta-napishti's wisdom is illustrated by the *Instructions of Shuruppak*, attested in Sumerian before 2500 B.C.E. and later translated into Akkadian. Here the wise old antediluvian Shuruppak counsels his son, the Flood hero-to-be.[73]

---

68. For the following, see Silva Castillo (1998), who stresses that Gilgamesh's wisdom ultimately derives from Ea.

69. George 2003: 445.

70. The Akkadian verb *emēqu* may have been chosen because of its specific combination of meanings 'to be deep, profound' and 'to be wise'.

71. Albright (1919) found this sense in some incantations. See George 2003: 520 n. 268.

72. George 2000: xlii.

73. For translations, see R. D. Biggs, "The Instructions of Shuruppak," *ANET* 594–95; Lambert, *BWL* 92–95. I do not have access to the edition by Alster (2001:

2. Gilgamesh: The Quest for Immortality

In the SB version that we owe to Sin-leqi-unninni, tablets VII–XI
deal with the death of Enkidu, Gilgamesh's mourning, his fear of
death, and his search for immortality.

> For his friend Enkidu Gilgamesh
> was weeping bitterly as he roamed the wild:
> "I shall die, and shall I not then be like Enkidu?
> Sorrow has entered my heart.
> I became afraid of death, so go roaming the wild,
> to Uta-napishti, son of Ubar-Tutu. . . ."
>
> (*GE* IX 1–6; George 2003: 666–67)[74]

Uta-napishti voices the same insight into the human condition.
Death is inescapable:

> No one sees death,
> no one sees the face [of death,]
> no one [hears] the voice of death:
> (yet) savage death is the one who hacks man down.
>
> (*GE* X 304–7; George 2003: 696–97)

Gilgamesh's intense quest for "life" is expressed by a number of different verbs:

- *še'û(m)*, a general verb for 'to search', I 41
- *erēšu(m)* II 'to request', 'wish for', 'demand', e.g., XI 213
- *bu''û(m)* 'look for', 'seek for', XI 208
- *saḫāru(m)* 'to go around', 'turn', 'search', Meissner-Millard frag.
  i 8; iii 2 (George 2003: 276–79)

Gilgamesh's quest for life took him along the dark Path of the Sun,
which stretches between the Twin Mountains at opposite extremes of
the earth—the mountains of sunrise and sunset (tablet IX 131–70).[75]
Having beaten Shamash, the sun, in a race against time (IX 170), he
arrived at the garden of jewels (IX 171–94).[76]

At last, Gilgamesh crossed the Waters of Death and reached Uta-
napishti, the "Exceeding-Wise."[77] He and his wife were the only hu-

---

chap. 1), to which Peter Machinist called my attention (personal communication).
74. See also X 70–71, 138–39, 147–48, 238–39.
75. On Mount Mashu ('Twin') in IX 37 as referring to the Twin Mountains at
opposite extremes of the world and on the dark path, see George 2003: 492–97.
76. For a discussion, see Stordalen 2000: 153–55; and George 2003: 497–98.
77. It is now clear that the "Stone Ones" in X (passim) are not anchors for kedg-
ing, an interpretation that I adopted in a previous work (Mettinger 2001: 101; see
George 2003: 501–2).

mans who had been granted immortality, and only they could reveal to Gilgamesh how to obtain this gift of the gods. There are two points of special interest to us in the description of the encounter between Gilgamesh and Uta-napishti. One is the role of the divine assembly as having power over life and death. The other is the secret of the magic herb.

Owing to the role of the divine assembly at the end of the Eden Narrative (Gen 3:22), the involvement of the same heavenly authority in *Gilgamesh* is noteworthy:

> The Anunnaki, the great gods, were in assembly,
> Mammitum, who creates destiny, made a decree with them:
> death and life they did establish,
> the day of death they did not reveal.
> (*GE* X 319–22; George 2003: 696–99)

The gods in assembly certainly have the authority to grant immortality. Gilgamesh asks Uta-napishti about the circumstances of his being made immortal (XI 7), and the answer is formulated as a key scene in the epic. Uta-napishti, the one who survived the Flood, tells the following story:

> Enlil came up into the boat,
> he took hold of my hands and brought me out.
> He brought out my woman, he made her kneel at my side,
> he touched our foreheads, standing between us to bless us:
> "In the past, Uta-napishti was [one of] mankind,
> but now Uta-napishti and his woman shall be like us gods!
> Uta-napishti shall dwell far away, at the mouth of the rivers!"
> (*GE* XI 199–205; George 2003: 716–17)

This is a scene of iconic, even emblematic qualities: the god stands in the middle, between the man and his spouse, who are genuflecting. In a gesture of blessing, he makes the human couple "like us gods," thus bestowing eternal life on them.

However, what happened to the antediluvian couple is the result of a special, one time, divine dispensation—a unique concession from the gods. The transfiguration from being one of humankind into being one of the gods is not to be experienced by Gilgamesh. Though semi-divine by virtue of his mother, the goddess Ninsun (and being two-thirds god and one-third human),[78] Gilgamesh will remain a human. Uta-napishti asks Gilgamesh:

---

78. See I 48; IX 51 and note also statements according to which Gilgamesh had the flesh of the gods in IX 49; X 7, 268. The divine determinative before the name

But now, who will bring the gods to assembly for you,
so you can find the life that you search for?

(*GE* XI 207–8; George 2003: 716–17)

The question, of course, is a rhetorical one. The implied answer is:
Nobody! Uta-napishti had immortality bestowed on him in unique
circumstances, never to be repeated. This episode also appears earlier,
in the *Sumerian Flood Story*, where the Flood hero, Ziusudra, prostrated
himself before An and Enlil, who "gave him life, like a god, elevated
him to eternal life, like a god."[79] The proper destiny of man is death,
not immortality. Only gods are immortal.

The role of the divine assemby as the authority that had power to
bestow immortality had long standing in the Gilgamesh tradition.
Thus, already as early as the Sumerian *Death of Bilgames* we find Bilgames at a meeting of the gods' council, convened to decide about the
destiny of the hero.[80] The gods review his heroic career, his journey to
the Cedar Forest, his killing of Humbaba, and his journey to the end of
the world to find the one who survived the Flood. Should Bilgames be
granted immortality? No! Bilgames was to descend to the Netherworld; but once there, he was to assume the position of chief of the
shades, sitting in judgment over the living and the dead, like Nin-
gishzida and Dumuzi.

Regarding the mortality of humans, there are two different traditions in Mesopotamia. According to one (note, for instance, the *Gilgamesh Epic*), man was mortal from the beginning. According to the
other (*Death of Bilgames*; *Atrahasis*), mortality was assigned to the human race on a later occasion.[81]

Note that both the Sumerian and the Akkadian name for the survivor of the Flood contains the element meaning 'life'. Sumerian Ziusudra means 'life of distant days', and the Akkadian name Uta-napishti
means 'I found my life'.[82] In addition, 'the Living One' (LÚ.TI.LA) in

---

Gilgamesh does not refer to the whole name but only to the first element in the
writing.

79. Quoted from Civil by Lambert and Millard 1969: 144–45, VI 255–57. My
thanks to Edward Lipiński, who reminded me of this passage (personal communication).

80. The Me-Turan version, lines 49–83, text in Cavigneaux and Al-Rawi 2000a:
27–28; French trans., pp. 56–57; English trans. in George 2000: 198–99. See also
Katz 2003: 371–73.

81. George 2003: 507–8.

82. George 2003: 152–54. The first element in Uta-napishti is a form of the verb
watāʾu(m) 'to find'.

the incipit of *Bilgames and Huwawa A* is probably the goal of the hero's quest, the immortal Ziusudra.[83] Though the element 'life' in these designations may primarily refer to surviving the Flood, one should not overlook the fact that the survivor of the Flood is the only one granted "life" par excellence, immortality.

It is thus clear, from the SB version and from the preceding tradition, that the divine assembly did not bestow immortality on Gilgamesh. The hero's inability to conquer death is illustrated by his inability to conquer sleep (XI 209–46). As a kind of test, Uta-napishti summons Gilgamesh: "Come, for six days and seven nights do not sleep" (line 209). But Gilgamesh falls asleep as soon as he sits down, and Uta-napishti notes: "See the fellow who demanded life! Sleep is wafting over him like a fog" (lines 213–14).[84]

On the instigation of his wife, however, Uta-napishti gives Gilgamesh a priceless farewell present: he reveals to him the secret of the magic herb to be found at the bottom of the Apsu (XI 273–86). Gilgamesh goes on a diving expedition and obtains the herb, which he refers to by two different designations: one is *šammu nikitti*, a designation that should now be understood as meaning the 'plant of heartbeat' (line 295);[85] the other is 'the Old Man Has Grown Young' (line 299). This herb will work miracles, says Gilgamesh; "I will eat some myself and go back to how I was in my youth!" (line 300). However, Gilgamesh finds the precious herb, only to lose it to a snake, who took the opportunity to snatch it while Gilgamesh was having a bath on his way back to Uruk (lines 305–7).

We can of course ask about the nature of the life that was to be granted by the magic plant. Is it immortality in the same sense as the life bestowed by the divine council on Uta-napishti? It seems to me that the magic herb represents the second best: although Gilgamesh could not attain immortality proper, he was at least given the possibility of reexperiencing or prolonging his youth.

---

83. Sumerian text in Edzard 1991: 167; English trans. in George 2000: 150. For the identification with Ziusudra, see Cavigneaux and Al-Rawi 2000b: 5–6 with n. 33; and George 2003: 17 and 97. The Living One is also mentioned in the Me-Turan version of *Bilgames and the Netherworld*; see George 2000: 190; and Cavigneaux and Al-Rawi 2000b: 5, line 29.

84. This is only the final peak of a number of occurrences of the sleep motif in the *Gilgamesh Epic*; see Vanstiphout 1990: 56–58.

85. Watanabe (1994: 583 n. 6) has found an attestation that favors *nikittu* as 'heartbeat, pulsating life' (*Herzschlag, pulsierendes Leben*).

On the level of narrative technique, the magic herb demonstrates that the story of Gilgamesh is similar to the story of Adapa. In both *Gilgamesh* and *Adapa*, the divine council or its chief deity, Anu, has the authority to grant immortal life. In both, deception plays a role: Adapa was deceived by Ea, and Gilgamesh by the cunning serpent. And, most importantly, in both, the protagonist only missed immortality by a very narrow margin.

We found that, in both the Eden Narrative and the Adapa myth, the protagonist stands out as a representative of humanity at large. In some sense, this is true of Gilgamesh as well. In his fruitless quest for immortality, Gilgamesh stands for the human creature of all times. George makes an interesting suggestion here, based on the difference between Gilgamesh and Uta-napishti: the mortal Gilgamesh represents "the individual Everyman," whereas the immortal Uta-napishti, blessed with a future of infinite years, "symbolizes the human race."[86]

It should be noted that I have so far refrained from defining the quest for immortality as the main theme of the *Gilgamesh Epic*. For the present purpose, a definite stance on this issue is not required. However, I would like to call attention to the worthwhile work on the literary aspects of the *Gilgamesh Epic* by Vanstiphout.[87]

What is the poem about? asks Vanstiphout. He finds several possible answers. Friendship is certainly an important aspect. Also, *Gilgamesh* may be said to be a dynastic epic; the hero is king of Uruk. Foundationally, however, Vanstiphout finds that the main theme of the poem is *la condition humaine* (the human condition). Gilgamesh's overall enterprise is the quest for eternal life and thereby for meaning. But, says Vanstiphout, unending life is only one aspect of meaning. He goes on to formulate the thesis that the meaning of life, and not immortality as such, is the central theme of the *Gilgamesh Epic*.

Vanstiphout finds this theme manifested on various levels in the poem. Thus, the Cedar Forest episode may be taken as an experiment in immortality through a heroic military enterprise. On another level, there is the idea that immortality may be granted to Gilgamesh through the great works that he has left to mankind. This is a salient feature at the beginning and end of the epic. In both, we find an invitation to come and inspect the great wall of Uruk, founded by the Seven Sages and built by Gilgamesh (I 18–21; XI 323–26).

---

86. George 2003: 528.
87. For the following, see Vanstiphout 1990: esp. pp. 61–68.

On a more profound level, Gilgamesh, like Horace, has left a *monumentum aere perennius*, "a monument lasting longer than bronze": not the wall of Uruk, but the poem he has given to the world.

According to the fiction upheld by the author of the poem, Sin-leqi-unninni, the epic derives from Gilgamesh himself. As we saw above, the introduction of the epic associates it with the genre of fictive autobiography, the *narû*-literature. This feature—immortality thanks to the great work of art, the poem—is stressed in the new prologue, added by Sin-leqi-unninni. Note that the *narû* records the labors of the hero (I 9–10).

In the *Gilgamesh Epic*, the idea of immortality undergoes a transfiguration: immortality is not manifested through the never-ending life of the body but through the bequeathing of an immortal piece of art to the rest of humanity. Hence, Vanstiphout maintains, in the *Gilgamesh Epic* the poem itself represents immortality in its transfigured shape.

Even so, I believe that the main theme of the poem may be defined as a quest for immortality. The *Gilgamesh Epic* depicts an inner development in the hero. The story about Gilgamesh's struggle against death and his pursuit of immortality begins with a quest for immortality through glorious deeds. After the death of his friend, Enkidu, Gilgamesh becomes involved in a quest for immortality in the sense of unending life in the body. The realization that this is out of question for any human after Uta-napishti leads to the conception of immortality through an everlasting masterpiece: the immortal poem that the hero purports to have left behind. The *Gilgamesh Epic* embodies both an "insistence on human values" and an "acceptance of human limitations."[88]

*   *   *

The Gilgamesh Epic: Conclusions. My perusal of *Gilgamesh* has led to the following insights.

1. The epic has a very long history, but I decided to focus on the late, Standard Babylonian version. This version contains a new prologue that lends added emphasis to the wisdom aspects of the epic.

2. Gilgamesh's wisdom is associated with the god Ea and is of antediluvian origin, being communicated to him by the survivor of the Flood, Uta-napishti.

---

88. Moran, quoted according to George 2000: xxxii–xxxiii. Moran was not available to me.

3. The basic theme of *Gilgamesh* is the hero's quest for immortality. However, immortality in the sense of everlasting life in the body is out of question for any human except for Uta-napishti, who was deified after the Flood. Ultimately, the epic transforms the idea of endless life into the notion of immortality through an everlasting masterpiece of art: the poem itself.

4. It is the divine assembly that has the authority to determine life and death and to grant immortality.

5. Gilgamesh stands out as a representative of humanity at large. His case is paradigmatic of the human condition.

6. Portions of the Middle Babylonian *Gilgamesh* have been found at Emar, Ugarit, and Megiddo. The epic was thus known in Late Bronze Age Syria and Palestine.

Chapter 7

Synthesis

We have now arrived at the end of our long and fascinating journey, investigating a text of cardinal importance to the Judeo-Christian tradition, a text that has left its imprint on innumerable pieces of art and literature in Western civilization, this biblical story of the first human revolt against God.

Genesis 2–3, a text of rare dimensions, has been read in a long series of dissimilar contexts and has consequently been understood in many different ways. A number of different themes have been found in the narrative. The history of its reception is thus a worthy topic for a monograph of its own. However, the task of writing a history of its reception falls outside the scope of this book. The nature of the present investigation has been that of a historical-critical study of the Eden Narrative. What I wanted to ascertain was what this narrative said in its own time, as far as this is possible to assess. I will now rehearse and comment on the outcome of the present project.

I formulated two questions that I wanted to answer: (1) What is the theme of the Eden Narrative? (2) Was there a prior tradition about the first man's expulsion from Eden and, if so, do the changes to that tradition made by the Eden Poet shed light on the theme of the Eden Narrative?

• The thematic analysis (chap. 3) demonstrates that the subject is the divine test, a notion with clear analogues in texts about God's testing of Israel, Abraham, and Job. Both trees have definite functions in this test. The theme is disobedience and its consequences.

• My narratological analysis (chap. 2) demonstrates that the narrative in its present shape is a well-integrated unit with the divine test as its focus. God gives his divine commandment, thereby confronting the first humans with a radical choice: obedience or disobedience? In the plot, one tree serves as the test case (the tree of knowledge) and the other as the symbol of the potential reward (the tree of life).

123

• A prior Adamic myth was retrieved by means of an analysis of Ezekiel 28. The changes carried out by the Eden Poet point up the focus of his composition: the divine test and the consequences of disobedience. The symbolism of the two trees is introduced by the Eden Poet to highlight the situation of radical choice.

• The role of wisdom and immortality in this Adamic myth can be understood against the background of their role in two major Mesopotamian compositions, *Adapa* and *Gilgamesh,* in which wisdom and immortality serve as the divine prerogatives *par préférence.*

Our definition of the subject as the divine test and the theme as disobedience and its consequences, worked out in chap. 3 above, is thus supported both by the analysis of the plot (chap. 2) and by the analysis of the changes made by the Eden Poet to the old Adamic myth that we retrieved from Ezekiel 28 (see above, chap. 5).

It should be clear by now that sound principles of paradisiacal forestry require an Eden Narrative with two special trees. The idea of a one-tree narrative that was subsequently enriched to include the other tree as well is no longer tenable. This is highly important to the way in which the theme of the narrative is to be defined.

7.1. The Two Main Traditions Alloyed

As far as I am aware, there was no self-contained narrative in the extrabiblical world that might have served as an epic pattern for the Eden Narrative. However, we did find a narrative of this sort in the Adamic myth (see chap. 5 above, on Ezekiel 28). When handling this myth, the Eden Poet left his fingerprints in a way that reveals his background in Deuteronomistic theology.

Thus, the luminosity of the Eden Narrative was caused by the high theological voltage of the two poles that a literary genius sparked together in this narrative: the Adamic myth and Deuteronomistic theology.

The Adamic myth was a story about the first man in the garden of Eden, of his aspirations to—or his claims to possess—wisdom and immortality, of sin as hubris, and of the expulsion from the garden. Exactly how Job 15:7–8 relates to this pattern is not quite clear. The Job passage alludes to the Adamic myth, maybe to a special version of it, and refers to the first man as a listener in the council of the gods. He then seizes wisdom in an inappropriate act of acquisition. Most likely, the *tradition* attested by the Job passage is prior to the Eden Narrative.[1] In any case, both the Genesis and the Job versions speak of wisdom attained by means of an illicit act of seizure.

The Eden Poet used *the plot* of the preliterary Adamic myth. His allegiance to the Deuteronomistic value system left its imprint on *the theme* of the Eden Narrative (chap. 3). Almost all of the changes carried out by the Eden Poet to the Adamic myth can be explained as being due to his thematic focus (chap. 5). They may thus be said to point up the theme as being the consequences of disobedience to the commandment (chap. 3).

In view of the preceding discussion, the tradition history behind the Eden Narrative may be illustrated as follows:

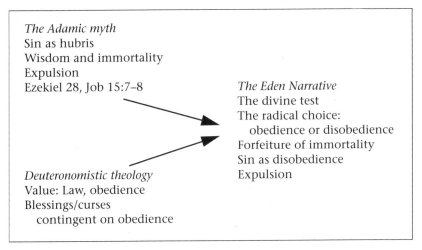

Fig. 9. The Eden Narrative entwines a number of traditions, of which the most important are the Adamic myth and Deuteronomistic theology.

Figure 9 indicates the aspects of the traditions that are of special importance for the present study. Other traditions contributed to the Eden Narrative as well: the chaos battle myth with the serpent was

---

1. Note that I speak of the *tradition*. Whether the *book* of Job is prior is a different matter. There are details in Job that point to knowledge of the primeval history (see Mettinger 1992: 236 n. 44). Details from Genesis 2–3 that appear in Job are: Gen 2:7, 3:19 (from dust to dust); see Job 1:21, 4:19, 10:9. Gen 2:7 (breath of life); see Job 27:3, 32:7–8, 33:4. Gen 2:21–24 (the rib); see Job 18:12 ("rib" stands for "wife"; see Gordis 1978: 191–92). Genesis 3 (the "fall"); see Job 31:33 ("Did I conceal my sins as Adam did?").

mentioned, and we should also remember the tradition about the creation of the first human being out of dust.

Before we leave the traditions used by the Eden Poet, another aspect should be mentioned. The question whether the Eden Poet was aware of using the myth genre was discussed above (§4.3, p. 76). I distinguished between texts that have a referential ambition and texts that strive for representativity (§4.1.1, p. 67). Against the background of my analysis of the Adamic tradition and the changes carried out by the Eden Poet (chap. 5), I find the conclusion obvious that the Eden Poet himself knew that he was the one who transformed the prior Adamic myth into a story about two trees and a divine test. He therefore must have known that he was not referring to a previous, one-time event in time and space—in other words, his ambition was not referential. Instead, it is clear that his ambition was to produce a text of maximal representativity, of universal validity. Though we do not know of any terms for "myth" or "symbol" in Biblical Hebrew, I believe that the Eden Poet was aware of proceeding on this level in the piece of literature that he produced.

7.2. The Conceptual Framework

In the ensuing section, I offer some comments on wisdom and immortality as constituting the ontological boundary between gods and humans.

1. The Ontological Boundary
The Eden Narrative shares the common ancient Near Eastern notion of wisdom and immortality as marking out the ontological boundary between gods and humans. The main evidence is as follows:[2]

1. In the chapter on *Adapa* and *Gilgamesh* above, we discovered that wisdom and immortality were considered divine prerogatives. The gods gave wisdom to humans, but they only granted immortality once, in the exceptional case of Ziusudra/Uta-napishti. Immortality is the ultimate divide between gods and humans.

2. The conflict between gods and humans in the Atrahasis myth is a further piece of evidence. We lack a few details on this matter, because the crucial passage (I 340–51) is very badly damaged. The statement in I 358–59 that the noise of humans disturbed the gods has

---

2. A fine discussion is found in Oden (1981), who concentrates on Atrahasis and Genesis 1–11 and hence does not deal with *Adapa* and *Gilgamesh*.

been discussed at length.[3] The Akkadian terms here are *rigmu* and *ḫubūru*, the first meaning 'cry', 'noise', and the second 'bustle', 'clamour'.[4] An interpretation put forward by Pettinato and then endorsed by von Soden is that the statement in these lines refers to noisy activities that marked a rebellious attitude on the part of the humans who were not content with their lot but wanted to encroach on the divine territory.[5]

3. Psalm 82 deals with Yʜwʜ (denoted as Elohim) and the other gods in the divine assembly. Wisdom and immortality stand out as the twin characteristics of deity, here denied to the gods (vv. 5, 7).[6]

4. The Adamic myth retrieved from Ezekiel 28 depicted the first man as claiming or aspiring to wisdom and immortality. These ambitions were denounced in the story (cf. Job 15:7–8).

5. The same stress on a borderline between the divine and human spheres is found in Genesis 1–11.[7] The passage on the Tower of Babel in Gen 11:1–9 presents "the tower whose top assaults the sky—a perfect and natural metaphor for the human assault on the divinely ordained cosmos," says Oden.[8] In Genesis 2–3, there are the statements by the serpent about becoming "like the gods" (3:5) and by God about the necessity of preventing the humans from becoming "like one of us" (3:22).

The "divine plurals" in Gen 1:26, 3:22, and 11:7 are particularly noteworthy in this connection, as was recently stressed by Lyle Eslinger.[9]

Gen 1:26   Let us make humankind in our image . . .

Gen 3:22   . . . like one of us, knowing good and evil.

Gen 11:7   Come, let us go down and confuse their language . . .

---

3. For the text, see Lambert and Millard 1969: 66–67.

4. See *CDA*, ad loc.

5. See Pettinato 1968: 184–90, esp. p. 190 ["Lärm der Empörung"] and pp. 193–94; and von Soden 1973: 353–55. Note also the discussion by Oden 1981: 197–210. On this motif of noise in *Erra and Ishum*, see Machinist (1983) and note his cautionary remark about the semantics as presented by Pettinato; Machinist notes that *rigmu* does not mean "sin, sin against the gods" per se; this is, rather, a contextual meaning (Machinist 1983: 225 n. 24).

6. I am grateful to Peter Machinist for calling my attention to this text (Machinist; personal communication).

7. On this, note Oden 1981: 210–16 and Hendel 1987.

8. Oden 1981: 211.

9. See Eslinger 2006.

"The first person plurals schematize 'we,' 'the gods,' versus 'them,' 'the humans,'" says Eslinger, and he considers all three statements to be sharing "a common rhetorical purpose: to mark out the ontological boundaries between gods and humans."[10] Moreover, "[t]he apodictic tonality . . . grows more prominent in the second and third occurrences."[11]

Consequently, the two main witnesses to the ontological boundary in the Primeval History of the Hebrew Bible are the Eden Narrative and the story about the Tower of Babel. There is a third passage worth mentioning, however, which is Gen 6:1–4. Ronald S. Hendel observes that this passage is in line with the other two, because it speaks about a problematic mixing of categories: the sons of God marrying the daughters of earthly humans.[12] Admittedly, the active party here is not the humans but the sons of God.

This view of the situation in Genesis 1–11 was questioned by Robert A. Di Vito.[13] I fail to see, however, that Di Vito has made his case. On the contrary, I think Hendel grasped the situation well:

> I suggest that the Primeval Cycle is characterized by a series of mythological transgressions of boundaries that result in a range of divine responses which slowly build up the present order of the cosmos.[14]

This notion of a line of demarcation between gods and humans helps us perceive important aspects of the Eden Narrative. The sin of the first humans in this narrative is not only disobedience in general but more exactly an infringement of the divinely prescribed boundaries, a conscious act of rebellion marked by utter hubris.

Wisdom and immortality are divine prerogatives. In Mesopotamian mythology, the gods grant wisdom to Adapa (and, via Uta-napishti, to Gilgamesh as well), but they retain immortality for themselves. In the Eden Narrative, the humans acquire wisdom (knowledge) by means of an illicit act of acquisition (as in Job 15:7–8). The God of the Eden Narrative had planned to grant immortality as a reward for obedience.

This may be illustrated by the following chart:

---

10. Eslinger 2006: 173–74.
11. Eslinger 2006: 176.
12. Hendel 1987: especially p. 23.
13. See Di Vito 1992.
14. Hendel 1987: 25.

	Mesopotamia	Israel
Wisdom	granted by the gods	seized by the human
Immortality	withheld by the gods	gift contemplated but withheld

Fig. 10. Wisdom and immortality take on new functions in the Eden Narrative. Here the human part is much more active, because man is confronted with a radical choice.

Having made these observations on the ontological borderline, I proceed to some observations about wisdom and immortality in the Eden Narrative.

2. Wisdom

In our narrative, wisdom is represented by the forbidden tree. To any post-Enlightenment reader, this creates an awkward problem: does the Eden Narrative thereby manifest a negative appreciation of wisdom/knowledge? Before jumping to conclusions on this issue, we must take into account certain circumstances.

First, in the ancient Near East, wisdom is otherwise a gift of the gods. Rainer Albertz perceptively notes that the prohibition in Gen 2:16–17 stands out as completely unparalleled (*ein Unikum*) against the background of the Sumerian-Babylonian tradition.[15]

Second, as Albertz also points out, the wisdom-related concepts found in Gen 3:4–7 are otherwise considered good in the Hebrew Bible (opening of the eyes, knowing "good and bad," and so on).[16]

Third, there is one thing that Albertz has overlooked, which is the thematic role of a radical choice between obedience and disobedience in the narrative and, in connection with this, the two notions of human hubris and the transgression of the ultimate ontological boundary found in the older Adamic myth (above, chap. 5). These notions are very much present in the Eden Narrative as well.[17]

---

15. Albertz 1993: 108, and note his survey on pp. 101–11.

16. Albertz 1992: 12–19.

17. Here I must confess to disagreeing with Albertz. Albertz anchors these notions of hubris and transgression of the borderline too exclusively in the *traditions* behind Gen 2:3 (Albertz 1992: 24).

The Eden Poet wanted to impress on his audience the importance of obedience to the divine commandment. He drew his plot from a tradition, the Adamic myth, in which wisdom and immortality were the two self-evident "Adamic" claims or aspirations. He wanted to present a divine test—a test with immortality as the potential reward. It was therefore clear that the other aspiration, wisdom, must be used for the test case.

Fundamentally, the question here concerns the intentions of the Eden Poet, what he wanted to communicate. Let me use an illustration: when we read on the calendar about the time of sunrise and sunset, we do not interpret the calendar as intending to communicate astronomical insights about the sun's movements in space.

Correspondingly, we should read the Eden Narrative in the light of its thematic focus: a divine test and a radical choice. We should ask just how much importance is being ascribed to the idea that knowledge is inherently illicit. Is this idea present at all? Could it be that the prohibition in Gen 2:17 is, so to speak, just the result of the "mechanics" of the plot?

To this consideration, I must add another, which is the potential reward for obedience: permission to eat from the tree of life. The logical implications of this interpretation of the text are considerable: the gift of free access to the tree of life would have made the first humans divine, with access to the heavenly council and the wisdom communicated there. This interpretation rests on what we have found in our study of *Adapa* and *Gilgamesh* and on the express statements in Job 15:7–8.

By their disobedience, the first humans attained wisdom but lost the chance for immortality. By obedience, they would have won both: immortality *and* wisdom. This observation shows me that the Eden Narrative is not a divine assessment of wisdom (knowledge) in negative terms but a divine lesson on the ultimate priorities that should prevail: first, obedience to the commandment, then all the rest following as a free gift (compare with Matt 6:33). In my first chapter, I quoted James Barr, who asked what was wrong with the knowledge of good and evil that God did not want the first humans to have it. My answer is: nothing! The narrator presents God as giving them the possibility of achieving both—by obedience to the divine commandment.

3. Immortality

We studied three narratives in which the possibility of immortality is forfeited by the respective protagonists, Adapa, Gilgamesh, and

"Adam." Of the three, only Gilgamesh actively strives for immortality. The other two are not even aware of the possibility. The reasons for missing immortality are quite different in the three stories:

- Adapa: his allegiance and obedience to Ea, whom he served
- Gilgamesh: (a) impossible for the divine assembly to grant him a favor exclusively given to Uta-napishti; (b) the serpent snatches the plant of heartbeat
- "Adam": disobedience to the divine commandment

The Eden Narrative evinces a double view of death, and this is due to the nature of the alloyed traditions and motifs. On the one hand, the Eden Poet uses the tradition about man's being created out of dust (Gen 2:7). From this perspective, death is the natural termination of human life. On the other hand, he creates a narrative with two trees, one of which is the tree of life—a narrative with immortality as a potential reward in case he passes the test of obedience. Here, the Eden Poet introduces a perspective in which death is seen as the ultimate evil, the perennial plague of humanity. Returning to dust is the punishment for disobedience (Gen 3:19).[18]

Surveying our results at large, we are able to make the following observations on the key notions of wisdom and immortality:

1. In the two Mesopotamian texts studied above, we found wisdom and immortality to be divine prerogatives.
2. In the Adamic myth, these two become the focal points of human hubris: the first man has wisdom from the outset and makes unsubstantiated claims to immortality (divine status).
3. In the Eden Narrative, wisdom and immortality take on a new function as key notions in the divine test: the tree of knowledge as the test case and the tree of life as the potential reward.

The Divine Assembly. Following our discussion of the ontological boundaries and of wisdom and immortality as divine prerogatives, I

---

18. In the story world of the Eden Poet, the first humans were not immortal from the beginning. The issue of immortality was open, the result depending on the outcome of the divine test. I think Barr was right in his observation that "Paul was not interpreting the story in and for itself; he was really *interpreting Christ* through the use of images from this story" (Barr 1993: 89). His main point was Adam as the antitype of Christ; see Rom 5:12–21 and 1 Cor 15:21–22. Paul's understanding of these matters is based on a tradition of interpretation attested in texts such as Wis 2:23; *4 Ezra* 3:21, and 7:116–18.

must append some remarks on the role of the divine assembly in this context. In our study of *Adapa* and *Gilgamesh,* we noted that in *Adapa* the god Anu was the head of the pantheon and chief of the divine assembly; he thus had the authority to offer Adapa the heavenly meal that would have made him immortal. In *Gilgamesh,* it was the convened divine assembly that accorded immortality to Uta-napishti. The same procedure, moreover, would be the only possible way for Gilgamesh to attain immortality.

In the Hebrew Bible, the divine assembly figures in a context in which the first man attains wisdom in the heavenly *sôd* (Job 15:7–8). The primeval history also contains allusions to the celestial court. The "divine plurals" provide an example (Gen 1:26, 3:22, 11:7). The words of the serpent supply another ("like the gods knowing good and evil," 3:5). Furthermore, there is the divine designation YHWH Elohim, which appears throughout chaps. 2–3 except in 3:1b–5. As Stordalen points out, this designation may imply a story world that features a class of *elohim* beings among whom YHWH is one.[19]

The study of óther major texts that appeared in the biblical ambit, such as *Gilgamesh* and *Adapa,* thus provides an improved understanding of the conceptual premises of the Eden Narrative. Its roots in the soil of the world of Near Eastern thought go deep, indeed.

4. Theodicy

I discussed theodicy above (§3.2.3, p. 58) and need only to add a few overarching comments here. Indeed, theodicy is "the touchstone of all religions."[20] The fundamental role of theodicy is rightly stressed by some of the finest scholars of sociology of religion: Max Weber, Peter Berger, and Thomas Luckmann.[21] Theodicy proper, says Berger, is "the religious legitimation of anomic phenomena," and by "anomic phenomena" he means the profound existential enigmas of human existence, foremost of which is death.[22] Theodicy is thus one of the most fundamental functions of symbolic universes, which are on principle nomic, or ordering, in character.[23] Because "mythology repre-

---

19. Stordalen 2000: 287. L'Hour does not discuss this possibility in his study (L'Hour 1974).

20. O'Flaherty 1988: 2.

21. Weber 1993: 138–50 (originally pub. in 1922); Berger and Luckmann 1985: 110–34 (originally pub. in 1966); Berger 1969: 53–80.

22. Berger 1969: 55. On the formation of the term "anomic," see p. 189 n. 23 and p. 190 n. 26.

23. Berger and Luckmann 1985: 115.

sents the most archaic form of universe-maintenance,"[24] we should not be surprised to find that theodicy is a vital aspect of the Eden Narrative.

We saw that Paul Ricoeur contrasted the Eden Narrative with the creation chaos myth (§4.4, p. 80). In chaos-battle mythology, evil is present in the world right from the beginning. Conversely, the Eden Narrative represents "the most extreme attempt to separate the origin of evil from the origin of the good."[25]

We also saw, with Eckhart Otto, that the Eden Narrative most likely presupposes and postdates the Priestly account of creation in Genesis 1 (§3.2.3, p. 59). With Ricoeur, we may say that Genesis 1 presents the fundamental reality of man, created good and destined for happiness, whereas Genesis 2–3 speaks of the actual modality of human existence, marked by suffering and death. Moreover, these chapters account for this transition, and they do so by means of a narrative.[26]

Max Weber sketched a typology for various forms of theodicy. He distinguished three basic types:

- predestination,
- dualism,
- retribution.[27]

What we have in Mesopotamia is a type of theodicy in which death is not the result of human guilt but is the way that the gods arranged human existence. If a label had to be applied, I would say that we have a sort of predestination here.

On the other hand, what we have in the Eden Narrative is a theodicy that derives the anomic phenomena from human guilt. Death is not what God intended but is the result of human sin. In Max Weber's typology, this seems to be a case of retribution theodicy.[28] However, the Eden Narrative is far from simplistic on this matter. We should not overlook the role of the serpent. Basically, our narrative is ambiguous on the issue of theodicy.

---

24. Berger and Luckmann 1985: 128.
25. Ricoeur 1969: 233.
26. Ricoeur 1969: 163.
27. Weber 1993: 138–50. With Berger (1969: 68–70), we could distinguish a fourth type: "future nomization," such as we find in messianism, millenarianism, and eschatology. For broader typologies of theodicy, see Laato and de Moor (2003: xx–xxx).
28. On retribution theodicy in the Hebrew Bible, see Laato and de Moor 2003: xxx–xxxviii.

7.3. Date and Literary Integrity

As was pointed out in the first chapter, it is now becoming commonplace to date the Eden Narrative to the late postexilic period. Without going into detail on the matter, let us now briefly summarize the main indications for this late dating, a dating that I fully endorse:

- The Eden Narrative probably presupposes the Priestly creation account in Genesis 1.[29]
- It is also clear that it presupposes the main tenets of Deuteronomistic theology. This has been recognized for some time and is now even more obvious from my observations about the divine experiment as a test in Deuteronomistic style.[30]
- In its view of death and, especially, the possibility of eternal life, it presupposes a development of ideas about YHWH and death that was not complete until postexilic times.[31]
- A late date for the Eden Narrative explains why there are no allusions to it whatsoever in the literature prior to the very late period. This has long been seen as an enigma; but once we realize that the Eden Narrative was too late for early allusions to appear, the problem vanishes.[32]

This narrative stands out as one literary unit. A vast amount of scholarly energy has gone into critical surgery, experiments that seriously maimed the patient. In contrast to this, I have argued that the text works excellently as a narrative about the failure of the first humans and the calamitous consequences of this failure. The tensions that may be found in the text hardly suffice to falsify this conclusion. Rather, they should be seen as resulting from the tradition-historical process that lies behind the narrative.

---

29. For this insight, see especially Otto 1996: 183–92. See also Sawyer 1992: 64–66. On the date of the Eden Narrative, note also Stordalen 2000: 206–13. On Gen 2:4 as an independent unit, a redactional link presupposing Genesis 1, see Stordalen 1992.

30. See above, §3.2.2 (p. 49).

31. See Day 2000: 116–27; Janowski: forthcoming. Day draws a line of development from Hos 6:2–3, via Isa 26:19, to Dan 12:2.

32. A mistake about the date of the narrative may have fatal consequences, as may be seen from Bechtel 1995. Bechtel obviously presupposes an early, preexilic date. Because she finds no allusions to the "sin and fall" interpretation in the Hebrew Scriptures, "despite the plentiful opportunities—particularly in the prophets," she believes that the "sin and fall" interpretation is alien to the text and "develops very slowly during the last few centuries of the first millennium B.C.E. in response to a general shift in society" (Bechtel 1995: 4). Into this disturbing blank, she introduces "a theme of maturation" (p. 5).

Thus, the passage about the rivers in Eden (Gen 2:10–14) is in my view a residue of the previous Adamic myth, in which the garden is on a mountain (as we reconstructed it from Ezekiel 28; note vv. 14, 16). In addition, the double closure of the Eden Narrative should be viewed from the same perspective. The original Adamic myth comprises the motif of expulsion that we now find at the very end of the Eden Narrative. The Eden Poet, steeped in Deuteronomistic theology, added the curses (Gen 3:14–19). The double closure results from twining together material from two different traditions in one and the same literary text.

*   *   *

The Eden Narrative is a sophisticated piece of literary art. It is a story about the divine commandment, without using any of the Hebrew words for commandment; about a divine test, without the Hebrew term (*nissâ*); and about sin, without any of the central terms for sin (verbs such as *pāšaʿ, ḥāṭāʾ, ʿāwâ*, etc.).[33] This reminds me of the deep truth in some lines by the Swedish writer Gunnar Ekelöf. He once wrote, in his poem "Poetics" in the collection *Opus Incertum* from 1959:

> It is to the silence you should listen
> the silence behind invocations, allusions
> the silence of rhetoric. . . .
> What I have written
> I have written between the lines[34]

---

33. This seems to have been overlooked by Mieke Bal when she said, "The woman was the leading actant; she did not exactly sin, she opted for reality. Therefore, it is not obvious that Jahweh's reaction should be considered as a punishment" (Bal 1985: 36).

34. I owe this translation to my colleague Lars-Håkan Svensson (University of Linköping).

References

Abrams, M. H.
  1998   *A Glossary of Literary Terms*. Fifth edition. Fort Worth: Holt, Rinehart
          & Winston.
Albertz, Rainer
  1992   "Ihr werdet sein wie Gott" (Gen 3,5). Pp. 11–27 in *Was ist der Mensch?*
          Beiträge zur Anthropologie des Alten Testaments: Hans Walter Wolff zum
          80. Geburtstag, ed. F. Crüsemann, Christoph Hardmeier, and Rainer
          Kessler. Munich: Chr. Kaiser.
  1993   "Ihr werdet sein wie Gott.": Gen 3,1–7 auf dem Hintergrund des alt-
          testamentlichen und des sumero-babylonischen Menschenbildes.
          WO 24: 89–111.
  2003   *Israel in Exile: The History and Literature of the Sixth Century* B.C.E.,
          trans. David Green. Studies in Biblical Literature 3. Atlanta: Society
          of Biblical Literature.
Albright, W. F.
  1919   The Mouth of the Rivers. *AJSL* 35: 161–95.
Allen, Douglas
  2002   *Myth and Religion in Mircea Eliade*. New York: Routledge.
Alster, Bendt
  2001   *Wisdom of Ancient Sumer*. Bethesda, MD: CDL.
Alter, Robert
  1981   *The Art of Biblical Narrative*. London: Allen & Unwin.
Anderson, Gary A.
  1988   The Cosmic Mountain: Eden and Its Early Interpreters in Syriac
          Christianity. Pp. 187–224 in *Genesis 1–3 in the History of Exegesis*, ed.
          G. A. Robbins. Studies in Women and Religion 27. Lewiston, NY: Ed-
          win Mellen.
  2001   *The Genesis of Perfection: Adam and Eve in Jewish and Christian Imagi-*
          nation. Louisville: Westminster John Knox.
Andersson, Greger
  2001   *The Book and Its Narratives: A Critical Examination of some Synchronic*
          Studies of the Book of Judges. Örebro Studies in Literary History and
          Criticism 1. Örebro: Universitetsbiblioteket.
Andreasen, Niels-Erik
  1981   Adam and Adapa: Two Anthropological Characters. *AUSS* 19: 179–
          94.
Assmann, Aleida, and Assmann, Jan
  1998   Mythos. Pp. 179–200 in vol. 4 of *Handbuch Religionswissenschaftlicher*
          Grundbegriffe, ed. Hubert Cancik, Burkhard Gladigow, and Matthias
          Laubscher. Stuttgart: Kohlhammer.

Assmann, Jan
2002 *Das Kulturelle Gedächtnis: Schrift, Erinnerung und politische Identität in frühen Hochkulturen.* Munich: Beck.
Auffret, Pierre
1982 *La sagesse a bâti sa maison.* OBO 49. Fribourg: Éditions Universitaires / Göttingen: Vandenhoeck & Ruprecht.
Aurelius, Erik
2003 *Zukunft jenseits des Gerichts: Eine redaktionsgeschichtliche Studie zum Enneateuch.* BZAW 319. Berlin: de Gruyter.
Bal, Mieke
1977 *Narratologie.* Paris: Klincksieck.
1985 Sexuality, Sin and Sorrow: The Emergence of the Female Character (A Reading of Genesis 1–3). *Poetics Today* 6: 19–42.
Bar-Efrat, Shimon
1989 *Narrative Art in the Bible.* JSOTSup 70. Sheffield: Almond.
Barr, James
1969 The Symbolism of Names in the Old Testament. *BJRL* 52: 11–29.
1992 'Thou Art the Cherub': Ezekiel 28.14 and the Post-Ezekiel Understanding of Genesis 2–3. Pp. 213–23 in *Priests, Prophets and Scribes: Essays on the Formation and Heritage of Second Temple Judaism in Honour of Joseph Blenkinsopp,* ed. Eugene Ulrich et al. JSOTSup 149. Sheffield: Sheffield Academic Press.
1993 *The Garden of Eden and the Hope of Immortality.* Minneapolis: Fortress.
Barthes, Roland
1970 *S/Z.* Paris: Seuil.
Barton, John
1984 *Reading the Old Testament: Method in Biblical Study.* Philadelphia: Westminster.
Bauer, Hans, and Leander, Pontus
1965 *Historische Grammatik der Hebräischen Sprache des Alten Testaments.* Olms Paperbacks 19. Hildesheim: Georg Olms.
Baxandall, Michael
1985 *Patterns of Intention: On the Historical Explanation of Pictures.* New Haven: Yale University Press.
Beardsley, Monroe C.
1958 *Aesthetics: Problems in the Philosophy of Criticism.* New York: Harcourt, Brace.
Bechtel, Lyn M.
1993 Rethinking the Interpretation of Genesis 2.4B–3.24. Pp. 77–117 in *The Feminist Companion to Genesis,* ed. Athalya Brenner. Sheffield: Sheffield Academic Press.
1995 Genesis 2.4B–3.24: A Myth about Human Maturation. *JSOT* 67: 3–26.
Begrich, Joachim
1932 Die Paradieserzählung. *ZAW* 50: 93–116.
Berger, Peter L.
1969 *The Sacred Canopy: Elements of a Sociological Theory of Religion.* Garden City, NY: Anchor.

Berger, Peter L., and Luckmann, Thomas
1985 *The Social Construction of Reality: A Treatise in the Sociology of Knowledge.* Harmondsworth: Penguin.

Berlin, Adele
1983 *Poetics and Interpretation of Biblical Narrative.* Bible and Literature 9. Sheffield: Almond. Repr. Winona Lake, IN: Eisenbrauns, 1994.

Bing, J. D.
1984 Adapa and Immortality. *UF* 16: 53–56.

Bird, Phyllis
1994 Genesis 3 in der gegenwärtigen biblischen Forschung. *Jahrbuch für Biblische Theologie* 9: 3–24.

Block, Per
1997 Kriterier för en vetenskaplig tolkning av Gamla testamentet. Pp. 96–121 in *Kristna tolkningar av Gamla testamentet,* ed. Birger Olsson. Stockholm: Verbum.

Blum, Erhard
1984 *Die Komposition der Vätergeschichte.* WMANT 57. Neukirchen-Vluyn: Neukirchener Verlag.

Böhl, Franz M. T. de Liagre
1950 Die Fahrt nach dem Lebenskraut. *AfO* 18: 107–22.
1959 Die Mythe vom weisen Adapa. *WO* 2: 416–31.

Bonnet, Corinne
1988 *Melqart: Cultes et mythes de l'Héraclès tyrien en Méditerranée.* Studia Phoenicia 8. Leuven: Peeters / Namur: Presses Universitaires.

Booth, Wayne C.
1991 *The Rhetoric of Fiction.* Second edition. Harmondsworth: Penguin.

Borger, Rykle
1974 Die Beschwörungsserie *Bit mēseri* und die Himmelfahrt Henochs. *JNES* 33: 183–96.

Börker-Klähn, Jutta
1982 *Altvorderasiatische Bildstelen und vergleichbare Felsreliefs.* 2 vols. Mainz am Rhein: von Zabern.

Boström, Lennart
1990 *The God of the Sages: The Portrayal of God in the Book of Proverbs.* ConBOT 29. Stockholm: Almqvist & Wiksell.

Bremond, Claude
1993 Concept and Theme. Pp. 46–59 in *The Return of Thematic Criticism,* ed. Werner Sollors. Cambridge: Harvard University Press.

Bright, John
1951 The Date of the Prose Sermons of Jeremiah. *JBL* 70: 15–35.

Brinker, Menahem
1993 Theme and Interpretation. Pp. 21–37 in *The Return of Thematic Criticism,* ed. Werner Sollors. Cambridge: Harvard University Press.

Brooks, Peter
1992 *Reading for the Plot: Design and Intention in Narrative.* Cambridge: Harvard University Press.

Buccellati, Giorgio
1973 Adapa, Genesis, and the Notion of Faith. *UF* 5: 61–66.

1981   Wisdom and Not: The Case of Mesopotamia. *JAOS* 101: 35–47.
Budde, Karl
1883   *Die Biblische Urgeschichte (Gen. 1–12,5)*. Giessen: Ricker'sche.
Burnett, Joel S.
2005   The Question of Divine Absence in Israelite and West Semitic Religion. *CBQ* 67: 215–35.
Callender, Dexter E., Jr.
2000   *Adam in Myth and History: Ancient Israelite Perspectives on the Primal Human.* HSS 48. Winona Lake, IN: Eisenbrauns.
Carr, David
1993   The Politics of Textual Subversion: A Diachronic Perspective on the Garden of Eden Story. *JBL* 112: 577–95.
Cavigneaux, Antoine, and Al-Rawi, Farouk
1993   New Sumerian Literary Texts from Tell Haddad (Ancient Meturan): A First Survey. *Iraq* 55: 91–105.
2000a   *Gilgameš et la mort: Textes de Tell Haddad VI.* . . . Cuneiform Monographs 19. Groningen: Styx.
2000b   La fin de Gilgameš, Enkidu et les enfers d'après les manuscrits d'Ur et de Meturan (Textes de Tell Haddad VIII). *Iraq* 62: 1–19.
Chatman, Seymour
1980   *Story and Discourse: Narrative Structure in Fiction and Film.* Ithaca, NY: Cornell University Press.
1983   On the Notion of Theme in Narrative. Pp. 161–79 in *Essays on Aesthetics: Perspectives on the Work of Monroe C. Beardsley,* ed. John Fisher. Philadelphia: Temple University Press.
1990   *Coming to Terms: The Rhetoric of Narrative in Fiction and Film.* Ithaca, NY: Cornell University Press.
Childs, Brevard S.
1968   *Myth and Reality in the Old Testament.* SBT 27. London: SCM.
Chrostowski, Waldemar
1996   *Ogród Eden.* Rozmowy i studia biblijne 1. Warsaw: Oficyna wydawnicza "Vocatio."
Clifford, Richard J.
1994   *Creation Accounts in the Ancient Near East and in the Bible.* CBQMS 26. Washington, DC: Catholic Biblical Association.
Clines, David
1976   Theme in Genesis 1–11. *CBQ* 38: 483–507.
Croatto, J. Severino
1998   On the Semiotic Reading of Genesis 1–3. *Semeia* 81: 187–210.
Culler, Jonathan
1986   *Structuralist Poetics: Structuralism, Linguistics and the Study of Literature.* London: Routledge.
1992   *The Pursuit of Signs: Semiotics, Literature, Deconstruction.* London: Routledge.
Dalley, Stephanie
1991   *Myths from Mesopotamia.* Oxford: Oxford University Press.
Dannenberg, Hilary P.
2005   Plot. Pp. 435–39 in *RENT.*

Davidsen, Ole
1982 The Mythical Foundation of History: A Religio-Semiotic Analysis of the Story of the Fall. *LB* 51: 23–36.
Day, John
2000 *Yahweh and the Gods and Goddesses of Canaan.* JSOTSup 265. Sheffield: Sheffield Academic Press.
Delitzsch, Franz
1887 *Neuer Kommentar über die Genesis.* Fifth ed. Leipzig: Dörffling & Franke.
Denning-Bolle, Sara
1992 *Wisdom in Akkadian Literature: Expression, Instruction, Dialogue.* Mededelingen en Verhandelingen van het Vooraziatisch–Egyptisch Genootschap "Ex Oriente Lux" 28. Leiden: Ex Oriente Lux.
Dietrich, Manfried
1984 Die Kosmogonie in Nippur und Eridu. *Jahrbuch für Anthropologie und Religionsgeschichte* 5: 155–84.
1985 Die Suche nach dem 'Kraut des Lebens' im Alten Vorderen Orient und im Alten China. *Forschungen für Anthropologie und Religionsgeschichte* 21: 49–73.
1991 Wurde Adapa um das 'Ewige Leben' betrogen? *Mitteilungen für Anthropologie und Religionsgeschichte* 6: 119–32.
1995 *"'ina ūmi ullûti', 'An jenen (fernen) Tagen'."* Pp. 57–72 in *Vom Alten Orient zum Alten Testament,* ed. M. Dietrich and O. Loretz. AOAT 240. Neukirchen-Vluyn: Neukirchener Verlag.
2001 Das biblische Paradies und der babylonische Tempelgarten. Pp. 281–323 in *Das biblische Weltbild und seine altorientalischen Kontexte,* ed. Bernd Janowski and Beate Ego. Tübingen: Mohr Siebeck.
Dijkstra, M., and Moor, J. C. de
1975 Problematical Passages in the Legend of Aqhatu. *UF* 7: 171–215.
Dillmann, August
1882 *Die Genesis erklärt.* Fourth edition. Leipzig: Hirzel.
Di Vito, Robert A.
1992 The Demarcation of Divine and Human Realms in Genesis 2–11. Pp. 39–56 in *Creation in the Biblical Traditions,* ed. Richard J. Clifford and John J. Collins. CBQMS 24. Washington, DC: Catholic Biblical Association.
Dohmen, Christoph
1996 *Schöpfung und Tod: Die Entfaltung theologischer und anthropologischer Konzeptionen in Gen 2/3.* Second edition. SBB 35. Stuttgart: Katholisches Bibelwerk.
Doty, William G.
1997 *Mythography: The Study of Myths and Rituals.* Tuscaloosa: University of Alabama Press.
Duff, David, ed.
2000 *Modern Genre Theory.* Harlow: Longman.
Eco, Umberto
2002 *Sulla letteratura.* Milan: Saggi Bompiani.

Edelman, Diana
2006 The Iconography of Wisdom. Pp. 149–53 in *Essays on Ancient Israel in Its Near Eastern Context: A Tribute to Nadav Na'aman,* ed. Yairah Amit et al. Winona Lake, IN: Eisenbrauns.

Edzard, D. O.
1991 Gilgamesh und Huwawa A. II. Teil. *ZA* 81: 165–233.
2002 Eas Doppelzügiger Rat an Adapa: Ein Lösungsversuch. *Or* 71: 415–16.

Engnell, Ivan
1955 "Knowledge" and "Life" in the Creation Story. Pp. 103–19 in *Wisdom in Israel and in the Ancient Near East: Presented to Professor Harold Henry Rowley,* ed. M. Noth and D. Winton Thomas. VTSup 3. Leiden: Brill.

Erikson, Gösta
1990 Adam och Adapa. *STK* 66: 122–28.

Eslinger, Lyle
2006 The Enigmatic Plurals like "One of Us" (Genesis I 26, III 22, and XI 7) in Hyperchronic Perspective. *VT* 56: 171–84.

Feldmann, Joseph
1913 *Paradies und Sündenfall: Der Sinn der biblischen Erzählung nach der Auffassung der Exegese und unter Berücksichtigung der ausserbiblischen Überlieferungen.* Alttestamentliche Abhandlungen 4. Münster i.W.: Aschendorffsche Verlagsbuchhandlung.

Fishelov, David
1993 *Metaphors of Genre: The Role of Analogies in Genre Theory.* University Park: Pennsylvania State University Press.

Fontenrose, Joseph
1966 *The Ritual Theory of Myth.* Berkeley: University of California Press.

Forster, E. M.
1927 *Aspects of the Novel.* London: Edward Arnold.

Foster, Benjamin R.
1974 Wisdom and the Gods in Ancient Mesopotamia. *Or* n.s. 43: 345–54.
1993 *Before the Muses: An Anthology of Akkadian Literature.* 2 vols. Bethesda, MD: CDL.

Fowler, Alastair
1982 *Kinds of Literature: An Introduction to the Theory of Genres and Modes.* Oxford: Clarendon.

Freytag, Gustav
1894 *Technique of the Drama,* trans. E. J. McEwan. Chicago: Scott.

Frymer-Kensky, Tikva
1992 *In the Wake of the Goddesses: Women, Culture, and the Biblical Transformation of Pagan Myth.* New York: Free Press.

Galter, Hannes D.
1983 *Der Gott Ea/Enki in der akkadischen Überlieferung.* Dissertationen der Karl-Franzens-Universität Graz 58.

Garr, W. Randall
2003 *In His Own Image and Likeness.* Culture and History of the Ancient Near East 15. Leiden: Brill.

Geertz, Clifford
1993   *The Interpretation of Cultures*. London: Fontana.
Genette, Gérard
1980   *Narrative Discourse: An Essay in Method*, trans. Jane E. Lewin. Ithaca, NY: Cornell University Press.
1982   *Palimpsestes: La littérature au second degré*. Paris: Seuil.
1988   *Narrative Discourse Revisited*, trans. Jane E. Lewin. Ithaca, NY: Cornell University Press.
George, Andrew R.
2000   *The Epic of Gilgamesh: The Babylonian Epic Poem and Other Texts in Akkadian and Sumerian. Translated and with an Introduction*. London: Penguin.
2003   *The Babylonian Gilgamesh Epic: Introduction, Critical Edition and Cuneiform Texts*. 2 vols. Oxford: Oxford University Press.
Gibbs, Raymond W., Jr.
2005   Intentionality. Pp. 247–49 in *RENT*.
Goodman, Nelson
1972   *Problems and Projects*. Indianapolis: Bobbs-Merrill.
Gordis, Robert
1957   The Knowledge of Good and Evil in the Old Testament and the Qumran Scrolls. *JBL* 76: 123–38.
1978   *The Book of Job: Commentary, New Translation, and Special Studies*. New York: Jewish Theological Seminary of America.
Gowan, Donald E.
1975   *When Man Becomes God: Humanism and Hybris in the Old Testament*. PTMS 6. Pittsburgh, PA: Pickwick.
Greenstein, Edward L.
2002   God's Golem: The Creation of the Human in Genesis 2. Pp. 219–39 in *Creation in Jewish and Christian Tradition*, ed. H. G. Reventlow and Y. Hoffman. JSOTSup 319. Sheffield: Sheffield Academic Press.
Gunkel, Hermann
1910   *Genesis übersetzt und erklärt*. HKAT 1/1. Göttingen: Vandenhoeck & Ruprecht.
Habel, Norman C.
1967   Ezekiel 28 and the Fall of the First Man. *CTM* 38: 516–24.
Haettner Aurelius, Eva
2003   Att förstå och definiera genrer: Ett semantiskt perspektiv på genreteori. Pp. 45–57 in *Genrer och genreproblem: Teoretiska och historiska perspektiv / Genres and Their Problems: Theoretical and Historical Perspectives*, ed. Beata Agrell and Ingela Nilsson. Gothenburg: Daidalos.
Haettner Aurelius, Eva, and Götselius, T., eds.
1997   *Genreteori*. Lund: Studentlitteratur.
Hallo, William W.
2004   Adapa Reconsidered: Life and Death in Contextual Perspective. *Scriptura: International Journal of Bible, Religion and Theology in Southern Africa* 87: 267–77.

Harris, Wendell V.
1992   *Dictionary of Concepts in Literary Criticism and Theory.* New York: Greenwood.
Hecker, Karl
1974   *Untersuchungen zur akkadischen Epik.* AOAT Sonderreihe 8. Kevelaer: Butzon & Bercker / Neukirchen-Vluyn: Neukirchener Verlag.
1994   Das akkadische Gilgamesh-Epos. Pp. 646–744 in vol. 3/4 of *TUAT.*
Hempfer, Klaus W.
1973   *Gattungstheorie.* Munich: Wilhelm Fink.
Hendel, Ronald S.
1987   Of Demigods and the Deluge: Toward an Interpretation of Genesis 6:1–4. *JBL* 106: 13–26.
Hermisson, H.-J.
1978   Observations on the Creation Theology in Wisdom. Pp. 43–57 in *Israelite Wisdom: Theological and Literary Essays in Honor of Samuel Terrien,* ed. J. G. Gammie et al. Missoula, MT: Scholars Press.
Hess, Richard S.
1990   Splitting the Adam: The Usage of *ʾādām* in Genesis I–V. Pp. 1–15 in *Studies in the Pentateuch,* ed. John Emerton et al. VTSup 41. Leiden: Brill.
Hess, Richard S., and Tsumura, David Toshio, eds.
1994   *"I Studied Inscriptions from before the Flood": Ancient Near Eastern, Literary, and Linguistic Approaches to Genesis 1–11.* SBTS 4. Winona Lake, IN: Eisenbrauns.
Hirsch, E. D., Jr.
1967   *Validity in Interpretation.* New Haven: Yale University Press.
Humbert, Paul
1936   Mythe de création et mythe paradisiaque dans le second chapitre de la Genèse. *RHPR* 16: 445–61.
1940   *Études sur le récit du paradis et de la chute dans la Genèse.* Mémoires de l'Université de Neuchâtel 14. Neuchâtel: Secrétariat de l'Université.
Hutter, Manfred
2003   Review of *Adapa and the South Wind,* by Shlomo Izreʾel. *BO* 60: 647–50.
Idinopoulos, T. A., and Yonan, E. A., eds.
1994   *Religion and Reductionism: Essays on Eliade, Segal, and the Challenge of the Social Sciences for the Study of Religion.* Studies in the History of Religions 62. Leiden: Brill.
Illman, Karl-Johan
1979   *Old Testament Formulas about Death.* Meddelanden från Stiftelsen för Åbo Akademi Forskningsinstitut 48. Åbo: Åbo Akademi.
Izreʾel, Shlomo
2001   *Adapa and the South Wind: Language Has the Power of Life and Death.* Mesopotamian Civilizations 10. Winona Lake, IN: Eisenbrauns.
Jacobsen, Thorkild
1976   *The Treasures of Darkness: A History of Mesopotamian Religion.* New Haven: Yale University Press.

Jahn, Manfred
2005   Focalization. Pp. 173–77 in *RENT.*
Janowski, Bernd
1994   Die Tat kehrt zum Täter zurück: Offene Fragen im Umkreis des "Tun-Ergehen-Zusammenhangs." *ZTK* 91: 247–71.
Forthcoming   Der Gott Israels und die Toten: Eine Religions- und theolo-giegeschichtliche Skizze. Lecture read at Israels Gott und die Götter der Völker: Symposium zum 80. Geburtstag von Klaus Koch, Ham-burg, 17–18 November 2006.
Jaroš, Karl
1980   Die Motive der Heiligen Bäume und der Schlange in Gen 2–3. *ZAW* 92: 204–15.
Jauss, Hans Robert
1982   *Toward an Aesthetic of Reception*, trans. Timothy Bahti. Theory and History of Literature 2. Brighton: Harvester.
2000   Theory of Genres and Medieval Literature. Pp. 127–47 in *Modern Genre Theory*, ed. David Duff. Harlow: Longman.
Jensen, Hans J. Lundager
1991   The Fall of the King. *SJOT* 1991: 121–47.
2004   *Den fortaerende ild: Strukturelle analyser af narrative og rituelle tekster i Det Gamle Testamente.* Aarhus: Aarhus Universitetsforlag.
Jeppesen, Knud
1991   You Are a Cherub, but No God. *SJOT* 1991: 83–94.
Jobling, David
1986   *The Sense of Biblical Narrative: Structural Analyses in the Hebrew Bible II.* JSOTSup 39. Sheffield: JSOT Press.
Juhl, P. D.
1980   *Interpretation: An Essay in the Philosophy of Literary Criticism.* Prince-ton: Princeton University Press.
Kalugila, Leonidas
1980   *The Wise King: Studies in Royal Wisdom as Divine Revelation in the Old Testament and Its Environment.* ConBOT 15. Lund: CWK Gleerup.
Kämmerer, Thomas R.
1998   *šimâ milka: Induktion und Reception der mittelbabylonischen Dichtung von Ugarit, Emār und Tell el-ʿAmārna.* AOAT 251. Münster: Ugarit–Verlag.
Katz, Dina
2003   *The Image of the Netherworld in the Sumerian Sources.* Bethesda, MD: CDL.
Kawashima, Robert S.
2006   A Revisionist Reading Revisited: On the Creation of Adam and Then Eve. *VT* 56: 46–57.
Kearns, Michael
2005a   Codes for Reading. Pp. 66–67 in *RENT.*
2005b   Genre Theory in Narrative Studies. Pp. 201–5 in *RENT.*
Keel, Othmar
1978   *The Symbolism of the Biblical World: Ancient Near Eastern Iconography and the Book of Psalms,* trans. Timothy J. Hallett. New York: Seabury. Repr. Winona Lake, IN: Eisenbrauns, 1997.

Kermode, Frank
1979   *The Genesis of Secrecy: On the Interpretation of Narrative.* Cambridge: Harvard University Press.
1983   *Essays on Fiction, 1971–1982.* London: Routledge.
Kienast, Burkhart
1973   Die Weisheit des Adapa von Eridu. Pp. 234–39 in *Symbolae Biblicae et Mesopotamicae Francisco . . . Böhl Dedicatae,* ed. M. A. Beek et al. Leiden: Brill.
Kirk, G. S.
1973   *Myth: Its Meaning and Functions in Ancient and Other Cultures.* Cambridge: Cambridge University Press.
Koch, Klaus
1989   Der Güter Gefährlichstes, die Sprache, dem Menschen gegeben . . . Überlegungen zu Gen 2,7. *BN* 48: 50–60.
2007   Vom Mythos zum Monotheismus im alten Israel. Pp. 321–56 in *Der Gott Israels und die Götter des Orients. Religionsgeschichtliche Studien II: Zum 80. Geburtstag von Klaus Koch,* ed. Friedhelm Hartenstein and Martin Rösel. FRLANT 216. Göttingen: Vandenhoeck & Ruprecht.
Korpel, Marjo
1990   *A Rift in the Clouds: Ugaritic and Hebrew Descriptions of the Divine.* Münster: Ugarit-Verlag.
Krašovec, Jože
1977   *Der Merismus im Biblisch-Hebräischen und Nordwestsemitischen.* Rome: Pontifical Biblical Institute.
Krausz, Michael, ed.
2002   *Is There a Single Right Interpretation?* University Park: Pennsylvania State University Press.
Krispenz, Jutta
2004   Wie viele Bäume braucht das Paradies: Erwägungen zu Gen II 4B–III 24. *VT* 54: 301–18.
Kronholm, Tryggve
1978   *Motifs from Genesis 1–11 in the Genuine Hymns of Ephrem the Syrian.* ConBOT 11. Lund: CWK Gleerup.
Kvanvig, Helge S.
1988   *Roots of Apocalyptic: The Mesopotamian Background of the Enoch Figure and of the Son of Man.* WMANT 61. Neukirchen-Vluyn: Neukirchener Verlag.
Laato, Antti, and de Moor, Johannes C.
2003   Introduction. Pp. vii–liv in *Theodicy in the World of the Bible,* ed. A. Laato and J. C. de Moor. Leiden: Brill.
Lambert, W. G.
1962   A Catalogue of Texts and Authors. *JCS* 16: 59–77.
1980   The Theology of Death. Pp. 53–66 in *Death in Mesopotamia: Papers Read at the XXVIᵉ Rencontre Assyriologique International,* ed. Bendt Alster. Mesopotamia 8. Copenhagen: Akademisk Forlag.
Lambert, W. G., and Millard, Alan
1969   *Atra-Ḫasīs: The Babylonian Story of the Flood with The Sumerian Flood Story by M. Civil.* London: Oxford University Press. Repr. Winona Lake, IN: Eisenbrauns, 1999.

Layton, Scott C.
1997   Remarks on the Canaanite Origin of Eve. *CBQ* 59: 22–32.
Leach, Edmund.
1970   Lévi-Strauss in the Garden of Eden: An Examination of Some Recent
        Developments in the Analysis of Myth. Pp. 47–60 in *Claude Lévi-
        Strauss: The Anthropologist as Hero,* ed. E. Nelson Hayes and Tanya
        Hayes. Cambridge, MA: M.I.T. Press.
Leach, Edmund, and Aycock, D. Alan
1983   *Structuralist Interpretations of Biblical Myth.* Cambridge: Cambridge
        University Press.
Levison, John R.
1988   *Portraits of Adam in Early Judaism: From Sirach to 2 Baruch.* JSPSup 1.
        Sheffield: JSOT Press.
Lévi-Strauss, Claude
1955   The Structural Study of Myth. *Journal of American Folklore* 68: 428–
        44.
L'Hour, J.
1974   Yahweh Elohim. *RB* 81: 524–56.
Lipiński, E.
2001   Review of W. Chrostowski, *Ogród Eden,* 1996. *Rocznik Orientalistyczny*
        54/2: 195.
Lodge, David
1992   *The Art of Fiction.* Harmondsworth: Penguin.
Lohfink, Norbert
1965   *Das Siegeslied am Schilfmeer.* Frankfurt am Main: Josef Knecht.
Long, Burke O.
1968   *The Problem of Etiological Narrative in the Old Testament.* BZAW 108.
        Berlin: Alfred Töpelmann.
Longman, Tremper, III
1991   *Fictional Akkadian Autobiography: A Generic and Comparative Study.*
        Winona Lake, IN: Eisenbrauns.
Loretz, Oswald
1968   *Schöpfung und Mythos: Mensch und Welt nach den Anfangskapiteln der
        Genesis.* SBS 32. Stuttgart: Katholisches Bibelwerk.
Louth, Andrew, and Conti, Marco, eds.
2001   *Genesis 1–11.* Ancient Christian Commentary on Scripture: Old Tes-
        tament 1. Downers Grove, IL: InterVarsity.
Machinist, Peter
1983   Rest and Violence in the Poem of Erra. *JAOS* 103: 221–26.
1986   On Self-Consciousness in Mesopotamia. Pp. 183–202 (text) and
        511–18 (notes) in *The Origins and Diversity of Axial Age Civilizations,*
        ed. S. N. Eisenstadt. Albany, NY: State University of New York Press.
2005   Order and Disorder: Some Mesopotamian Reflections. Pp. 31–61 in
        Genesis and Regeneration: Essays on Conceptions of Origins, ed. Shaul
        Shaked. Jerusalem: Israel Academy of Sciences and Humanities.
Machinist, Peter, and Tadmor, Hayim
1993   Heavenly Wisdom. Pp. 146–51 in *The Tablet and the Scroll: Near East-
        ern Studies in Honor of William W. Hallo,* ed. Mark E. Cohen, Daniel C.
        Snell, and David B. Weisberg. Bethesda, MD: CDL.

Maier, John, ed.
1997   *Gilgamesh: A Reader.* Wauconda, IL: Bolchazy-Carducci.
Malinowski, Bronislaw
1926   *Myth in Primitive Psychology.* London: Kegan Paul.
Mayer, Werner R.
1987   Ein Mythos von der Erschaffung des Menschen und des Königs. *Or* 56: 55–68.
McCarthy, D. J.
1967   Creation Motifs in Ancient Hebrew Poetry. *CBQ* 29: 393–406.
Mettinger, Tryggve N. D.
1976   *King and Messiah: The Civil and Sacral Legitimation of the Israelite Kings.* ConBOT 8. Lund: CWK Gleerup.
1988   *In Search of God: The Meaning and Message of the Everlasting Names,* trans. Frederick Cryer. Philadelphia: Fortress.
1990   The Elusive Essence: YHWH, El and Baal and the Distinctiveness of Israelite Faith. Pp. 393–417 in *Die Hebräische Bibel und ihre zweifache Nachgeschichte: Festschrift für Rolf Rendtorff zum 65 Geburtstag,* ed. Erhard Blum et al. Neukirchen-Vluyn: Neukirchener Verlag.
1992   The God of Job: Avenger, Tyrant, or Victor? Pp. 39–49 (text) and 233–36 (notes) in *The Voice from the Whirlwind: Interpreting the Book of Job,* ed. Leo G. Perdue and W. Clark Gilpin. Nashville: Abingdon.
1993   Intertextuality: Allusion and Vertical Context Systems in Some Job Passages. Pp. 257–80 in *Of Prophets' Visions and the Wisdom of Sages: Essays in Honour of R. Norman Whybray on His Seventieth Birthday,* ed. Heather A. McKay and David Clines. JSOTSup 162. Sheffield: JSOT Press.
2001   *The Riddle of Resurrection: "Dying and Rising Gods" in the Ancient Near East.* ConBOT 50. Stockholm: Almqvist & Wiksell.
2003   Review of Terje Stordalen, *Echoes of Eden,* 2000. *STK* 79: 63–64.
2005   Cui Bono? The Prophecy of Nathan (2 Sam. 7) as a Piece of Political Rhetoric. *SEÅ* 70: 193–214.
Metzger, Martin
1959   *Die Paradieseserzählung: Die Geschichte ihrer Auslegung von J. Clericus bis W. M. L. de Wette.* Abhandlungen zur Philosophie, Psychologie und Pedagogik 16. Bonn: H. Bouvier.
1983a   Eigentumsdeklaration und Schöpfungsaussage. Pp. 37–51 in *"Wenn nicht jetzt, wann dann?": Aufsätze für Hans-Joachim Kraus zum 65. Geburtstag,* ed. H.-G. Geyer et al. Neukirchen-Vluyn: Neukirchener Verlag.
1983b   Gottheit, Berg und Vegetation in vorderorientalischer Bildtradition. *ZDPV* 99: 54–94.
Michalowski, Piotr
1980   Adapa and the Ritual Process. *Rocznik Orientalistyczny* 41/2: 77–82.
Michel, Andreas
1997   *Theologie aus der Peripherie: Die gespaltene Koordination im Biblischen Hebräisch.* BZAW 257. Berlin: de Gruyter.
Michel, Diethelm
1997   *Studien zur Überlieferungsgeschichte alttestamentlicher Texte,* ed. Andreas Wagner et al. TB 93. Munich: Chr. Kaiser.

Millard, A. R.
1984   The Etymology of Eden. *VT* 34: 103–6.
Miller, James E.
1993   The Maelaek of Tyre (Ezekiel 28,11–19). *ZAW* 105: 497–501.
Moberly, R. W. L.
1988   Did the Serpent Get It Right? *JTS* 39: 1–27.
Moran, William L.
1980   Rilke and the Gilgamesh Epic. *JCS* 32: 208–10.
Morris, Brian
1998   *Anthropological Studies of Religion: An Introductory Text.* Cambridge: Cambridge University Press.
Müller, H.-P.
1983   Mythos als Gattung archaischen Erzählens und die Geschichte von Adapa. *AfO* 29–30: 75–89.
1990   Parallelen zu Gen 2f. und Ez 28 aus dem Gilgamesh-Epos. *ZAH* 3:167–78.
1991a   Drei Deutungen des Todes: Genesis 3, der Mythos von Adapa und die Sage von Gilgamesh. *Jahrbuch für biblische Theologie* 6: 117–34.
1991b   *Mythos—Kerygma—Wahrheit: Gesammelte Aufsätze zum Alten Testament in seiner Umwelt und zur Biblischen Theologie.* BZAW 200. Berlin: de Gruyter.
Niditch, Susan
1985   *Chaos to Cosmos: Studies in Biblical Patterns of Creation.* Chico, CA: Scholars Press.
Nielsen, Eduard
1972   Creation and the Fall of Man: A Cross-Disciplinary Investigation. *HUCA* 43: 13–22.
Norin, Stig
2002   *Aqedat jiṣḥaq*—1 Mos 22:1–19: På jakt efter ett retoriskt centrum. *SEÅ* 67: 5–25.
Obbink, H. T.
1928   The Tree of Life in Eden. *ZAW* 46: 105–12.
Oden, Robert A., Jr.
1981   Divine Aspirations in Atrahasis and in Genesis 1–11. *ZAW* 93: 197–216.
O'Flaherty, Wendy Doniger
1988   *The Origins of Evil in Hindu Mythology.* Delhi: Motilal Banarsidass.
Olsson, Tord
1977   The Social Usage of Mythical Elements among the Maasai. *Temenos* 13: 118–27.
Orr, Mary
2003   *Intertextuality: Debates and Contexts.* Cambridge: Polity.
Otto, Eckart
1996   Die Paradieserzählung Genesis 2–3: Eine nachpriesterschriftliche Lehrerzählung in ihrem religionshistorischem Kontext. Pp. 167–92 in *"Jedes Ding hat seine Zeit . . .": Studien zur israelitischen und altorientalischen Weishet Diethelm Michel zum 65. Geburtstag,* ed. Anja A. Diesel et al. BZAW 241. Berlin: de Gruyter.

1999   Woher weiss der Mensch um Gut und Böse? Philosophische An-
          näherungen der ägyptischen und biblischen Weisheit an ein Grund-
          problem der Ethik. Pp. 207–31 in *Recht und Ethos im Alten Testa-
          ment—Gestalt und Wirkung: Festschrift für Horst Seebass zum 65 Ge-
          burtstag*, ed. Stefan Beyerle, Günther Mayer, and Hans Strauss.
          Neukirchen-Vluyn: Neukirchener Verlag.
Ottosson, Magnus
1988   Eden and the Land of Promise. Pp. 177–88 in *Congress Volume: Jeru-
          salem, 1986*, ed. John Emerton. VTSup 40. Leiden: Brill.
Otzen, Benedikt
1993   The Paradise Trees in Jewish Apocalyptic. Pp. 141–54 in *Apocryphon
          Severini Presented to Sören Giversen*, ed. Per Bilde, Helge Kjaer Nielsen,
          and Jörgen Podemann Sörensen. Aarhus: Aarhus University Press.
Otzen, Benedikt; Gottlieb, Hans; and Jeppesen, Knud
1980   *Myths in the Old Testament*. London: SCM.
Palm, Anders
2004   Innan kvinnan fanns: Om förhållandena i Paradiset och Kåseberga.
          Pp. 15–25 in *Från Eden till Damavdelningen: Studier om kvinnan i litte-
          raturen. En vänbok till Christina Sjöblad*, ed. B. Jonsson, K. Nykvist,
          and B. Sjöberg. Lund: Litteraturvetenskapliga Institutionen.
Panofsky, Erwin
1955   *Meaning in the Visual Arts*. Garden City, NY: Doubleday.
Parpola, Simo
1997   *The Standard Babylonian Epic of Gilgamesh: Cuneiform Text, Translit-
          eration, Glossary, Indices and Sign List*. SAACT 1. Helsinki: The Neo-
          Assyrian Text Corpus Project.
Patte, D.
1980   One Text: Several Structures. Pp. 1–22 in *Genesis 2 and 3: Kaleido-
          scopic Structural Readings*. Semeia 18. Chico, CA: Scholars Press.
Patte, D., ed.
1980   *Genesis 2 and 3: Kaleidoscopic Structural Readings*. Semeia 18. Chico,
          CA: Scholars Press.
1998   *Thinking in Signs: Semiotics and Biblical Studies . . . Thirty Years After*.
          Semeia 81. Atlanta: Scholars Press.
Pedersen, Johs
1955a   The Fall of Man. Pp.162–72 in *Interpretationes ad Vetus Testamentum
          pertinentes Sigmundo Mowinckel septuagenario missae*. Oslo: Land og
          Kirke.
1955b   Wisdom and Immortality. Pp. 238–46 in *Wisdom in Israel and in the
          Ancient Near East: Presented to Professor Harold Henry Rowley*, ed. M.
          Noth and D. Winton Thomas. VTSup 3. Leiden: Brill.
Pettersson, Anders
2000   *Verbal Art: A Philosophy of Literature and Literary Experience*. Montreal:
          McGill–Queen's University Press.
2006   Conclusion: A Pragmatic Perspective on Genres and Theories of
          Genre. Pp. 279–305 in *Literary History: Towards a Global Perspective,
          Volume 2: Literary Genres: An Intercultural Approach*, ed. Gunilla Lind-
          berg-Wada. Berlin: de Gruyter.

Pettersson, Torsten
1988   *Literary Interpretation: Current Models and a New Departure.* Åbo: Åbo Academy Press.
2002   The Literary Work as a Pliable Entity: Combining Realism and Pluralism. Pp. 211–30 in *Is There a Single Right Interpretation?* ed. Michael Krausz. Philadelphia: Pennsylvania State University Press.
2005   Bibelns relation till verkligheten: En principiell jämförelse med sakprosan och skönlitteraturen. Pp. 219–35 in *Litteraturen og det hellige: Urtekst—Intertekst—Kontekst,* ed. Ole Davidsen. Acta Jutlandica 80/1. Teologisk serie 21. Aarhus: Aarhus Universitetsforlag.

Pettinato, Giovanni
1968   Die Bestrafung des Menschengeschlechts durch die Sintflut. *Or* 37: 165–200.
1977   *Das altorientalische Menschenbild und die sumerischen und akkadischen Schöpfungsmythen.* AHAW Phil.-hist. Klasse 1971: 1. Heidelberg: Carl Winter Universitätsverlag.

Pfeiffer, Henrik
2000   Der Baum in der Mitte des Gartens: Zum überlieferungsgeschichtlichen Ursprung der Paradieserzählung (Gen 2:4b–3:24). Teil 1. *ZAW* 112: 487–500.
2001   Der Baum in der Mitte des Gartens: Zum überlieferungsgeschichtlichen Ursprung der Paradieserzählung (Gen 2:4b–3:24). Teil 2. *ZAW* 113: 2–16.

Pfister, Manfred
1985   Zur Systemreferenz. Pp. 52–58 in *Intertextualität: Formen, Funktionen, anglistische Fallstudien,* ed. Ulrich Broich and Manfred Pfister. Tübingen: Max Niemeyer.

Picchioni, S. A.
1981   *Il Poemetto di Adapa.* Budapest: Eötvös Loránd Tudományegyetem.

Pope, Marvin H.
1955   *El in the Ugaritic Texts.* VTSup 2. Leiden: Brill.

Prince, Gerald
1985   Thématiser. *Poétique* 64: 425–33.
1992   *Narrative as Theme.* Lincoln: University of Nebraska Press.
2003   *A Dictionary of Narratology.* Revised edition. Lincoln: University of Nebraska Press.
2005   Point of View (Literary). Pp. 442–43 in *RENT.*

Rad, Gerhard von
1961   *Genesis: A Commentary,* trans. John H. Marks. London: SCM.

Rankin, O. S.
1936   *Israel's Wisdom Literature.* Edinburgh: T. & T. Clark / New York: Schocken.

Reiner, Erica
1961   The Etiological Myth of the "Seven Sages." *Or* 30: 1–11.

Reiser, W.
1960   Die Verwandtschaftsformel in Gen 2:23. *TZ* 16: 1–4.

Ricoeur, Paul
1969   *The Symbolism of Evil,* trans. Emerson Buchanan. Boston: Beacon.

1987   Evil. Pp. 199–208 in vol. 5 of *ER*.
Rimmon-Kenan, Shlomith
1985   Qu'est-ce qu'un thème? *Poétique* 64: 397–406.
2005   *Narrative Fiction: Contemporary Poetics.* Second edition. London: Routledge.
Ringgren, Helmer
1977   גרע, *gāraʿ*. Cols. 70–72 in vol. 2 of *TWAT*.
Robbins, Gregory Allen, ed.
1988   *Genesis 1–3 in the History of Exegesis: Intrigue in the Garden.* Studies in Women and Religion 27. Lewiston, NY: Edwin Mellen.
Rogerson, J. W.
1974   *Myth in Old Testament Interpretation.* BZAW 134. Berlin: de Gruyter.
1991   *Genesis 1–11.* OTG. Sheffield: JSOT Press.
Rottzoll, Dirk U.
1997   Die Schöpfungs- und Fallerzählung in Gen 2f. Teil 1. *ZAW* 109: 481–99.
1998   Die Schöpfungs- und Fallerzählung in Gen 2f. Teil 2. *ZAW* 110: 1–15.
Roux, Georges
1961   Adapa, le vent et l'eau. *RA* 55: 13–33.
Ryle, Gilbert
1933   'About.' *Analysis* 1: 10–12.
Sawyer, John F. A.
1967   Root-Meanings in Hebrew. *JSS* 12: 37–50.
1992   The Image of God, the wisdom of serpents and the knowledge of good and evil. Pp. 64–73 in *A Walk in the Garden: Biblical, Iconographical and Literary Images of Eden,* ed. Paul Morris and Deborah Sawyer. JSOTSup 136. Sheffield: JSOT Press.
Schmid, Konrad
2002   Die Unteilbarkeit der Weisheit: Überlegungen zur sogenannten Paradieserzählung Gen 2f. und ihrer theologischen Tendenz. *ZAW* 114: 21–39.
Schüle, Andreas
2005   Made in the 'Image of God': The Concept of Divine Images in Gen 1–3. *ZAW* 117: 1–20.
Segal, Robert A.
2004   *Myth: A Very Short Introduction.* Oxford: Oxford University Press.
2005   Myth: Theoretical Approaches. Pp. 330–35 in *RENT*.
Sharon, Diane M.
1998   The Doom of Paradise: Literary Patterns in Accounts of Paradise and Mortality in the Hebrew Bible and the Ancient Near East. Pp. 53–80 in *Genesis,* ed. A. Brenner. A Feminist Companion to the Bible (Second Series) 1. Sheffield: Sheffield Academic Press.
Shea, W. H.
1977   Adam in Ancient Mesopotamian Traditions. *AUSS* 15: 27–41.
Silva Castillo, Jorge
1998   *Nagbu:* Totality or Abyss in the First Verse of Gilgamesh. *Iraq* 60: 219–21.

Sjöberg, Åke W.
  1984   Eve and the Chameleon. Pp. 217–25 in *In the Shelter of Elyon: Essays on Ancient Palestinian Life and Literature in Honor of G. W. Ahlström*, ed. W. Boyd Barrick and John R. Spencer. JSOTSup 31. Sheffield: JSOT Press.
Ska, Jean-Louis
  1990   *"Our Fathers Have Told Us": Introduction to the Analysis of Hebrew Narratives.* SubB: 13. Rome: Pontifical Biblical Institute.
Slivniak, Dmitri M.
  2003   The Garden of Double Messages: Deconstructing Hierarchical Oppositions in the Garden Story. *JSOT* 27: 439–60.
Smith, Barbara Herrnstein
  1968   *Poetic Closure: A Study of How Poems End.* Chicago: University of Chicago Press.
Soden, Wolfram von
  1973   Der Mensch Bescheidet sich nicht: Überlegungen zu Schöpfungserzählungen in Babylonien und Israel. Pp. 349–58 in *Symbolae Biblicae et Mesopotamicae Francisco Mario Theodoro de Liagre Böhl Dedicatae*, ed. M. A. Beek et al. Leiden: Brill.
Sollors, Werner, ed.
  1993   *The Return of Thematic Criticism.* Cambridge: Harvard University Press.
Steck, Odil Hannes
  1970   *Die Paradieserzählung: Eine Auslegung von Genesis 2,4b–3,24.* BibS(N) 60. Neukirchen-Vluyn: Neukirchener Verlag.
Sternberg, Meir
  1978   *Expositional Modes and Temporal Ordering in Fiction.* Baltimore: Johns Hopkins University Press.
  1987   *The Poetics of Biblical Narrative: Ideological Literature and the Drama of Reading.* Bloomington: Indiana University Press.
Stolz, Fritz
  1972   Die Bäume des Gottesgartens auf dem Libanon. *ZAW* 84: 141–56.
Stordalen, Terje
  1992   Genesis 2,4: Restudying a *locus classicus*. *ZAW* 104: 163–77.
  1998   Mytebegrepet i bibelforskningen. *TTKi* 69: 279–308.
  2000   *Echoes of Eden: Genesis 2–3 and Symbolism of the Eden Garden in Biblical Hebrew Literature.* Biblical Exegesis and Theology 25. Leuven: Peeters.
Streck, Maximilian
  1916   *Assurbanipal und die letzten assyrischen Könige bis zum Untergange Ninivehs. II. Teil: Texte: Die Inschriften Assurbanipals und der letzten assyrischen Könige.* Leipzig: Hinrichs.
Strenski, Ivan
  1987   *Four Theories of Myth in Twentieth Century History: Cassirer, Eliade, Lévi-Strauss and Malinowski.* London: Macmillan.
Tigay, Jeffrey H.
  1982   *The Evolution of the Gilgamesh Epic.* Philadelphia: University of Pennsylvania Press.

Tournay, Raymond Jacques, and Shaffer, Aaron
1994   *L'épopée de Gilgamesh: Introduction, traduction et notes.* Paris: Cerf.
Trible, Phyllis
1985   *God and the Rhetoric of Sexuality.* OBT 2. Philadelphia: Fortress.
Trommler, Frank
1995   *Thematics Reconsidered: Essays in Honor of Horst S. Daemmrich.* Internationale Forschungen zur allgemeinen und vergleichenden Literaturwissenschaft 9. Amsterdam: Rodopi.
Van Dyk, P. J.
1990   The Function of So-Called Etiological Elements in Narratives. *ZAW* 102: 19–33.
Vanhoozer, Kevin J.
1998   *Is There a Meaning in This Text? The Bible, the Reader and the Morality of Literary Knowledge.* Leicester: Apollos.
Van Seters, John
1989   The Creation of Man and the Creation of the King. *ZAW* 101: 333–42.
1992   *Prologue to History: The Yahwist as Historian in Genesis.* Louisville: Westminster John Knox.
Vanstiphout, H. L. J.
1990   The Craftmanship of *Sîn-leqi-unninni.* *OLP* 21: 45–79.
Veijola, Timo
1988   Das Opfer des Abraham: Paradigma des Glaubens aus dem nachexilischen Zeitalter. *ZTK* 85: 129–64.
2002   Abraham und Hiob: Das literarische und theologische Verhältnis von Gen 22 und der Hiob-Novelle. Pp. 127–44 in *Vergegenwärtigung des Alten Testaments: Beiträge zur biblischen Hermeneutik. Festschrift für Rudolf Smend zum 70. Geburtstag,* ed. Christoph Bultmann, Walter Dietrich, and Christoph Levin. Göttingen: Vandenhoeck & Ruprecht.
Vermes, Geza
1992   Genesis 1–3 in Post-Biblical Hebrew and Aramaic Literature before the Mishnah. *JJS* 43: 221–25.
Vogels, Walter
1998   "Like one of us, knowing *ṭôb* and *ra‘*" (Gen 3:22). *Semeia* 81: 145–57.
Vulpe, Nicola
1994   Irony and the Unity of the *Gilgamesh Epic.* *JNES* 53: 275–83.
Walker, C. B. F.
1981   The Second Tablet of *ṭupšenna pitema*: An Old Babylonian Naram-Sin Legend? *JCS* 33: 191–95.
Wallace, Howard N.
1985   *The Eden Narrative.* HSM 32. Atlanta: Scholars Press.
Walsh, Jerome T.
1994   Genesis 2:4b–3:24: A Synchronic Approach. Pp. 362–82 in *"I Studied Inscriptions from before the Flood": Ancient Near Eastern, Literary, and Linguistic Approaches to Genesis 1–11,* ed. Richard S. Hess and David Toshio Tsumura. SBTS 4. Winona Lake, IN: Eisenbrauns.

Watanabe, Kazuko
1994 Lebenspendende und Todbringende Substanzen in Altmesopotamien. *BaghM* 25: 579–96.

Watson, Wilfred G. E.
1986 *Classical Hebrew Poetry: A Guide to Its Techniques.* JSOTSup 26. Sheffield: JSOT Press.

Weber, Max
1993 *The Sociology of Religion,* trans. E. Fischoff. Boston: Beacon. [German original, 1922]

Weippert, Manfred
1973 Fragen des israelitischen Geschichtsbewusstseins. *VT* 23: 415–42.

Wellhausen, J.
1895 *Prolegomena zur Geschichte Israels.* Fourth edition. Berlin: Georg Reimer.
1961 *Prolegomena to the History of Ancient Israel,* trans. J. S. Black and A. Menzies. Cleveland: World.

Wenham, Gordon
1987 *Genesis. Vol. 1.* WBC. Waco, TX: Word.

Westermann, Claus
1972 *Genesis 1–11.* Erträge der Forschung 7. Darmstadt: Wissenschaftliche Buchgesellschaft.
1976 *Genesis. 1. Teilband: Genesis 1–11.* BKAT 1/1. Neukirchen-Vluyn: Neukirchener Verlag.
1984 *Genesis 1–11,* trans. John J. Scullion. Minneapolis: Augsburg.

White, Hugh C.
1991 *Narration and Discourse in the Book of Genesis.* Cambridge: Cambridge University Press.

Wilcke, Claus
1977 Die Anfänge der akkadischen Epen. *ZA* 67: 153–216.
1991 Göttliche und menschliche Weisheit im Alten Orient. Pp. 259–70 in *Weisheit: Archäologie der literarischen Kommunikation III,* ed. Aleida Assmann. Munich: Wilhelm Fink.

Wilson, R. R.
1987 The Death of the King of Tyre: The Editorial History of Ezekiel 28. Pp. 211–18 in *Love and Death in the Ancient Near East: Essays in Honor of Marvin H. Pope,* ed. John H. Marks and Robert M. Good. Guilford, CT: Four Quarters.

Winter, Urs
1986 "Der Lebensbaum" in der altorientalischen Bildsymbolik. Pp. 57–88 in *". . . Bäume braucht man doch!": Das Symbol des Baumes zwischen Hoffnung und Zerstörung,* ed. Harald Schweizer. Sigmaringen: Jan Thorbecke.

Wiseman, D. J.
1975 A Gilgamesh Epic Fragment from Nimrud. *Iraq* 37: 157–63.

Witte, Markus
1998 *Die biblische Urgeschichte: Redaktions- und theologiegeschichtliche Beobachtungen zu Genesis 1,1–11,26.* BZAW 265. Berlin: de Gruyter.

Wolde, Ellen van
    1989   *A Semiotic Analysis of Genesis 2–3.* SSN 25. Assen: Van Gorcum.
    1994   *Words Become Worlds: Semantic Studies of Genesis 1–11.* Biblical Interpretation 6. Leiden: Brill.
Wright, David P.
    1996   Holiness, Sex, and Death in the Garden of Eden. *Bib* 77: 305–29.
Xella, Paolo
    1973   L'"inganno" di Ea nel mito di Adapa. *OrAnt* 12: 257–66.
Zimmerli, Walther
    1969   *Ezechiel: 2. Teilband.* BKAT 13/2. Neukirchen-Vluyn: Neukirchener Verlag.

Index of Authors

Albertz, R.   72, 129
Albright, W. F.   115
Al-Rawi, F.   100, 118–119
Alster, B.   115
Anderson, G. A.   2, 94
Andersson, G.   xiii, 65
Andreasen, N.-E.   107–108
Assmann, A.   68
Assmann, J.   68–69
Auffret, P.   17
Aurelius, E.   51

Bakhtin, M.   77
Bal, M.   12, 33, 135
Bar-Efrat, S.   17–18, 29
Barr, J.   3, 9, 20, 30, 62, 85, 87, 130–131
Barthes, R.   28, 38–39
Barton, J.   79
Bauer, H.   87
Bavinck, H.   68
Baxandall, M.   66, 96
Beardsley, M. C.   42–44, 46
Bechtel, L. M.   4, 62, 134
Begrich, J.   23
Berger, P. L.   73, 132–133
Berlin, A.   29–30, 32
Biggs, R. D.   115
Bing, J. D.   106
Block, P.   42, 46
Blum, E.   53–54
Böhl, F. M. T.   104
Bonnet, C.   88–89
Booth, W. C.   12
Borger, R.   103
Börker-Klähn, J.   15
Boström, L.   58
Bremond, C.   42, 45–46
Bright, J.   51
Brinker, M.   42, 45
Brooks, P.   21, 28

Buccellati, G.   102, 104, 106
Budde, K.   xi, 7–9
Burnett, J. S.   25

Callender, D. E., Jr.   85, 92
Campbell, J.   70
Carr, D.   8
Cavigneaux, A.   100, 118–119
Chatman, S.   18, 29, 32, 42–43, 45
Childs, B. S.   68, 83
Chrostowski, W.   xiv, 96
Clines, D.   42, 44, 46
Conti, M.   2
Croatto, J. S.   75
Culler, J.   12, 32, 44, 79

Dalley, S.   100, 110
Dannenberg, H. P.   18
Davidsen, O.   75
Day, J.   16, 94, 134
Delitzsch, Franz   40
Denning-Bolle, S.   102–103
Di Vito, R. A.   128
Dietrich, M.   xiv, 15–16, 69, 100–101, 105–107
Dijkstra, M.   27
Dohmen, C.   8, 61
Doty, W. G.   68, 70, 74, 76
Duff, D.   77–78
Durkheim, É.   70

Eco, U.   65
Edelman, D.   61
Edzard, D. O.   104, 119
Eidevall, G.   xiv, 50
Eliade, M.   70
Engnell, I.   39, 62
Erikson, G.   107–108
Eslinger, L.   127–128

Feldmann, J.   2

Fishelov, D. 78
Flaubert, G. 33–34
Fontenrose, J. 69
Forster, E. M. 30
Foster, B. R. 100–101, 107
Fowler, A. 66, 77–78
Freytag, G. 23

Galter, H. D. 102, 105
Garr, W. R. 24, 55
Geertz, C. 60
Genette, G. 12, 32–33, 77, 114
George, A. R. 106, 110–121
Goodman, N. 45
Gordis, R. 26, 62, 125
Görtz-Wrisberg, I. von xiv
Götselius, T. 77
Gottlieb, H. 68
Gowan, D. E. 85
Grayson, A. K. 110
Greenstein, E. L. 15, 29, 36
Greimas, A.-J. 74–75
Gunkel, H. 2, 4, 7, 16, 68–69, 85, 107

Habel, N. C. 85, 90
Haettner Aurelius, E. 77–78
Hallo, W. W. 39, 69, 100, 103, 107–108
Harris, W. V. 38
Hecker, K. 110
Hempfer, K. W. 77–78
Hendel, R. S. 127–128
Hermisson, H.-J. 81
Hess, R. S. 30
Hidal, S. xiv
Hirsch, E. D., Jr. 66, 79
Humbert, P. 5, 8–9, 20, 22, 40, 48–49, 63
Hutter, M. 105

Idinopoulos, T. A. 70
Illman, K.-J. 22
Izre'el, S. 99–102, 106–107

Jacobsen, T. 105, 110
Jahn, M. 32–33
Janowski, B. 58, 134

Jauss, H. R. 77–78
Jensen, H. J. L. 1–2, 74, 76, 87
Jeppesen, K. 68, 85
Jobling, D. 75–76
Juhl, P. D. 66

Kämmerer, T. R. 100, 106
Katz, D. 118
Kawashima, R. S. 31
Kearns, M. 28, 77
Keel, O. 15
Kermode, F. 65–66, 73
Kienast, B. 100
Kirk, G. S. 76
Koch, K. 31
Korpel, M. 68
Krasovec, J. 63
Krausz, M. 66
Krispenz, J. 10
Kronholm, T. 2
Kvanvig, H. S. 103

Laato, A. 133
Lambert, W. G. 102–103, 105, 111, 115, 118, 127
Layton, S. C. 26, 108
Leach, E. 70–71, 74
Leander, P. 87
Levison, J. R. 2
Lévi-Strauss, C. 74
L'Hour, J. 14, 58, 132
Lipiński, E. xiv, 96, 118
Lodge, D. 38
Lohfink, N. 49–50, 52, 56
Long, B. O. 72
Longman, T., III 113–114
Louth, A. 2
Luckmann, T. 73, 132–133

Machinist, P. xiv, 102–103, 113–114, 116, 127
Maier, J. 109
Malinowski, B. 70, 80
Mayer, W. R. 87
McCarthy, D. J. 29
Meissner, B. 106, 110, 112, 116
Mettinger, T. N. D. xiii, 30, 43, 50, 68, 82–83, 85, 87, 116, 125

Metzger, M.   2, 15, 82
Michel, A.   22, 36, 41
Michel, D.   62
Millard, A. R.   15, 67, 106, 110, 112, 116, 118, 127
Moberly, R. W. L.   23, 57
Moor, J. C. de   27, 133
Moran, W. L.   109, 121
Muilenburg, J.   4
Müller, H.-P.   69, 104, 107–108

Nielsen, E.   10
Norin, S.   53

Obbink, H. T.   20
Oden, R. A., Jr.   126–127
O'Flaherty, W. D.   132
Olsson, T.   xiv, 80
Oppenheim, A. L.   112
Orr, M.   83, 96
Otto, E.   11, 13, 23, 50–52, 56, 59, 62–63, 69, 71, 87, 133–134
Otzen, B.   68

Palm, A.   xi, xiii, 35, 39
Panofsky, E.   66
Parpola, S.   110
Patte, D.   75
Pedersen, J.   99, 107
Peirce, C. S.   75
Pettersson, A.   42, 45, 78
Pettersson, T.   xiii, 43, 45, 66–67
Pettinato, G.   127
Pfeiffer, H.   8
Picchioni, S. A.   100, 102–104, 107
Pope, M. H.   85, 87
Prince, G.   18, 23, 27–28, 32, 42, 44, 63
Propp, V.   74–75

Rad, G. von   ix, 2–3, 56, 62–63, 72
Rankin, O. S.   58
Reiner, E.   103
Reiser, W.   72
Ricoeur, P.   1, 52, 67–68, 72, 81–82, 133
Rimmon-Kenan, S.   12, 18, 29, 32–33
Ringgren, H.   92

Rogerson, J. W.   68, 74, 82
Rottzoll, D. U.   8
Roux, G.   102
Ryle, G.   45

Sawyer, J. F. A.   11, 30, 59, 71, 134
Schmid, K.   10, 24
Schüle, A.   59, 71
Segal, R. A.   68, 70, 74
Shaffer, A.   110, 113
Shea, W. H.   107
Silva Castillo, J.   115
Sjöberg, Å. W.   61
Ska, J.-L.   17
Slivniak, D. M.   75
Smith, B. H.   47
Soden, W. von   127
Sollors, W.   42
Speiser, E. A.   100, 110
Steck, O. H.   3, 9, 62, 68
Sternberg, M.   12, 17, 27, 29–30, 32, 34–35, 37
Stordalen, T.   xiii, 2–4, 9–20, 23, 29, 31, 35, 39, 51, 59, 67–69, 71, 85, 107, 116, 132, 134
Streck, M.   103
Strenski, I.   70
Svensson, L.-H.   ix, 135

Tadmor, H.   103
Tigay, J. H.   109, 111–114
Todorov, T.   77
Tournay, R. J.   110
Trible, P.   4, 12–13, 16–17, 24, 31, 37
Trommler, F.   42
Troy, L.   xiv

Van Dyk, P. J.   72
Vanhoozer, K. J.   66
Van Seters, J.   50, 52, 56, 85, 87
Vanstiphout, H. L. J.   110, 119–121
Veijola, T.   53–54
Vulpe, N.   111

Walker, C. B. F.   113
Wallace, H. N.   7–8, 61–62
Walsh, J. T.   12, 16
Watanabe, K.   61, 119

Watson, W. G. E. 63
Weber, M. 132–133
Weippert, M. 58
Wellhausen, J. 56, 63
Wenham, G. 2, 14, 16, 23, 58
Westermann, C. 2, 6–7, 9, 15–16, 18, 60, 62–63, 72, 85, 107
White, H. C. 12, 21, 28
Wikander, O. xiv
Wilcke, C. 100, 102–103, 105, 113
Wilson, R. R. 85, 90

Winter, U. 6, 61
Wiseman, D. J. 113
Witte, M. 8
Wolde, E. van 4, 6, 35, 61–62, 75–76, 82–83
Wright, D. P. 88–89

Yonan, E. A. 70

Zetterholm, M. xiv
Zimmerli, W. 85, 90

Index of Scripture

Genesis

1   11, 13, 59, 71, 95,
        133–134
1–11   44, 46, 75, 96–
        97, 126–128
1:1–2:3   13
1:1–2:4   75
1:26   24, 55, 127,
        132
1:31   59
2   13, 15–16, 18, 29
2–3   iii, xii–xiii, 1–2,
        5, 8–10, 14, 17–18,
        23, 29–30, 33–34,
        37, 42, 50, 53, 55–
        57, 59–60, 68, 71,
        74–76, 81, 85, 88,
        90, 92, 94, 96, 99,
        108, 111, 123, 125,
        127, 132–133
2:3   129
2:4   13, 16, 59, 69,
        134
2:4–6   4
2:4–7   5
2:4–17   17
2:4–24   13
2:4–25   75
2:4–3:24   1
2:5   13, 18, 69
2:5–7   17–19, 28
2:5–24   18
2:5–3:24   13
2:7   13–14, 31, 47,
        125, 131
2:7–24   5, 16
2:7–25   4
2:8   8, 14
2:8–15   19
2:8–16   19

Genesis (cont.)

2:8–17   17, 28
2:9   5–8, 14, 21–24,
        36–39, 41, 47, 49,
        54, 61–62
2:10–14   8, 15–16,
        28, 88, 94, 135
2:15   8, 13, 15, 50
2:15–17   16
2:16   51
2:16–17   19, 22, 24,
        26, 37, 51, 54, 129
2:17   5–7, 18, 22–23,
        61, 130
2:18   18
2:18–20   31
2:18–24   17, 19, 28
2:18–25   17
2:19   13, 48
2:20   30
2:21–24   125
2:22   29
2:23–24   19, 72
2:24   2, 4
2:24–3:24   13
2:25–3:7   5, 16–17,
        19, 24, 28
3   18, 82–83, 125
3:1   29–30, 82
3:1–5   16, 132
3:1–6   19
3:1–7   4, 14, 26, 33,
        51
3:1–13   17
3:1–24   75
3:2   7
3:2–3   38
3:3   5–7, 22, 24, 36–
        39, 41
3:4–6   37

Genesis (cont.)

3:4–7   129
3:5   7, 24–25, 27, 30,
        48, 55, 60, 127,
        132
3:6   5, 23–25
3:6–8   16
3:8–13   17, 19, 28, 33
3:8–19   17
3:8–24   4–5, 16
3:11   5, 7, 26, 51
3:12   7, 31
3:14–19   17, 19, 25,
        28, 47, 52, 72–73,
        135
3:14–21   17
3:17   6, 26, 30, 51,
        54, 73
3:17–19   19
3:18   9
3:19   25, 47–48, 56,
        72–73, 125, 131
3:20   14
3:20–21   16
3:20–24   14, 26, 28,
        68
3:21   19, 32
3:22   3, 6–7, 14, 19–
        20, 23, 25, 27, 36,
        39–40, 47–48, 55,
        60, 107, 117, 127,
        132
3:22–24   7, 9, 17, 48,
        55, 72
3:23   7, 13, 47–48
3:24   6–7, 13–14, 36,
        47, 72, 89
4   66
4:9   25
4:16   66

160

Genesis (cont.)
4:25 30
5 55
5:1 13, 30
5:3–5 30
6 55
6:1–4 24, 55, 75, 128
6:3 7
6:5–9:19 75
6:11–13 59
11:1–9 56, 75, 127
11:7 24, 55, 127, 132
18:9–15 34
18:12–14 34
22 53–54, 57, 64, 71
22:1 54
22:12 54
22:18 5428
28:13 88
29:14 72

Exodus
1:9–10 20
5:8 92
5:11 92
5:19 92
10:28 22
15 53
15:25 51
15:25–26 53, 64
16:4 64
19:5 51
24:4 22
28:17–20 89

Numbers
3:1 13
24:15–16 92
30:6 22
30:9 22
30:13 22

Deuteronomy
1:39 4
4:2 92
8 53–54, 64, 71
8:1–3 53

Deuteronomy (cont.)
8:3 53
8:20 51
11:26–28 52, 58
13:1 92
13:5 50
13:19 51
15:5 51
26:14 51
26:17 51
27:10 51
28:1 51
28:2 51
28:15 51
28:45 51
28:62 51
30:8 51
30:10 51
30:15–20 52, 58
33:15 14
33:27 14

Judges
2:20 51
9:2–3 72

Ruth
4:5 22

1 Samuel
13:19 20
26:16 25

2 Samuel
5:1 72
7 43
12:27–28 20
19:13–14 72

1 Kings
2:37 22
2:42 22

2 Kings
18:12 51

1 Chronicles
1:1 30

2 Chronicles
32:31 54

Job
1:8–9 54
1:9 54–55, 64
1:21 125
4:19 125
10:9 125
11:12 91
15 85
15:7 88, 93
15:7–8 16, 56, 60, 85, 89, 92, 97, 124–125, 128, 130, 132
18:12 125
26:13 82
27:3 125
29:8 63
31:33 125
32:7–8 125
33:4 125
34:10 91
35:10 25
38:11 81

Psalms
24:1–2 82
26:2 54
68:34 14
74:12–17 81–82
82 127
82:5 127
82:7 127
89:10–13 82
89:10–14 81
93 81
95:5 63, 82
104:9 81
104:29 31

Proverbs
3:18 61
11:30 61
13:12 61
15:4 61
30:3 92

Qoheleth
  3:6   89

Song of Songs
  4:9   91
  7:11   73

Isaiah
  1:6   63
  14:13   16, 88, 94
  14:14   91
  15:2   92
  26:19   134
  27:1   82
  27:1–3   30
  51:3   15
  65:22   61

Jeremiah
  3:25   51
  5:22   81
  7:28   51
  22:16   61, 64
  23:1   89
  40:3   51
  48:37   92
  51:51   89

Ezekiel
  14:12–23   54
  28   xii–xiii, 28, 56,
    81, 85, 87–91, 93–
    94, 96, 124–125,
    127, 135
  28:1–10   85
  28:1–19   90, 97
  28:2   56, 88–89, 91,
    93
  28:2–10   87
  28:3   108
  28:3–5   90–91
  28:5   56, 89
  28:6   56, 91
  28:7   90–91
  28:8   88
  28:9   56, 89, 93
  28:9–10   93
  28:11–19   85
  28:12   85, 91
  28:12–19   87
  28:13   15, 88
  28:14   16, 87, 92,
    135
  28:15   88–89, 95

Ezekiel (cont.)
  28:16   16, 87, 89, 92,
    95, 135
  28:17   56, 90–91
  28:18   88–89
  28:19   93
  31:8–9   88
  31:11   89
  31:16   88
  31:18   88

Daniel
  12:2   134

Hosea
  4:11   91
  6:2–3   134

Micah
  5:1   14

Habakkuk
  1:12   14

Malachi
  2:17   25

New Testament

Matthew
  6:33   130

Romans
  5:12–21   131

1 Corinthians
  15:21–22   131

Apocrypha

Ben Sira
  17:6   91
  24:1–2   92

Ben Sira (cont.)
  49:16   30

Wisdom of Solomon
  2:23   131

Index of Other Ancient Sources

Pseudepigrapha

4 Ezra
  3:21   131
  7:116–18   131

Ancient Near Eastern Texts

Adad-guppi Autobiography   113
Adapa and the South Wind   100
  A   100–101, 105, 109
        3–4   101, 105–106
        5   69
        5–8   102
        6–15   102
        7   103
        8   103
  B   100, 105, 109
        14   105
        28–34   104
        57–59   101
        60–63   104
        67–68   106
        68   106
  C   101
  D
        9–10   102, 109
Atrahasis   118
  I 340–51   126
  I 358–59   126
  III vi 47–50 (Old Babylonian)   105

Bilgames and Huwawa A   114, 119
Bilgames and the Netherworld, Me-
    Turan version, line 29   119

Catalog of Texts and Authors
    (Lambert 1962)   103
Cuthean Legend of Naram-Sin   114

Death of Bilgamesh   118
  Me-Turan version, 49–83   118

Erra and Ishum   127

Gilgamesh Epic
  Sumerian   112
  Old Babylonian   108, 112, 114
    OB III = Yale Tablet
      v 188   114
    Pennsylvania Tablet
      OB II   113
  Middle Babylonian   112
  Standard Babylonian   112
  I–V   111
  I
      1–10   115
      1–28   113–114
      4   115
      6   115
      8   115
      9–10   121
      10   113
      10, 24–28   113
      18–21   114, 120
      24–28   113
      29   113
      29–46   113
      41   116
      48   117
      241–42   115
  III
      104   115
  VI   110–111
  VII–XI   111, 116
  IX
      1–6   116
      37   116
      49   117
      51   117
      131–70   116
      170   116
      171–94   116

Gilgamesh Epic (cont.)
  X 116
      7 117
      70–71 116
      138–39 116
      147–48 116
      238–39 116
      268 117
      304–7 116
      319–22 117
  XI 114–115
      7 117
      49 115
      197 115
      199–205 117
      205 115
      207–8 118
      208 116
      209 119
      209–46 119
      213 116
      213–14 119
      273–86 119

Gilgamesh Epic (cont.)
      287–93 115
      295 119
      299 119
      300 119
      305–7 119
      323–26 114, 120
  XII 111
  Meissner-Millard frag.
    i 8 116
    iii 2 116
    iii 2–5 106, 110
  Meissner-Millard tablet (Old
    Babylonian) 106

Instructions of Shuruppak 115

Kirta (CAT 1.16.IV:2) 108

Persian Verse Account 103

Sennacherib Autobiography 114
Sumerian King List 112

Index of Terms, Mainly Literary

aboutness 45
alimentary (nutritional) code 74
anagnorisis 27
apkallu 103
authorial intention 66
chaos battle drama of creation 80
chaos, myth of 81
character-focalizer 32
code 28
Deuteronomistic affinities 49
discourse 12
divine prerogatives 126
drama of discovery 27
emic designation 80
etic designation 80
etiological narrative 68
exposition 17
extradiegetic 34
fall 1, 81
  of man 81
focalization (point of view) 32
function of the myth: explanatory,
    etiological 72
functionalist approach to the
    myth 70
generic awareness 80
genre 65, 76
  ontological status of 78
genre-bound character of
    understanding 79
hermeneutic code 28
hubris 55
implied author 12
intention, authorial 66
intertextuality 83
literary competence 79
merismus 63
myth 66, 68
  Adamic 85
  as counter-present 69
  as explanation 69

myth (cont.)
  aspects of 68
  as validation 69
names as generic signals 66
narratological analysis 12
narrator 12
narrator-focalizer 32
narû-literature 113, 121
omniscience 34
ontological boundary 126
peripeteia 24
plot 18, 21, 44
plot segments 18
pragmatic dimension 65
proairetic code 28
referential ambition 67
representativity 67
retribution 58
scenes 16
sociofunctionalist
    interpretation 70
sociology of knowledge 73
split coordination 21, 36
story 12, 18
story narration 19
story significance 19
structuralist approaches 74
structuralist-semiotic tradition 75
subject 43
symbol 60
symbolic universes 73
symbolism of names 30
test 23, 53
thematic fields 45
theme 42
theodicy 58, 132
tradition 96, 124
validation of social values 72
voice 32, 33
wisdom 102, 129

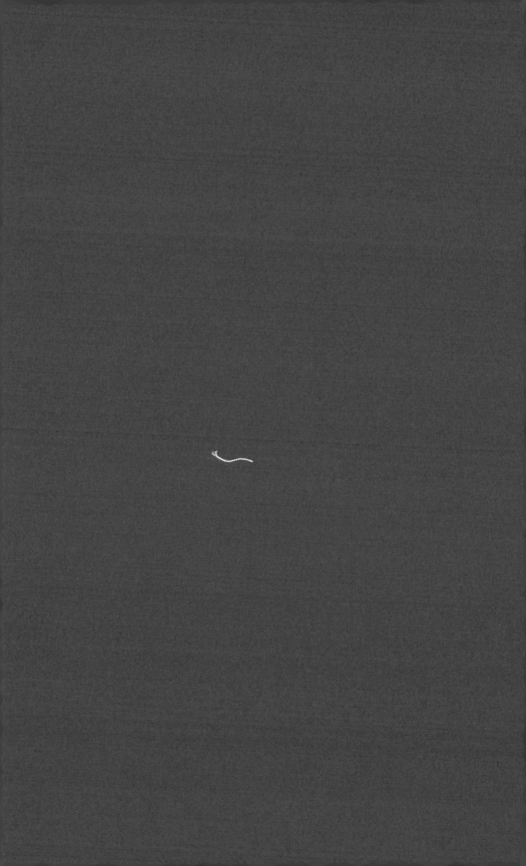